Complete Guitar Care & Maintenance:
The Ultimate Owner's Guide

By Jonny Blackwood

Discover other books available from the author (paperback and digital editions):

How to Setup Your Guitar Like A Pro: An Easy Guide for Beginners

How to Build & Setup Guitar Kits Like A Pro: An Easy Guide for Bolt-on Neck Guitars

How to Start and Run a Successful Guitar Repair Business: Practical Tips for the New Entrepreneur

How to Do Fretwork Like A Pro: An Easy Guide for Beginners (coming soon)

Discover the *"Guitar Setup Pro"* app, featuring the *"Guitar Setup Calculator"* at your favourite App Store.

Complete Guitar Care & Maintenance: The Ultimate Owner's Guide

By Jonny Blackwood

Published by Blackwood Guitarworks

Email: info@blackwoodguitarworks.com

Copyright © 2020 Jonny Blackwood

All rights reserved. No part of this book may be reproduced in any form,

without written permission, except in the case of brief quotations embodied in articles and reviews.

Published 2020

ISBN 978-1-989514-01-6 Print edition

ISBN 978-1-989514-02-3 Hardcover edition

Disclaimer

All trademarks, service marks, trade names and copyrights present in this book are trademarks, registered trademarks, or copyrights of their respective owners. Fender®, Strat®, Stratocaster®, Telecaster®, Tele®, P-Bass®, and J-Bass® are registered trademarks of Fender Musical Instruments Corporation. Floyd Rose® is a registered trademark of Floyd Rose Industries. Gibson® and Les Paul® are registered trademarks of Gibson Guitar Corp. Gretsch® is a registered trademark of Fred Gretsch® Enterprises. Learn-GuitarSetups.com, it's agents or authors are not affiliated with Fender®, Gibson®, Gretsch®, Floyd Rose®, or any other Brand, copyright or trademark listed in this Book. No warranty of any kind applies. Information in this book is for educational purposes only, and the publisher, author, website owner, affiliates, and any other person associated with the distribution, marketing or advertising of this book publication will not be held liable for any damages of any kind as a result of action taken from the content within this book. The information contained in this book is provided in good faith by the author for general guidance on matters of interest only.

FOR MORE TIPS, TRICKS, & TOOLS

VISIT US AT:

Guitar Setup & Repair Tutorials

Guitar Setup & Repair Classes

Check out our exclusive (and the worlds' first)

Guitar Setup Calculator

- Factory Setup Settings

- JB Custom Setup Specs for All Guitar Types

- Electric, Acoustic & Bass GUITAR

- Mix and Match Your Own Settings

- SIGN UP ONLINE FOR **FREE ACCESS**

TABLE OF CONTENTS

INTRODUCTION 1
HOW TO USE THIS BOOK 3
PARTS OF THE GUITAR 4
GENERAL GUITAR MAINTENANCE 6
   CHANGING THE STRINGS 7
      Removing the Old Strings 7
      Removing Strings on a Tremolo Bridge 10
      Removing Strings on a Floyd Rose-Style Bridge 11
      Removing Strings on an Archtop Floating Bridge 15
      Removing Strings on an Acoustic Guitar Bridge 16
   HOW TO INSTALL NEW STRINGS 17
      Fender-Style Guitars 17
      Gibson-Style Guitars 18
      Standard Tuners 19
      Slot-head Tuners 21
      Locking Tuners 22
      Floyd Rose-Style Bridges 23
      Acoustic Guitars 26
      Nylon String Guitars 28
      Tuning Tips 31
      Guitar String Gauges 33
      Tunings – Standard & Alternate 35
   CLEANING 37
      Cleaning the Body 38
      Cleaning the Fretboard 39
      Cleaning the Neck 42
      Cleaning the Strings 42
      Cleaning the Hardware 43
      Repairing Scratches 44
   GENERAL HARDWARE ADJUSTMENTS 45
      How to Fix Loose Strap Buttons 46
      How to Remove the Control Knobs 47
      How to Clean Dirty Potentiometers and Controls 51
      How to Check Battery Voltage 52
SETUPS & ADJUSTMENTS 53
   ADJUST THE NECK RELIEF (BOW) 58
      How to Measure Neck Relief 61
      How to Adjust the Truss Rod 65
      How to Remove the Neck for a Truss Rod Access 67
      How to Adjust the Neck Alignment 68
   ADJUST THE STRING HEIGHT AT THE BRIDGE 71
      About Fretboard Radius 71
      Gibson-style Hard-tail Bridges (Tune-o-matic) 73
      Fender-style Hard-tail Bridges 75
      How to Adjust Individual Saddle Height 76
      How to Use Under-String Radius Gauges 78
      Vintage-Style Tremolo Bridges 81
      Modern Tremolo Bridges 82
      How to Adjust Tremolo Bridge Angle 84
      Floyd Rose Bridges 86
      Acoustic Guitars 88

- ADJUST THE STRING HEIGHT AT THE NUT 91
  - How to File Nut Slots 92
  - Nut Removal & Replacement 97
- ADJUST THE PICKUP HEIGHT 101
- ADJUST THE INTONATION 102
- WIRING & ELECTRONICS 103
  - How to Solder 107
  - Repairing Guitar Electronics 110
  - Wiring Tips 118
- GUITAR CARE 120
  - Humidity & Environment 120
  - Humidity Symptoms Chart 126
  - Instrument Storage 127
  - Shipping Guitars 129
- BUYERS GUIDE 130
- TROUBLESHOOTING 136
  - String Buzz, Rattle, & Noise 136
  - Common Tuning Issues 137
  - Common Bridge & Saddle Problems 139
  - Common Truss Rod Issues 140
  - Common Electronics Issues 142
- TOOL TEMPLATES 145
- SETUP SPEC SHEETS 152
- MANUFACTURER PICKUP HEIGHT SPECS 157
- MEASUREMENT CONVERSION CHART 158
- WIRING DIAGRAMS 159
- FURTHER RESOURCES 171
- ABOUT THE AUTHOR 172
- ONE LAST THING 173

INTRODUCTION

Thank you for buying *"Guitar Complete Care & Maintenance: The Ultimate Owners Manual."* After many years of working in the repair business, I noticed a large number of instruments I worked on were commonly neglected of simple upkeep and care. Owning a musical instrument is not unlike owning a car, and requires seasonal checkups and maintenance to ensure everything keeps running tiptop, year after year. Even the frequent task of restringing the guitar has its role in play & performance. These things aren't always talked about by the salesperson at the guitar store, the guitar instructor, or friends. Like many things, we usually react to problems as they come up, but a little knowhow can prevent most common issues from ever happening.

This guide has been designed to fill in all the blanks between routine maintenance, improving its playability, and to doing the odd repair. All of this, combined into a concise manual, means fewer trips to the repair shop and more time playing and understanding your instrument. Procedures are described in a step-by-step manner so that you can easily follow along, no matter where you are, and no matter what your experience level.

I wish you all the best in your guitar playing journey, and I hope this manual provides all the key information you will ever need in maintaining and caring for your instrument.

Connect with me on Facebook (www.facebook.com/blackwoodguitarworks), Instagram (@blackwoodguitarworks) or through my website (https://www.blackwoodguitarworks.com/) and let me know how it's worked out.

Cheers,

-JB

HOW TO USE THIS BOOK

This book is written in a particular sequence to assist the reader through professional guitar maintenance, setup, and repair, using step-by-step instructions. For those new to the subject, it is best to read the book from beginning to end, for a broad overview of the entire operation. Each step is described in detail for each guitar type that would be applicable, with subsequent sections on related topics. Thumb through the sections as needed, try different setup specifications, and when you're ready, tackle something new, such as nut slot cutting.

NOTE: The work described in this guide is intended for individuals with basic mechanical skills. If you do not understand the described procedures or are uncomfortable using tools, please leave this kind of work to a qualified technician.

PARTS OF THE GUITAR

To do a successful setup, let's get familiar with all the working parts of a guitar.

Body: The body of the guitar contributes to its comfort, style, and resonant tonal quality. Often made from select tonewoods, laminates or in rarer cases, composite materials.

Neck: The neck of the guitar also contributes to the overall comfort of playing and can vary in thickness, width, and length. Guitar necks are generally made from hard tonewoods such as maple or mahogany, or a select combination of different tonewoods.

Fretboard: The fretboard is the main playing surface and is often made from hard tonewoods most popularly maple, rosewood, or ebony.

Frets: Fret size and fret wear condition can play a role in the comfort of playing and ultimately affect the end-result of the setup. There are tips on this throughout the book, but we will not dive into fretwork as it is an advanced-level topic.

Head or headstock: The headstock is the upper-end of the neck, where the tuners and strings are anchored.

Tuners: The tuners wind up and change the pitch of the strings. One misconception is they also keep the strings in tune, but that is not entirely correct. When there is a problem with a string losing its pitch, or going out of tune, it is more often because of another issue.

Nut: The nut keeps the strings aligned across the fretboard, up to the tuners. Like the bridge saddle, it is a crucial area for string height and playing comfort. Nuts are often made from bone, plastic, or some composite material. Occasionally you will also see them in brass or steel.

Truss rod: A truss rod is a steel rod that runs down the interior of the guitar neck. Its purpose is to counteract the pull of the strings by applying a counterforce within the neck. It is generally accessible at the headstock or the butt-end of the neck.

Pickups: The pickups amplify the strings of the guitar. Electric guitar pickups can be adjusted for sensitivity, which we'll cover later.

Bridge: The bridge anchors the strings to the guitar body. The bridge style and design will significantly vary. We will cover the most common styles and how they can be adjusted for the setup.

Bridge saddles: The bridge saddle(s) will most often determine the string height and length. Depending on guitar design, the bridge saddle(s) may or may not be fixed to the bridge.

Controls: General controls for volume and tone shaping.

Pickguard: The pickguard (not pictured), if applicable, generally protects the guitar from wear but may also house electronics in some cases.

Strap button: This is for attaching your strap.

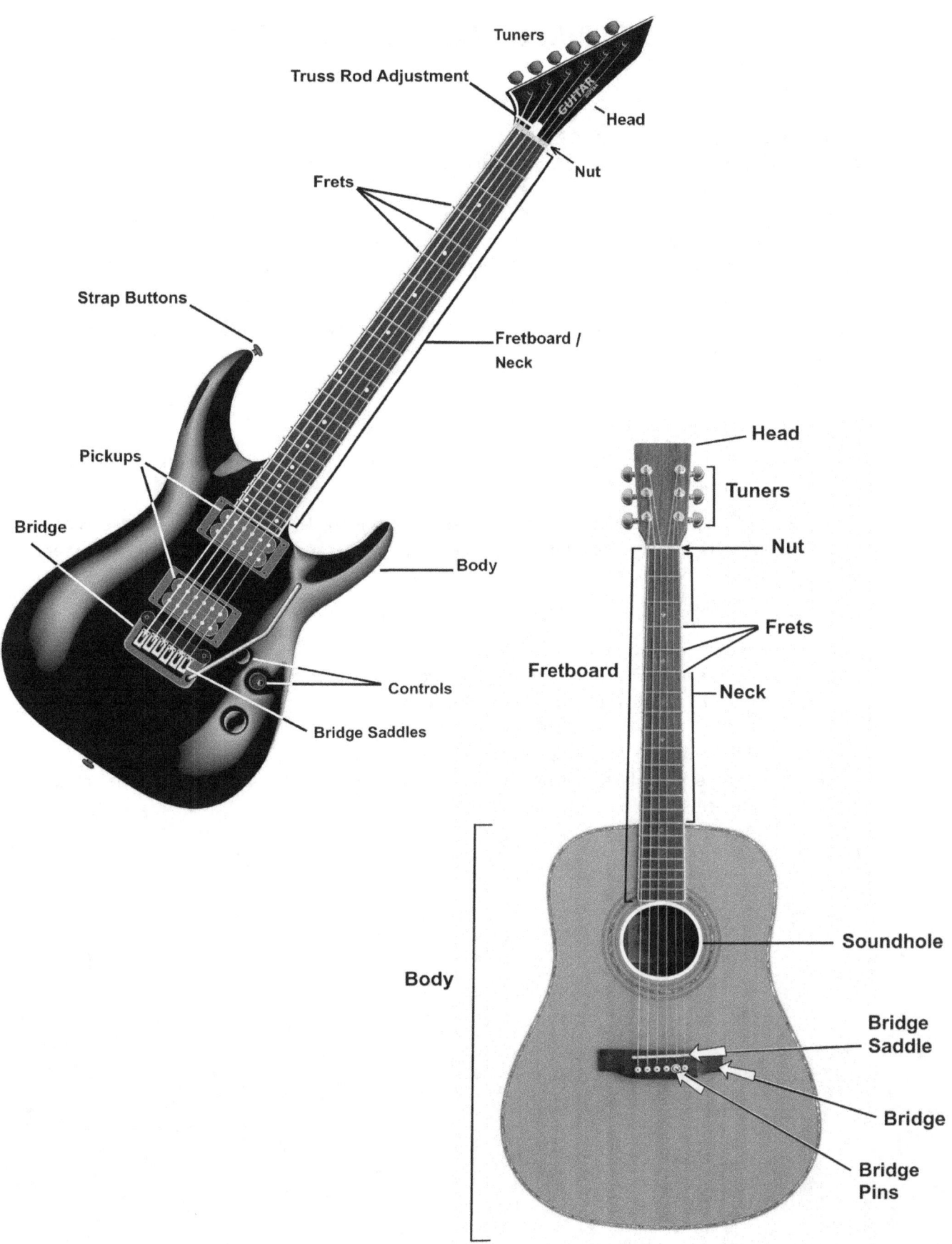

GENERAL GUITAR MAINTENANCE

What Is Guitar Maintenance?

Maintenance can be defined as the act of cleaning, inspecting or testing, and servicing as needed. On a guitar, this would consist of changing the strings, cleaning the fretboard and body, and making any necessary mechanical adjustments for optimum playability. A set up can be learnt by anyone and will benefit the user in his or her understanding of the instrument considerably. Regularly maintaining your guitar will help retain its condition and functionality of the guitar for many years to come.

Whether you received an owner's manual with your guitar or not, this guide will have you covered in all aspects of guitar maintenance, including instrument setup and the occasional minor repair when needed. So, let's dive right in!

Why Maintain Your Guitar?

Guitar maintenance is an important, but often overlooked aspect of guitar ownership. A properly maintained guitar will perform its best, no matter what quality it is.

A regular maintenance schedule can be as simple as cleaning it regularly, or as comprehensive as a full mechanical setup. Let's look at the common areas needing attention and the methods you can use to keep your guitar in its best working order.

In this guide, we will cover in detail the following aspects of guitar maintenance:

- Cleaning the instrument regularly and after use
- Checking for loose connections or hardware every time you change the strings
- Changing the strings regularly on a schedule that suits how often it is needed
- Conducting a basic setup once or twice a year as needed
- Repairing or replacing any deteriorating parts
- Keeping the instrument properly stored when not in use and always within a suitable and safe environment

CHANGING THE STRINGS

Why Should I Change My Strings?

Guitar strings have a direct relationship to how the guitar sounds and performs. Over time, guitar strings get worn and dirty, which will have an ill-effect on the tone, feel, functionality and overall life expectancy of the strings. Dirty strings will also wear down your frets faster. The oxidized dirt becomes corrosive and jagged, much like having little files grinding down on your frets while playing. Fret repair is expensive, but you can postpone that trip to the shop for a long time, just by cleaning and changing those strings regularly.

How Often Should I Change My Strings?

For strings to stay in tune, they should be changed regularly. Old, dirty strings will not hold their intonation or tune very well.

String changes should be based on the needs of the player and the condition of the strings. Many touring pros will change a set of strings either every night or every other night, but someone who plays casually at home may get three months out of a set. So, other than when they start breaking, how do you know it's time to change them?

If you run a finger underneath the strings and feel dirt, rust, or flat spots, it is time to change them.

If your hands sweat a lot when you play, this will speed up the corrosion of the strings. You can prolong the life of the strings by simply cleaning them after each use. You can use a dry cloth to wipe them down, or you can purchase a product like The String Cleaner, which is designed to clip above and below your strings to clean them from all angles. Another method is to use a string cleaning lubricant such as Fender Speed Slick Guitar String Cleaner, MusicNomad Fuel-String Cleaner and Lubricant, the D'Addario XLR8, or GHS Fast Fret. These products are designed to clean your strings so that they are like new again, with the additional benefit of lubricating the string as well, for a lightning fast feel.

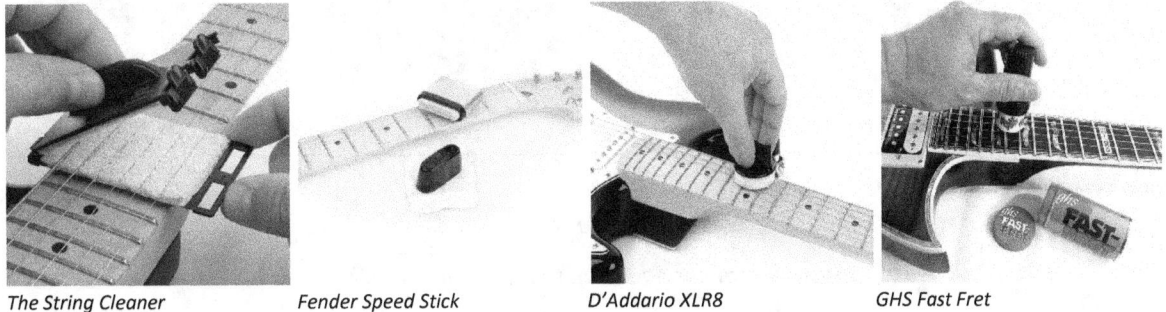

The String Cleaner *Fender Speed Stick* *D'Addario XLR8* *GHS Fast Fret*

Removing the Old Strings

This is also the best time to inspect the hardware and electronics more closely. If any of the controls are noisy or intermittent, we would need access to clean them, as well as to take care of any other issues, such as changing batteries (if applicable). When planning on using under-string radius gauges for the setup, measuring the fretboard radius is easiest at this stage (more on this later).

Lay the guitar down and prop up the neck, so you have access to the tuners on the headstock. You can use a rolled-up towel if you don't have a neck rest designed for the job. Starting with either the 6th or 1st string, loosen the string and remove it from string post. If you have some side cutters, clip the string near the bridge and remove each end of the string carefully. Cutting the string will make it easier to remove from the tuner, and the bridge saddles with minimal wear on the hardware- especially on tremolo equipped guitars.

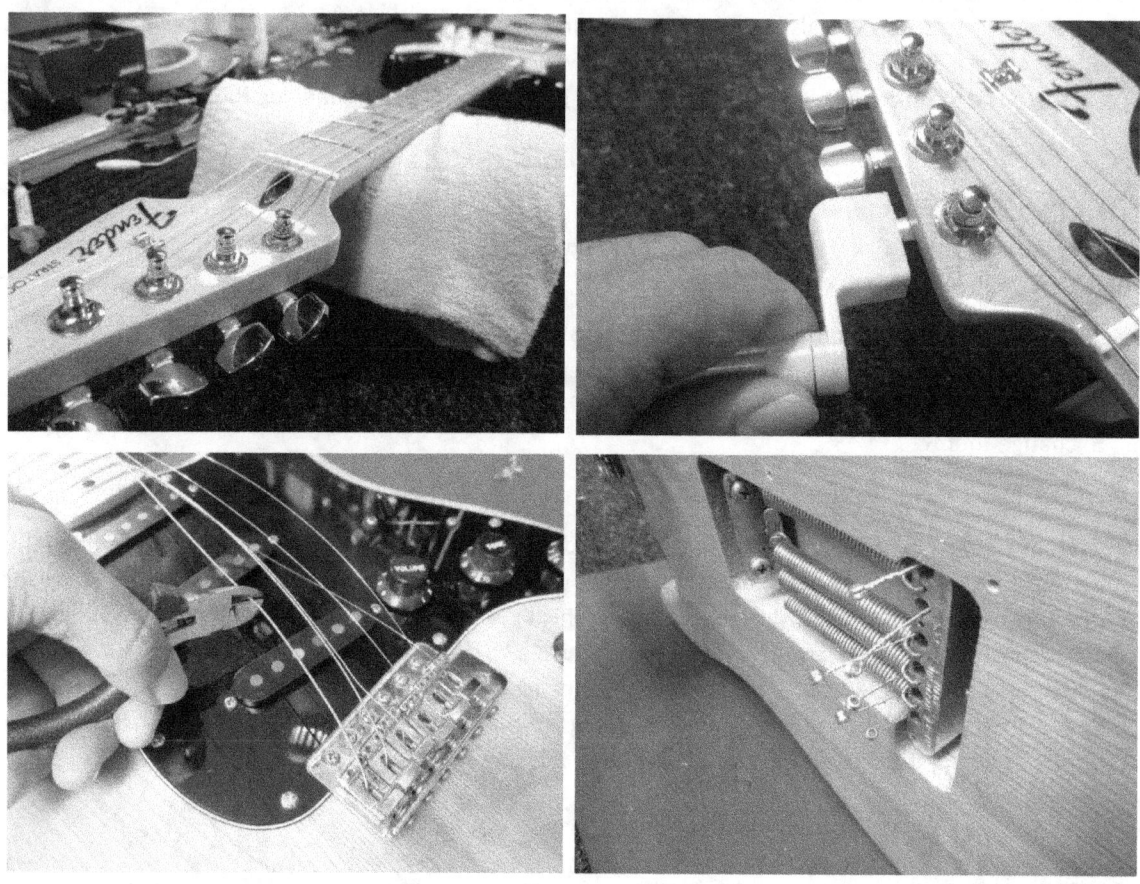

"But isn't removing all the strings bad for the neck?

Won't that change something on my guitar?"

I am asked this a lot, and there's no harm in removing all the strings at once. It seems like there's some debate on this topic, but this is how it is done in any shop, or factory, or even on the road by professional guitar techs and luthiers. Regardless, if you don't feel comfortable changing strings as recommended, skip the section on cleaning and jump ahead to **RESTRINGING**.

> *"But what about on tremolo bridges?*
>
> *Won't removing the strings cause the tremolo bridge to sink into the body?*

Often the bridge can be blocked or held in place when changing strings. Here are a few hacks that will make restringing a breeze.

Removing Strings on a Tremolo Bridge

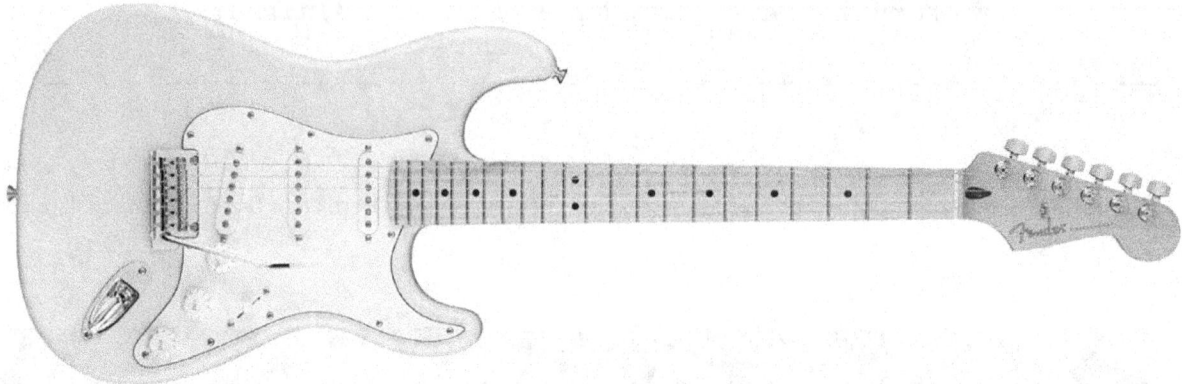

The tremolo bridge usually sits above the guitar body and is balanced by the string tension and the tremolo springs (more on this later). When the strings are loosened for removal, the bridge falls back to the body since there is no longer any tension holding it in place. Once the new strings are installed, re-tuning is a slow, tedious process as it takes several attempts to build up the optimum tension for the bridge to regain its position.

HACK: Put a tremolo cavity cover, notepad or magazine under the bridge when detuning and removing the strings. Once the new strings are installed, retuning to pitch will be much faster because the bridge angle will already be in its playing position (or close to it). For best results, find a spacer that perfectly fits underneath the bridge plate when the guitar is tuned to pitch.

Removing Strings on a Floyd Rose-Style Bridge

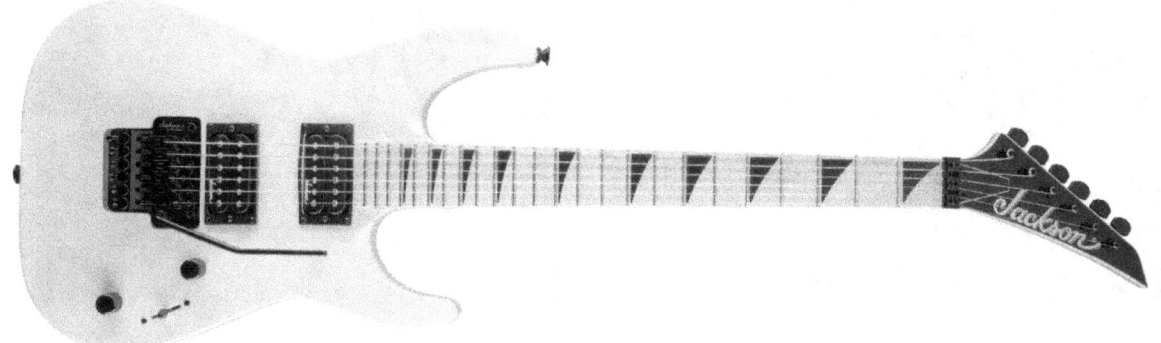

Floyd Rose-style double-locking bridges are completely other beasts. String tension holds the bridge angle similarly, as mentioned before, but the difference is that the bridge sits either above or within a routed cavity on the guitar. So, when restringing from scratch, the tuning and resetting of the bridge angle can take an incredible amount of patience when balancing and rebalancing the tension- you know what I'm talking about if you have ever done this yourself (more on this later).

HACK: For bridges that sit in a recessed cavity, you can use some round wood dowel from the hardware store. Cut it in length to fit under the tremolo bridge plate. Now you can loosen and change the strings while the bridge remains blocked. As soon as the new strings are tuned up, the dowel will become loose again as the bridge returns to tension.

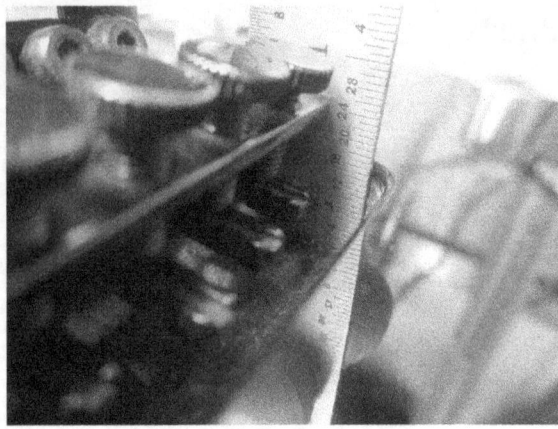 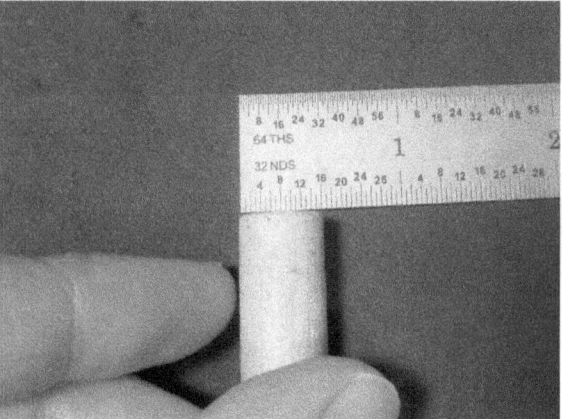

Find the correct dowel diameter size by placing a ruler behind the bridge and into the cavity to measure the depth. Use the size that closely matches the depth of the cavity, and this will block the bridge in the same position as when it's tuned to pitch.

To insert the dowel, push down on the whammy bar, so the bridge raises high enough to allow it to drop into the bridge cavity.

> *NOTE: The dowel shouldn't influence the bridge position upwards- it should be an exact fit. If you can't get it exact, try to get it as close as possible- it will save you quite a headache when retuning.*

To get a closer fit, you can apply masking tape around the dowel to increase its diameter.

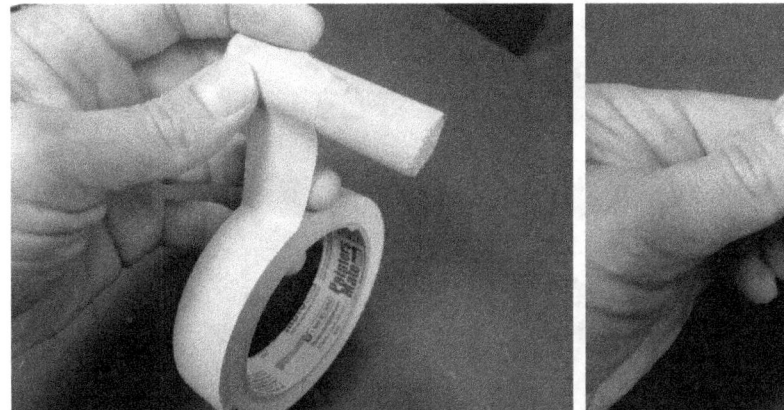
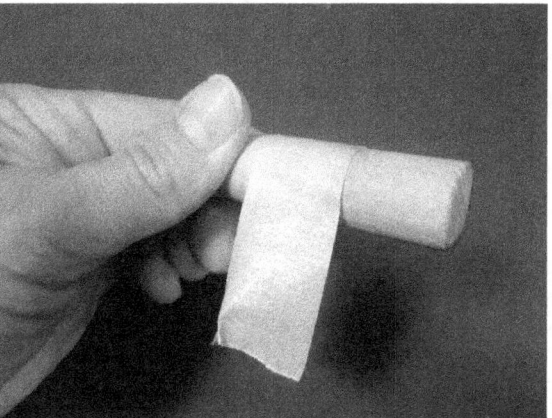

With double-locking bridges that sit *above* the body, you can wedge the backplate or something similar under the bridge to keep it stable while changing strings. *TIP: Flat cork works really well and won't scratch or damage the guitar.*

Floyd Rose String Removal

Loosen and remove the nut lock clamps. *TIP: Keep them in the same order to be reinstalled. If there is any wear on the clamps, they will function the best on the same strings.*

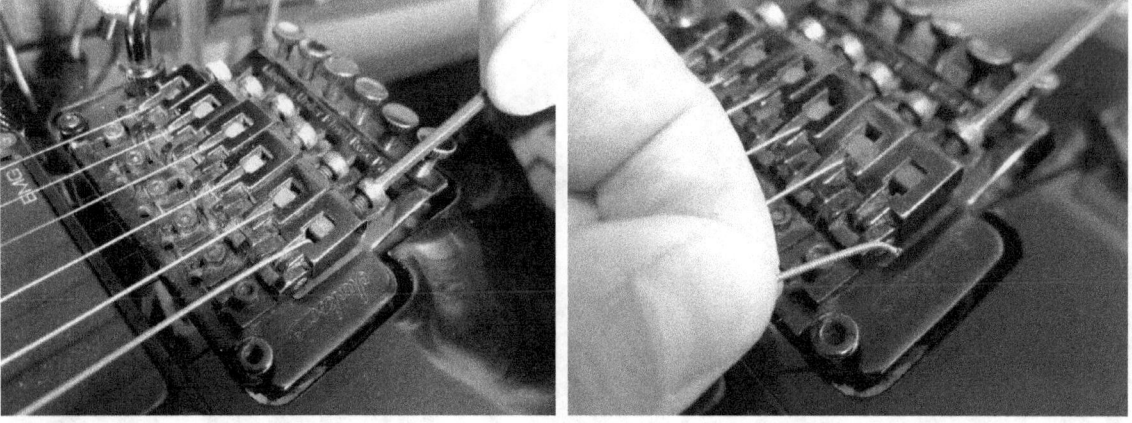

Loosen the clamp at the saddle with the appropriate hex key or tool and remove the string.

Removing Strings on an Archtop Floating Bridge

"On my archtop guitar, isn't the string tension holding the bridge in place? If I remove all the strings, the bridge will fall off!"

Archtop guitar bridges such as those pictured below are often held in place by the string tension alone – hence the term "floating" bridge. Some manufacturers will "pin" them in place – such as on certain Gretsch guitars. Other times, the guitar owner may have the bridge glued in place by a qualified luthier or guitar technician. The easiest way to keep the bridge stationary when changing strings is to apply a couple of pieces of low-tack painters masking tape to the bridge legs (*do not put tape on delicate or cracked finishes*). The lowest tack tape you can find is the best choice. Always remove the tape at an angle slowly and carefully.

HACK: Lower the tack or stickiness of any tape by applying a piece onto your clothing- such as a cotton t-shirt or your pants. The tape will pick up any fuzz or lint and will become less sticky in the process. Do this several times over to make it safer for a guitar finish.

Removing Strings on an Acoustic Guitar Bridge

Bridge pins can be easily damaged by incorrect removal. Sometimes they are bent upwards or pulled on, and this may damage them over time (especially plastic ones). If you have a bridge pin puller, they are designed to remove the pins by pulling straight upwards.

If you don't have a specific tool, you can use some side cutters like those pictured below. Place the cutter on the bridge saddle with its jaws cradled *gently* around the head of the bridge pin (don't tighten or grip hard). Use a little leverage off of the saddle and gently push down on the handle so that the jaws pull up on the bridge pin.

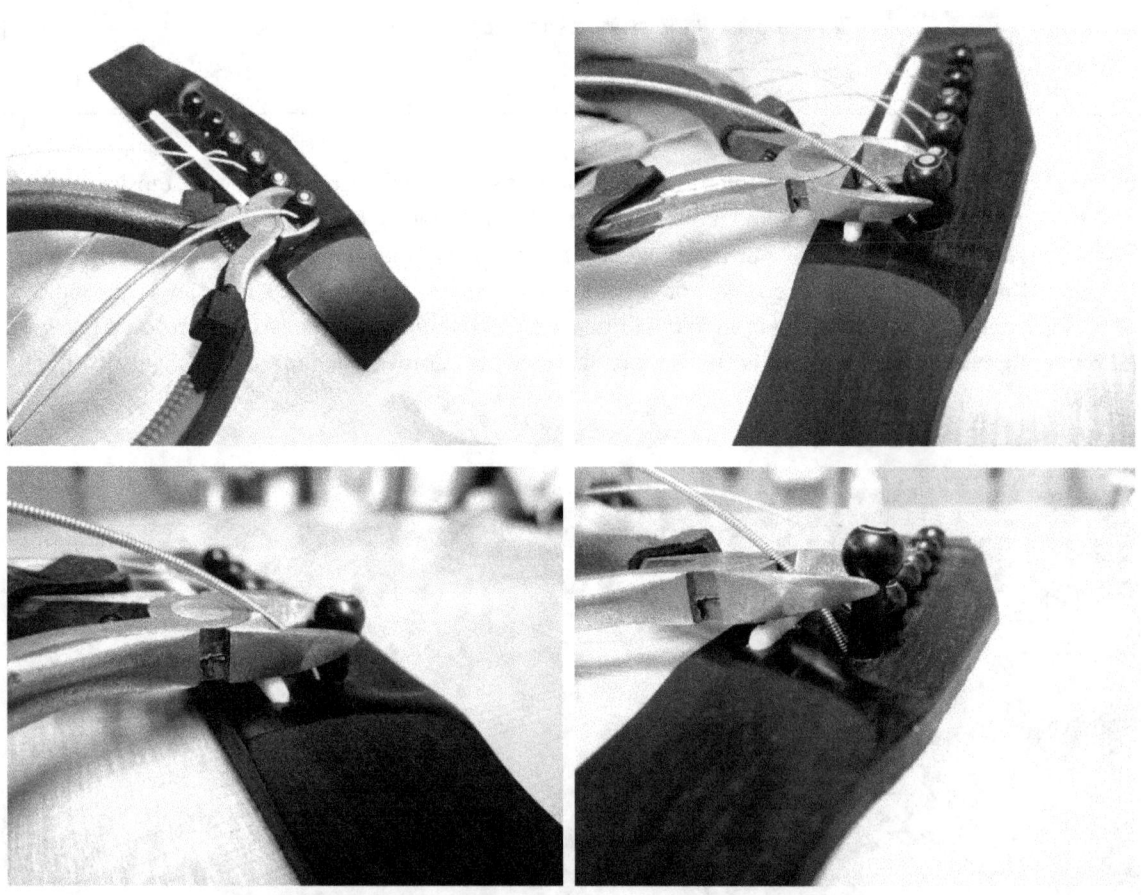

HOW TO INSTALL NEW STRINGS

Fender-Style Guitars

Fender-style guitars are often loaded from the rear. A Telecaster typically has a rear-loaded fixed bridge, which is called a "string-thru" design- the strings are inserted into the body through small holes on the back. The string passes up through the body and out at the top before being pulled over the saddles.

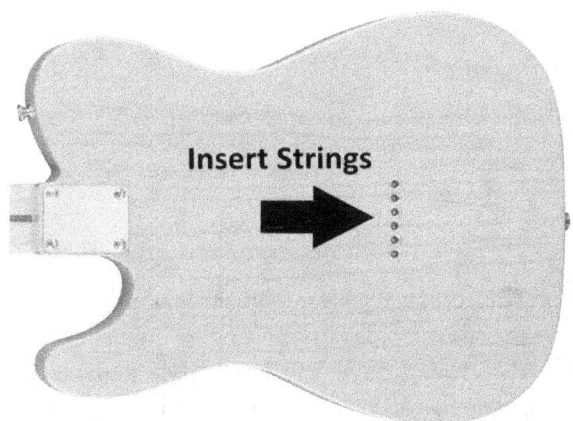

Strat-style guitars are often back-loaded as well but through the tremolo bridge. Vintage style tremolos can be set up to either sit flat on the body or to float. When setting these types of bridges up, it is important to set the tension correctly to maintain string tuning **(read more about this in Guitar Setups/Vintage Tremolos)**.

Gibson-Style Guitars

Most Gibson-style guitars have a 2-piece bridge made up of a tailpiece and a bridge with saddles. These are known as Tune-o-matic bridges.

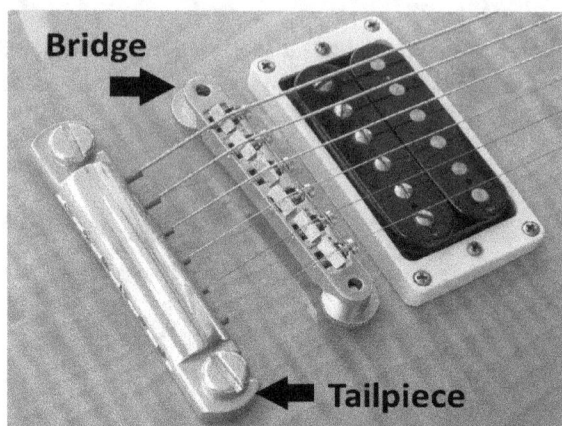

Pass the strings through the tailpiece towards the headstock and pull them over the appropriate saddle. Seat the string in the nut slot and wind it around the tuning peg, as mentioned previously.

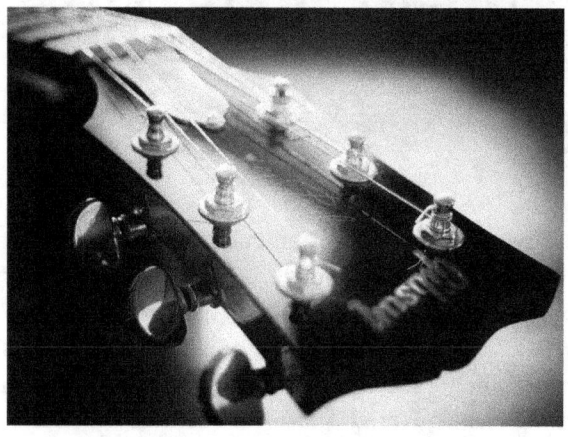

Many Gibson-style guitars have three tuning pegs per side of the headstock as opposed to the usual 6 in a line style found on most Fender-style guitars. This changes the direction that you wrap the strings at the headstock end. The E, A and D strings are wound counter-clockwise, and the G, B and high E strings are wound clockwise.

Image courtesy Keith Ellwood.

TIP: Take care when removing all the strings from a Gibson-style guitar as the tailpiece and bridge are both held in place by the string tension. The tailpiece will often fall off its posts once the strings are removed.

Standard Tuners

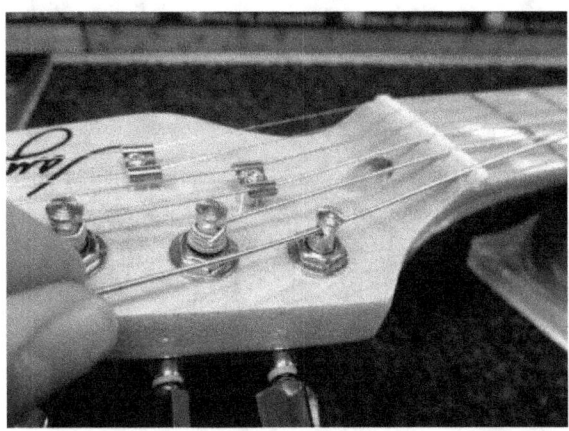

1) Start by inserting the string into the tuner. Pull it through until you have between 2 and 2½ inches of slack past the tuner (on Fender-style guitars, that distance is equal to pulling it past two tuners.

2) Keep the string pinched in your left hand and pull it back towards the string post to hold the amount of slack.

3) Put a kink in the string at a right angle from the inside, and an opposite kink on the outside like a reversed 'Z.'

4) Loop one wrap around the top and wind the remaining slack underneath the loop, feeding the string downwards. Gently keep some tension on the backside of the string while winding up.

5) Tune-up to pitch and trim the excess. Three windings per string are sufficient on wound strings. Treble strings may have more.

Slot-head Tuners

If you have vintage-style slot-head tuners, the process is similar. Measure the slack like in the previous example but add another half of an inch or so. The extra slack will account for the portion of the string inserted into the top of the tuner. Cut the string and insert it as pictured.

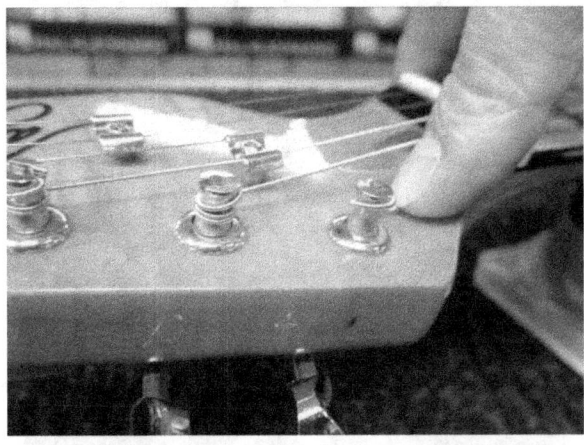 

Loop the excess string around the post and wind the rest downward, again keeping some tension on the backside of the string. The more windings there are, the lower the string will be pushed down towards the base of the string post.

Locking Tuners

Locking tuners generally do not require windings around the post as traditional tuners do. Some designs don't even allow it. Therefore, you can feed the string in through the tuner, lock it in place and then tune to pitch. Once it is locked, it's a good idea to put a 90-degree kink the string. It will further help prevent it from slipping. Once the string is tuned to pitch, cut the excess string at the tuner.

PRO TIP: On all the examples given, you can cut the excess string right at the string post or alternatively, loop it around the tuner once, and then cut it. Now the string end is like a spring, and because it has some give, it is less likely to poke your hands (my biggest pet peeve!). They will also be less likely to poke holes in your gig bag, bandmate, girlfriend/boyfriend, etc.

Floyd Rose-Style Bridges

Floyd Rose-style bridges are more time consuming to restring due to their tension balanced, floating bridge system. The strings lock at the bridge and nut while the bridge floats by the balanced tension of the strings and tremolo springs.

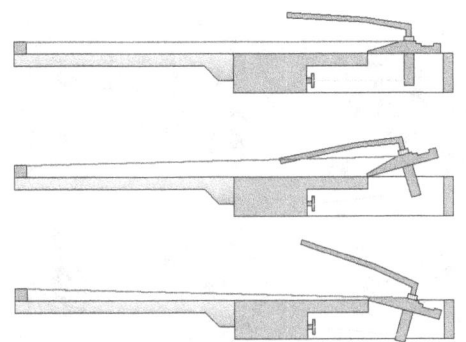

When restringing, you will block the bridge, as mentioned in the previous section, "Removing Strings," or you will change the strings individually.

Before starting, notice the position of the bridge. Many Floyd Rose style bridges are designed to remain parallel with the body of the guitar. When the strings have all been changed, the bridge should return to the same position as when you started. If it doesn't, a further adjustment will be necessary **(read more in Guitar Setups/Floyd Rose Bridges).**

Floyd Rose and similar style tremolos often require you to cut the ball end off of the string before clamping the string into the saddle. Once the string has been inserted and clamped, feed the other end of the string into the appropriate nut slot, followed by the tuning post. Wrap the string around the tuning post, as mentioned previously and tune to pitch.

Repeat this for each string, balancing the bridge each time and re-checking each string tuning as you work. By the time you've put on all six strings, the bridge should be level with the strings in-tune. Keep in mind that further adjustment is often necessary, which we cover in the **Guitar Setups section**.

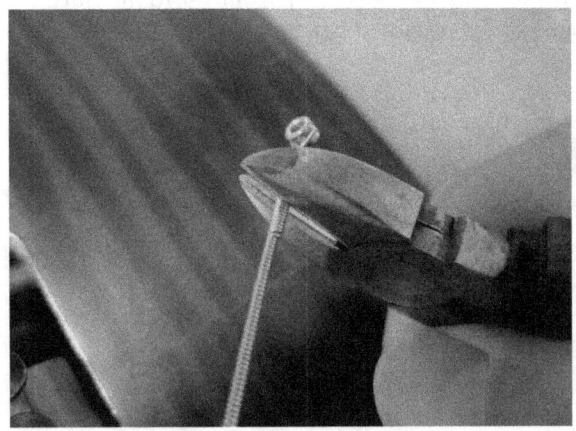
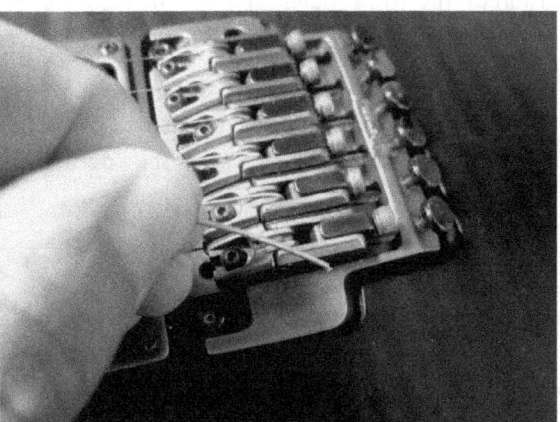

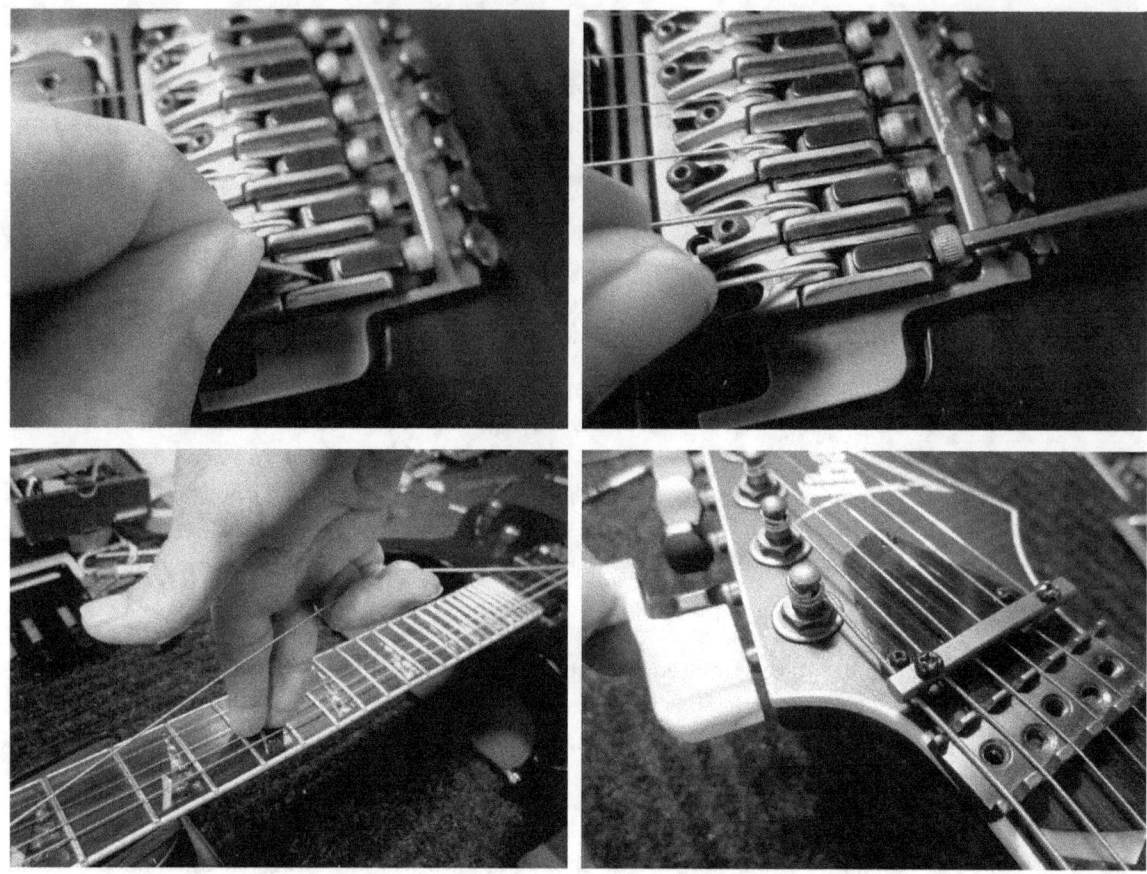

Another way to measure the correct amount of string slack is by using your hand as a ruler. With slight tension on the string, pull it up from the centre of the fretboard and use your index finger to measure the slack. For those with average-size hands, this will give you the equivalent of 2 to 2½ inches passed the string post.

Once the new strings have been installed, continue to the next section on tuning. You can keep the nut clamps off the guitar until you are entirely done the setup.

PRO TIP: Guitars with a locking nut may also have a string retainer bar behind the nut. The purpose of the bar is to direct the string angle downwards, behind the nut. If the pitch of the string(s) goes sharp after the nut clamps are tightened, adjust the bar lower by tightening the two screws.

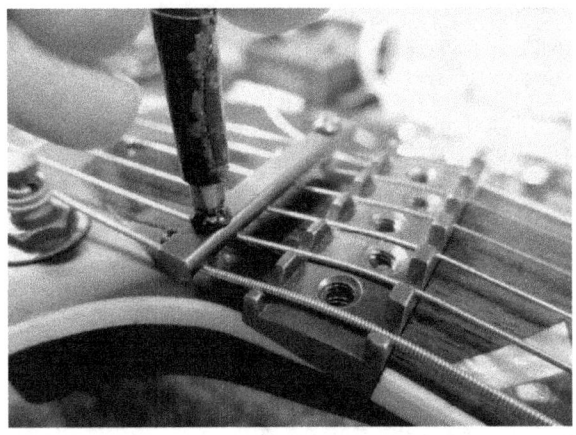 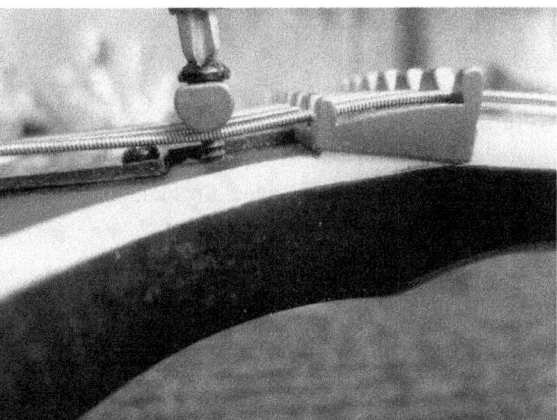

Tuning Floyd Rose Equipped Guitars

Since many people have difficulty tuning their Floyd Rose equipped guitar, I've included this section directly from the Floyd Rose Service Dept.

"Tuning your Floyd Rose bridge is certainly a tricky business when the bridge is floating. This is because the total tension of the strings must balance the total tension of the tremolo springs with the base plate of the bridge parallel to the face of the guitar- with the strings tuned to the desired pitch. So, follow these steps, and it will start to make sense."

Step 1: Loosen the three string clamps at the nut

Step 2: Set the fine tuner screws on the bridge to the middle of their adjustment range.

Step 3: Tune the strings to your desired pitch (this can be drop tuning, open tuning, or standard pitch, the procedure is the same for any tuning) with an electronic tuner starting with the low 'E' (#6 string).

Step 4: When you have finished tuning all of the strings, check the tuning on the low 'E' again. If the low 'E' is now flat, re-tune the strings starting again with the low 'E' but this time tune the E, A, D, G, and B strings a little bit sharp, then the high 'E' (#1 string) to pitch. If the low 'E' is sharp, re-tune as just described only tuning the first five strings a little flat. You must tune the strings a little sharp or flat to get to your tuning because every time you change the tension (or pitch) of one string, the other strings change pitch in the opposite direction.

Step 5: Repeat step 4 (remembering to stretch the strings simultaneously) until all the strings are at the desired pitch.

Step 6: When the strings are at the desired pitch, check to see if the bridge base plate is sitting parallel with the top surface of the guitar. If the base plate is tilted forward away from the body, you must tighten the tremolo springs' tension by turning the spring claw screws clockwise and repeat step 4. If the base plate is tilted back toward the body, you must loosen the tremolo springs' tension by turning the spring claw screws counter-clockwise and repeat step 4.

Step 7: When the bridge is sitting parallel to the face of the guitar, and the strings are tuned to the desired pitch, re-clamp the three nut clamps and re-tune (if necessary) once again using only the fine tuners.

Step 8: When tuning is complete, any changes in action will slightly change the tuning. If the fine tuners run out of range, you must repeat steps 1 through 7.

Acoustic Guitars

Restringing an acoustic guitar has some distinct differences to electrics, so let's discuss the other end of the string now: the ball end. When installing the ball end, be sure that it is wedged up against the bridge plate on the inside of the guitar.

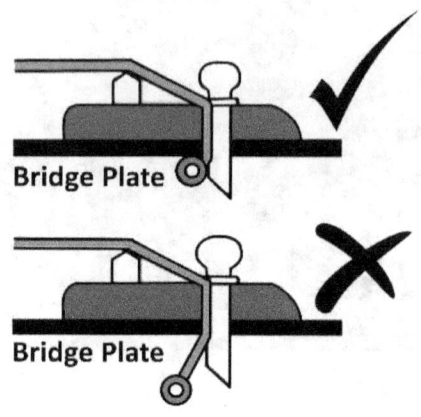

The bridge pin's job is to push the ball end to the underside of the guitar when under tension. It is a misconception that the pin itself holds the string down. If you ever notice a pin on the guitar popping up regularly, the string may not be installed correctly. It could also be due to a damaged or worn-out bridge plate, which coincidentally happens over time when strings are not installed correctly.

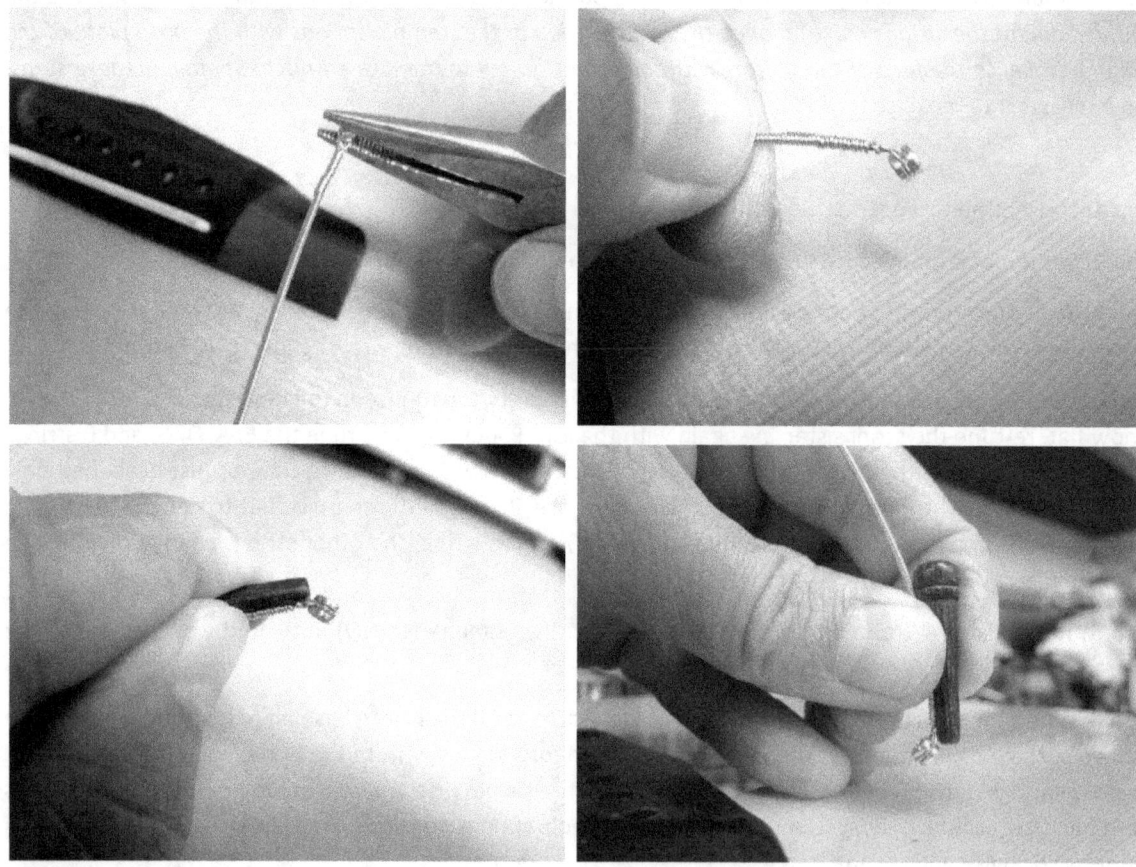

PRO TIP: Before installing the string, bend the ball end forward slightly. This will assist the string in seating properly under the bridge plate.

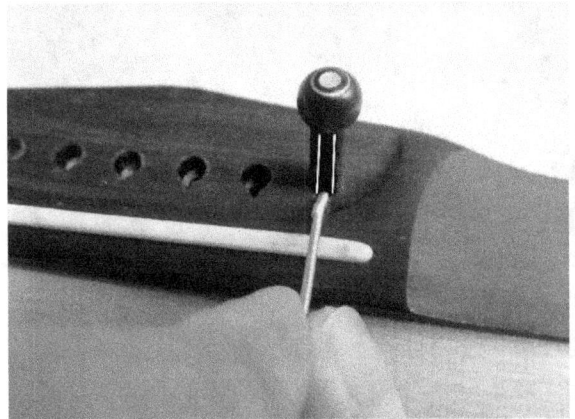 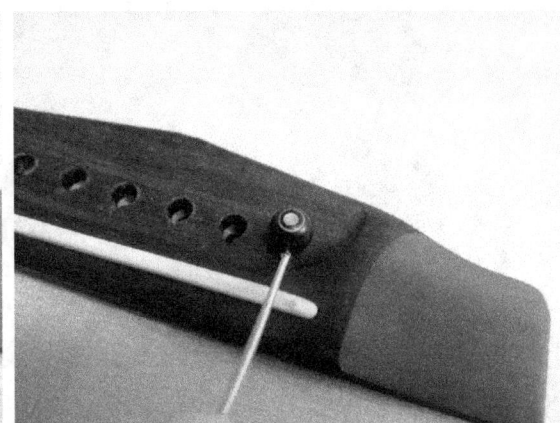

Install the string, so the groove of the bridge pin is pointed towards the neck.

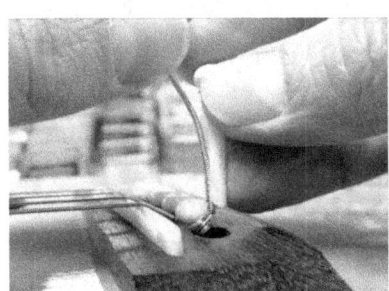  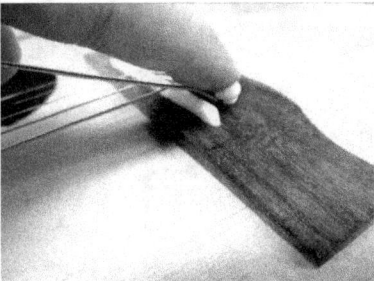

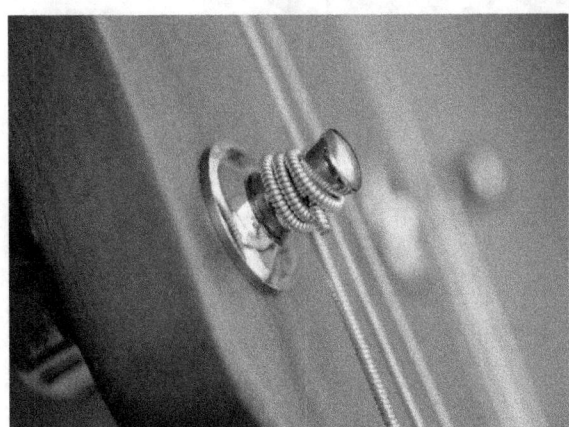

Hold the pin and gently pull on the string until you feel the ball catch under the bridge. Feed the string through the tuner post and tune the string to pitch as described previously.

Nylon String Guitars

On classical guitars, the restringing process is entirely different from previously mentioned. I will demonstrate a useful tie and lock method that can be used on these kinds of guitars.

Pull the end of the string through the hole in the bridge then loop it back towards the neck. Bring it *under* and then back around, and feed it into the loop just created.

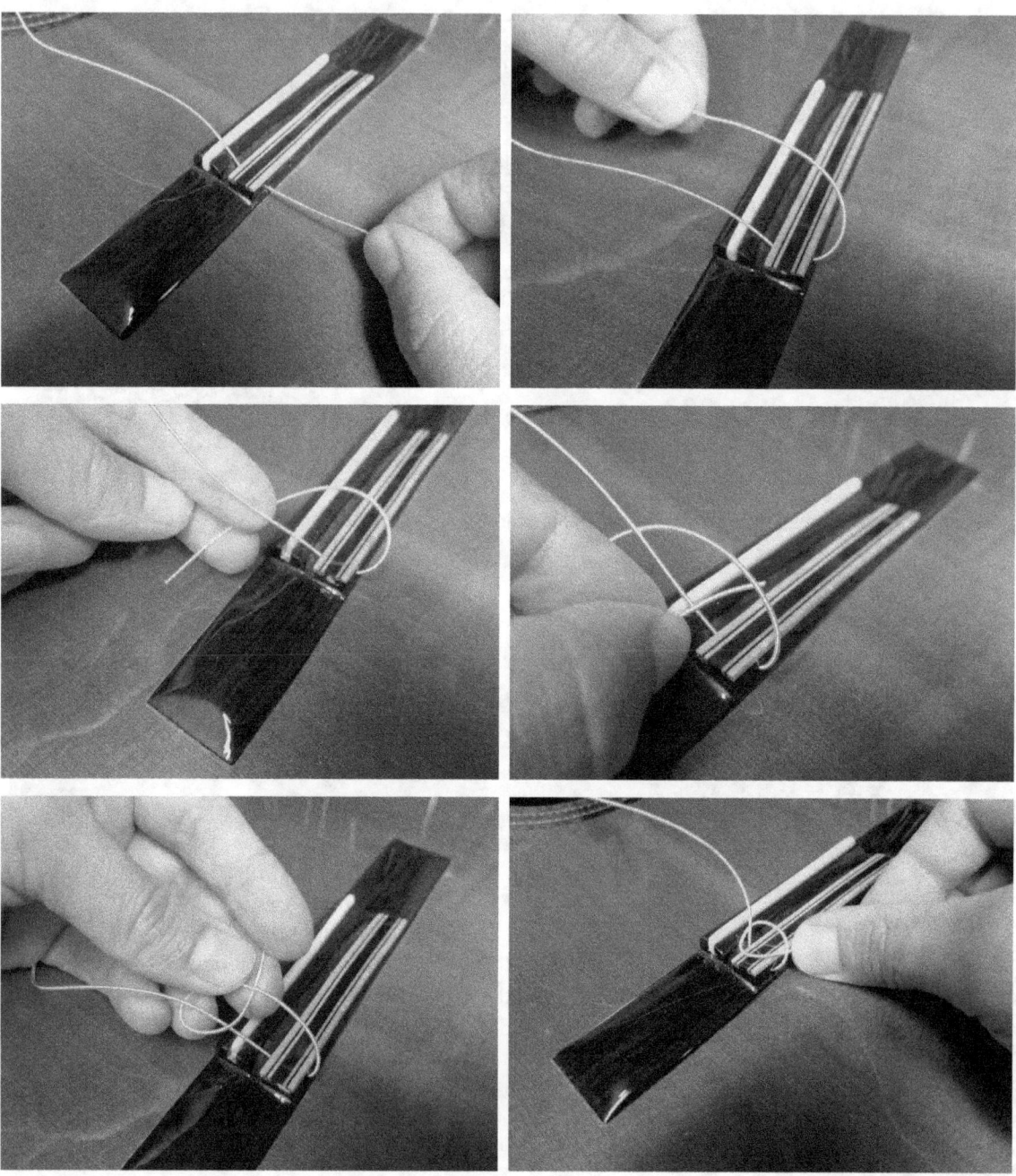

Hold the loop at the very back edge of the bridge with one hand. With the other hand, pull the opposite end of the string so that the loop tightens into a knot.

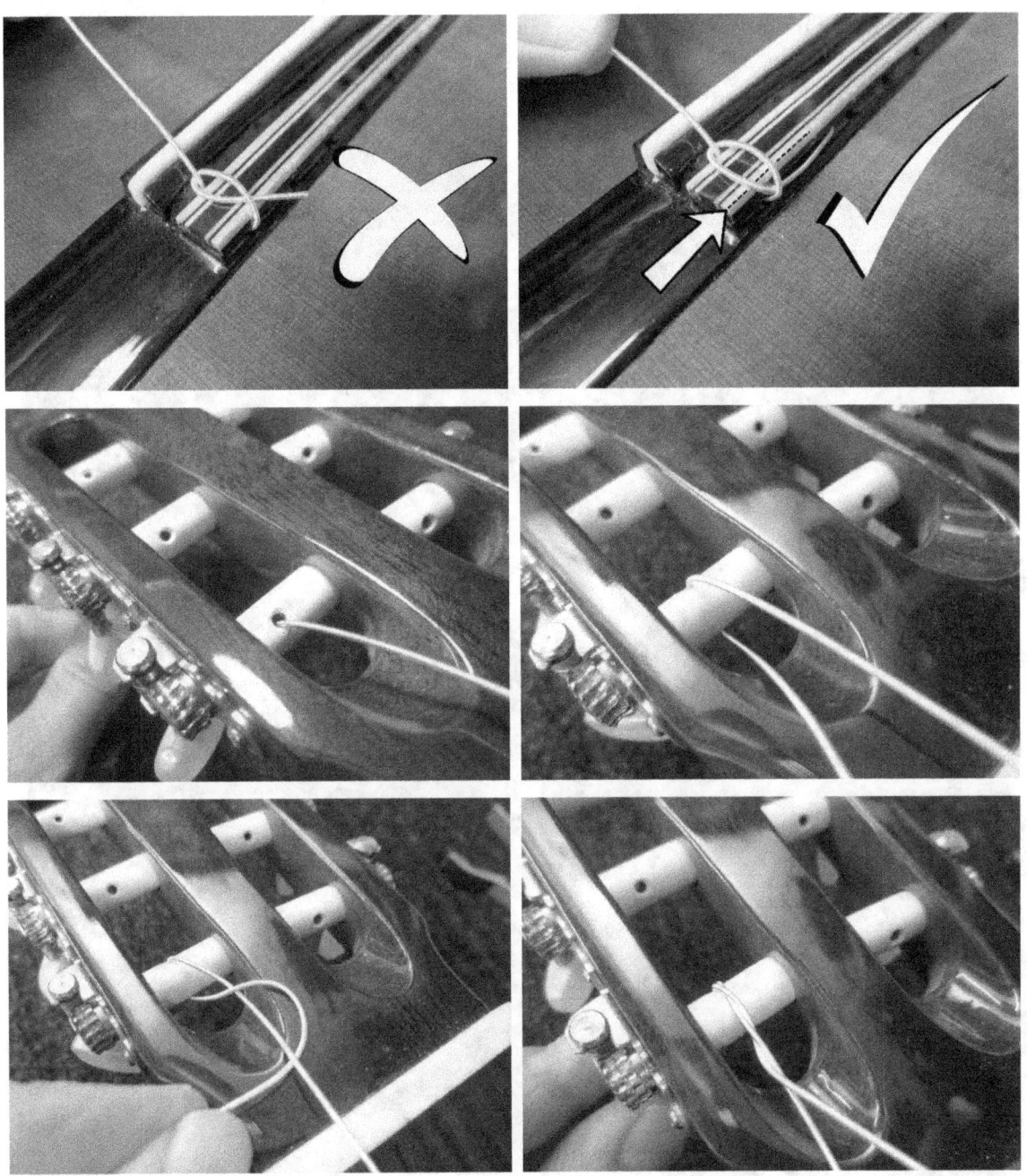

To keep the string from slipping, the knot must tighten at the back edge of the bridge. If it slips out of place during the process, you can reposition it and try again. Once it is tied, you will need to keep constant tension on the knot so that it does not loosen off.

Now feed the other end of the string into the tuning post. You can create another knot here to avoid excessive string windings and to bring it to pitch quickly.

Bring the string back towards the nut and loop it around itself once. Pull the string and the looped end, away from the string post to keep some back-tension on it. The knot will become tied as soon as you start winding it up.

Tune it up to pitch like this, keeping firm back-pressure on the string. For the treble strings, the process is similar, although you will loop not once, but twice both at the bridge and string post. The additional loop will help ensure the string does not slip or become untied.

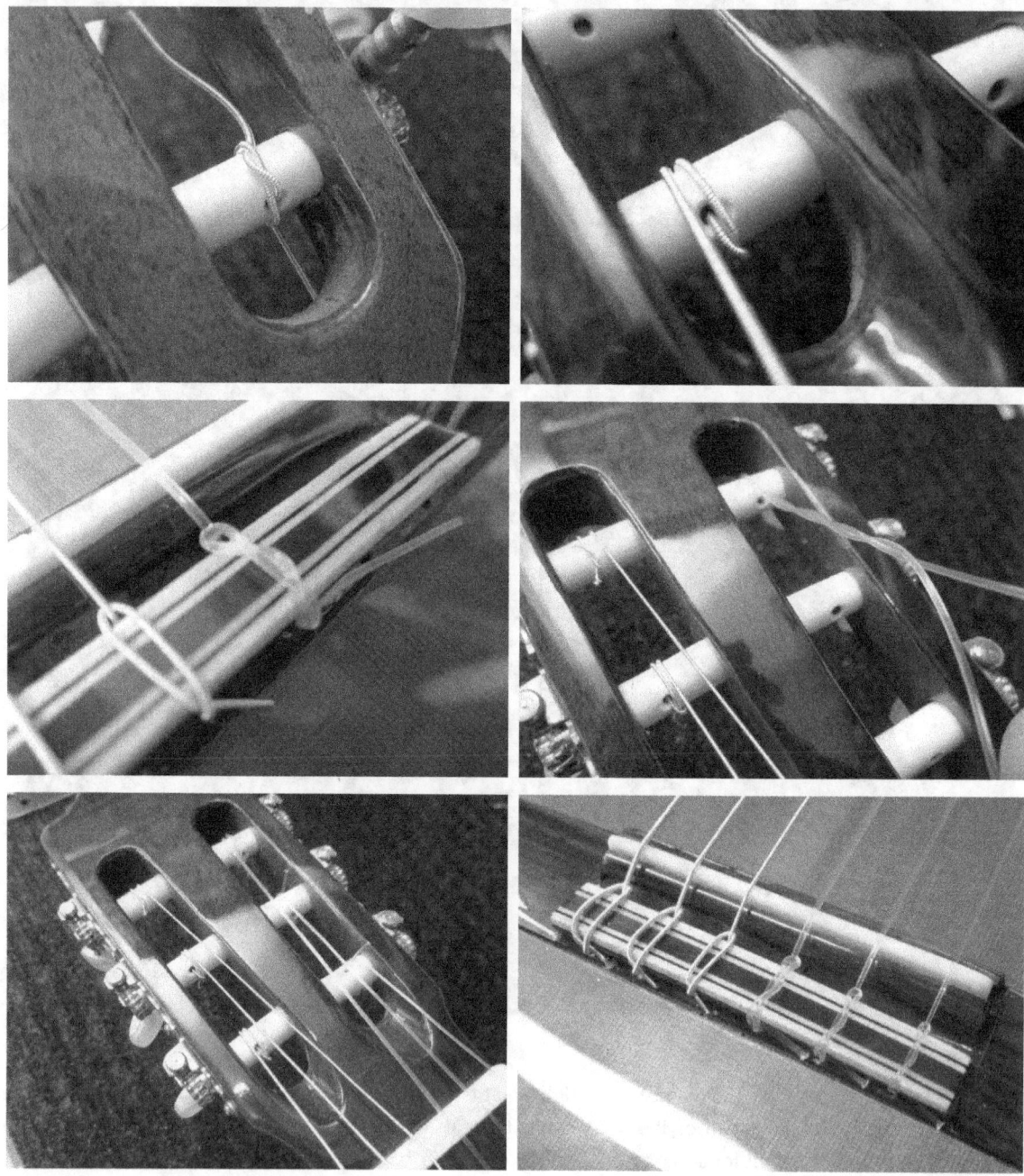

Tuning Tips

Stretch the Strings

Stretch the strings thoroughly after restringing. All new strings, no matter the quality, require stretching and seating for optimum tuning stability. Stretching will pull out any gaps between the saddle and the tuning peg winding to ensure the string is stable and holds tension.

Tune and stretch them until they stop losing pitch. Grab the string and pull up on it slightly with your fingers while pushing down with your thumb using moderate pressure. Run your hand up and down the string a few times while doing this. Retune after stretching the entire length. Once the pitch remains stable, move on to the next string. Be careful not to pull too hard, or you may break one (especially the #1 string)!

Lubricate the Nut Slots

The nut on the guitar can be a source of tuning problems and is often overlooked. A string can bind and become stuck in the slot, causing the tuning to jump around wildly, which is very frustrating.

If you have ever tuned a guitar and heard a distinct 'pinging' sound, you have heard the sound of a string binding within the nut slot. Tremolo equipped guitars are especially at risk. Besides taking a trip down to your local guitar tech, how can you remedy this problem?

After restringing, add some Vaseline or graphite in each nut slot. You can also find products specifically for this at your local music store, such as Big Bends Nut Sauce. Another option is to use some pencil lead- it works great! Lubricating the nut slots will minimize any string binding at the nut and provide all-around better performance.

Tune "Up" to The Note
Always tune *"up"* to the desired pitch. A string is prone to slipping out of tune if not held under tension. Start below the desired note and tune up to the pitch- never down. For example, if you are tuning the low 'E' of the guitar down to a 'D', detune it slightly below the 'D' note, and then back up to the target note. Doing so will help prevent the string from slipping and going flat during play.

Break the Strings In
Guitar strings stretch and shrink as the temperature changes. It is one reason you may need to retune after playing for several minutes. As the strings warm up and expand, the pitch changes.

Guitar String Gauges

There are several different gauges, or sizes, of guitar strings available. The term is referring to the diameter of the string.

There are standard gauges in several sizes, such as light, medium, and heavy. Each, when properly tuned, will exert a different tension on the guitar's neck. Different sizes will affect playability, feel, and tone. For those just starting, light strings are generally recommended. The lighter the strings, the easier they are to play, and the heavier, the more difficult. You can always purchase the same sized-set that came on your guitar. If you are unsure of which sizes are standard, hang on to those old strings and bring them into the guitar store with you. Their guitar tech can measure the string sizes so you can be sure they are the same.

How Strings Affect Your Tone & Playing

There must be some reason why some people would use heavy strings, even though they are not as easy to play on. It comes down to the tone and volume they produce. The heavier the string, the more volume it produces, which can also equate to thicker-sounding tones. For some, this is worth moving up a string gauge or two. Heavier strings have less "give"- meaning, they have more tension then lighter strings. They don't move as much when played on, and they respond much differently to lighter strings. If you have ever picked up an acoustic guitar right after playing an electric, or vice versa, you will know what I mean.

On the other end of the spectrum, a thinner string will produce less volume, which may also equate to less bass and more treble. Lighter strings move more and may be prone to string rattling as a result.

DIFFERENT KINDS OF STRINGS

Electric Guitar

Most of the major guitar string manufacturers offer a range of strings, each with their own tonal and feel characteristics.

The typical electric guitar string will be nickel wound, which is accepted as the standard and offers a balanced sound and feel. With many guitar players seeking other options when it comes to tone, feel and durability, companies have begun offering alternatives.

Ernie Ball, for instance, offers a diverse selection of string types including:

- Paradigm – Superior break-resistance and unparalleled durability
- Cobalt – Increased clarity and higher output
- M-Steel – Extra low end, ultra-high output
- Classic Pure Nickel – Vintage, warmer tone
- RPS Coated Titanium – Brighter tone, longer life
- Stainless Steel – Brighter tone, classic feel

Whichever brand of strings you choose, you will be presented with a similar range of options. Different string materials and coatings will offer a range of performance and durability options.

Acoustic Guitar

Acoustic guitar strings, much like their electric counterparts, come with a range of coatings and types offering a range of tonal and durability options. Typically, acoustic strings come in 2 alloys:

- Phosphor Bronze – Warm and well-rounded
- 80/20 Bronze – Brighter overall tone

Phosphor Bronze strings are made from Bronze with phosphor added to the alloy. These strings have a warmer overall sound and typically are longer lasting than the 80/20 strings. 80/20 Bronze strings are made from an alloy made from 80% copper and 20% zinc.

Classical Guitars

Classical and Spanish style guitars are generally strung with nylon, fluorocarbon, or some other synthetic string. The bass strings may have a threaded or solid core which is covered with windings of various metals and nylon. There are still some classical guitar strings on the market made of traditional gut and silk materials as well, such as the Pyramid Gut and Gut/Nylon.

The sound of classical guitar strings varies extensively, depending upon the materials used and the manufacturing techniques involved. In general nylon-based strings offer a warmer sonic colour and more sustain, while the fluorocarbon-based strings generally provide a brighter sonic colour and offer a more powerfully projecting sound with less sustain.

Nylon strings greatly differ to steel strings by both sound and feel. They also have much less tension than a standard steel set, which is why many Classical guitars will not have a truss rod in the neck **(read more**

about this in Guitar Setups/ How to Adjust the Truss Rod). Because of this, never put a set of steel strings on a guitar built for nylon. It will do irreversible damage to the neck, soundboard, and bridge.

Differences in Gauges & Tuning

The string gauge is the measured thickness of each string. The numbers you see on the string packet refers to the thickness of each string as measured in thousandths of an inch (.001").

Many people refer to the size of a set by the 1st or thinnest string. For example, a .009-.042" set of strings would be called 9's. A .010-.046", would be called 10's, and so on.

Fender guitars come with a standard string gauge of .009-.042", while most Gibson's come with .010-.046". Many players gravitate towards a 9-gauge or a 10-gauge set with 10's being popular as finger strength increases. 10's would be categorized as "regular" or "medium" and are very well balanced in both tension and tone on many instruments.

If you play "down-tuned" music, using a thicker gauge string will provide better tone and sustain, as it will compensate for the loss of tension that comes from detuning. For example, a set of 11's or 12's on the electric guitar may be a suitable gauge, depending on the chosen tuning and guitar type.

Acoustic guitars generally use heavier strings. A set of 11s is considered extra-light on an acoustic, whereas a set of 12s is considered standard. Lighter and heavier strings are available to match whatever needs you may have.

Nylon strings are generally offered in different tensions, as opposed to gauges.

Tunings – Standard & Alternate

There is a wide range of tunings for the guitar, all with different sounds and purposes. Standard tuning is widely accepted as the norm and is what would be considered the most common.

Standard Tuning: E A D G B E (low to high)

Standard tuning is also referred to as A440 tuning because the "A" note is tuned to the frequency of 440Hz.

Changing the tuning can change the sound of the guitar. You can manipulate a standard tuning in to a range of other tunings. Here is a list of some alternate tunings and a few examples of songs that use them:

- Drop D (D A D G B E) – *Heart Shaped Box (Nirvana), Killing in The Name Of (Rage Against the Machine), Rocky Mountain High (John Denver), Ten Years Gone (Led Zeppelin)*
- Drop C (C G C F A D) – *Isolation (Alter Bridge), Tears Don't Fall (Bullet for my Valentine), Animal I Have Become (Three Days Grace)*
- Half Step Down (Eb Ab Db Gb Bb Eb) – *Sweet Child O' Mine (Guns N' Roses), Voodoo Child (Jimi Hendrix), You Really Got Me (Van Halen)*
- Full Step Down (D G C F A D) – *Come as You Are (Nirvana), Kickstart my Heart (Motley Crue), Sad But True (Metallica)*

You may also have heard of a group of tunings called "Open Tunings." An open tuning consists of each string being tuned to a note of a specific chord.

- Open G (D G D G B D) – *Honky Tonk Women (Rolling Stones), Fearless (Pink Floyd), Dancing Days (Led Zeppelin), Bad to the Bone (George Thorogood), Jealous Again (The Black Crowes)*

- Open D (D A D F# A D) – *Place to Be (Nick Drake), The Cave (Mumford and Sons), Little Martha (Allman Brothers)*
- DADGAD – *Kashmir (Led Zeppelin), Photograph-Live (Ed Sheeran), Tell Her This (Del Amitri)*
- Open E (E B E G# B E) – *Big Yellow Taxi (Joni Mitchell), She Talks to Angels (The Black Crowes), Jumpin' Jack Flash (Rolling Stones)*
- Open C (C G C G C E) – *Friends (Led Zeppelin), Townsend Shuffle (William Ackerman)*
- Open A (E A E A C# E) – *Seven Nation Army (The White Stripes), In My Time of Dying (Led Zeppelin)*

Conclusion

One of the coolest things about the guitar is how unique it can become. Simply changing the tuning can transform its sonic personality, inspiring new ideas and collaborations. Experiment with some of these tunings today and discover some new sounds!

CLEANING

One of the easiest things you can do to prolong the life of your guitar is to simply clean it. Over time, sweat, dirt and your skin's natural oils tend to build-up on the various parts of the guitar. The areas impacted the most are the strings, fretboard, and the finish.

The build-up of all that dirt and grime can eventually corrode and damage the hardware as well as tarnish the finish on your instrument. Metal components such as saddles and bridges on electric guitars can rust and seize, whereas grime buildup on frets and the fretboard itself can impede playability and deteriorate the playing surface.

Regularly cleaning your guitar will keep it in its best condition for years of enjoyment.

What You'll Need:
- A lint-free polish cloth
- Guitar polish/cleaner
- Lemon oil (for rosewood or ebony fretboards)
- String cleaner (optional)

The best time to clean your guitar is when you're changing the strings. This way, you have unrestricted access to the instrument, including the bridge and the fretboard. In most cases, a damp cloth and a bit of elbow grease are all it takes to remove dirt or grime from your instrument.

Tips for Cleaning Your Guitar:

1. Wipe the strings, neck and bridge often with a lint-free cloth.
2. Wipe metal parts clean with a soft, dry polishing cloth.
3. Clean the body of the instrument with cleaning products made specifically for guitars (available at most guitar stores).
4. Do not use anything other than products designed for guitars. Do not use glass cleaner (or anything with ammonia in it), household cleaners, or products containing abrasives, silicon, or waxes.
5. Do not expose lacquered finishes to plastics, synthetics or surgical rubber tubings such as that used on many guitar stands and straps. All of these react adversely with lacquer, and can literally melt the finish off your guitar if left for too long.

Tips on Keeping Your Guitar Clean
- Wash your hands before you play – it's a simple and effective way of reducing grime on your guitar and getting the most life out of a set of strings.
- Wipe your guitar down with a cloth after use.
- Store your guitar in its case after use.

TIP: Before you start cleaning, consider what type of finish is on your guitar. Certain cleaning materials may have adverse effects on specific finish types. Always check the label before using and do not use household cleaners or waxes, as they may contain additives that can impregnate and wreck the finish on your guitar.

Guitar Polish

When reaching for a guitar polish, get one specifically for your brand, or one that is safe for all finish types. For example, Gibson Guitars makes a great polish for Nitrocellulose Lacquer, which would cover their product line, but may not be as suitable for other finishes. Whereas Planet Waves/ D'Addario makes a cleaner/polish suitable for all modern finish types. If in doubt, check the label! Or keep it safe and use no product at all- try a _very_ slightly damp cloth to clean the dirt and grime away.

> NOTE: if you have an old or vintage guitar with a fragile, aged, cracked finish, play it safe and don't use a guitar polish on it. The polish can seep through the cracks, and impregnate the wood, and otherwise make a bigger mess of that old mess of a finish. Play it safe on old guitars.

Cleaning the Body

Pictured below is a small selection of popular brand name polishes and cleaners available. Stop by your local music store and pick some up. Use a lint-free cloth designed for guitar polishing or an old cotton t-shirt. You may also find some ultra-soft microfiber cloths that work really well.

Spray a small amount of cleaner/polish onto the cloth and wipe the guitar in a circular pattern. Wipe around the pickups, bridge and controls. Most of these cleaners are also safe to use on the backside of the guitar neck, as well as the hardware, but read the label to be sure. If your guitar has a satin finish, find a cleaner specifically for that finish type. If you prefer not to use a commercial product, as previously mentioned, a slightly damp cloth will do the trick.

Another alternative is to use lighter fluid (naphtha) as an effective way to remove grease and fingerprints. It evaporates quickly and is safe to apply to most finishes. Again, steer clear of household or automotive polishes as they may have waxes or silicone in them, which may impregnate and ultimately wreck the finish of your guitar.

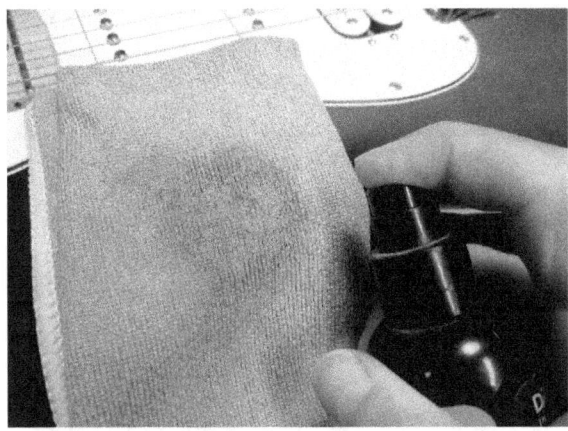 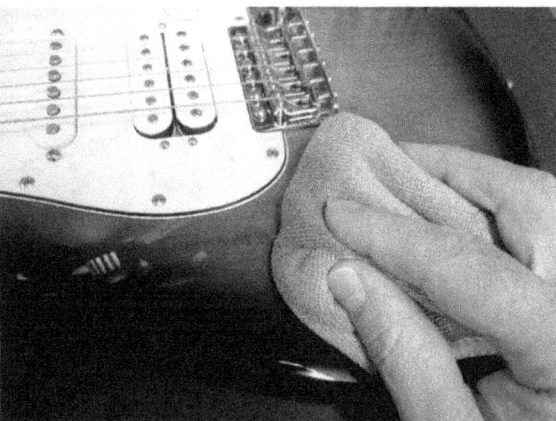

Cleaning the Fretboard

There are plenty of cleaning products available on the market, and as such, multiple methods to clean the fretboard. Some people will use a mild wood cleaner, others may use a lemon or mineral oil, and some may use a specially formulated guitar cleaning product from their local music store. I prefer to steer away from cleaners or excess oil on fretboards, as I find they are rarely needed- although not to say they don't have their place at times.

The safest methods to clean the instrument do not include any cleaners or detergents. Using a slightly damp cloth with a little elbow grease works quite well, not only on the fretboard but also on the body of the instrument. Glossy finishes buff up exceptionally well by simply huffing a little breathe over the finish and buffing it out with a dry cloth.

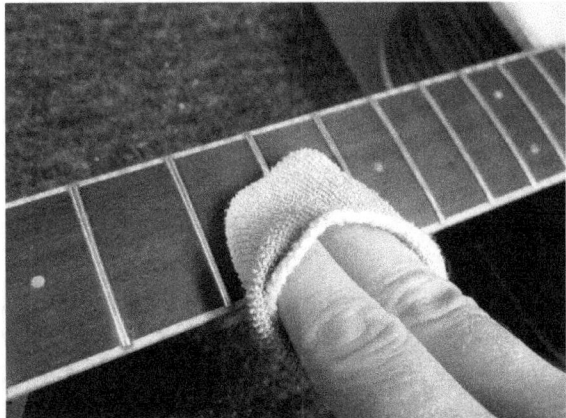 

If the fretboard on the guitar has grime and dirt accumulating on it, you can use <u>ultrafine</u>-grade steel wool (#0000) to remove the buildup safely. Using the steel wool will also give your fretboard and frets a nice polished look. Always go with the grain, which is most often length-wise with the neck. Be careful not to scratch large fretboard inlays in the process (lighten up the amount of pressure used around these sensitive areas). Some people will use a scraper to clean off the gunk buildup, then follow up with the steel wool, and that works too. Steel wool is messy, so tape off the guitar to protect it from debris and scratching. The pickups, being magnetic, will attract all the loose steel wool fibres, so tape them off well. Also, for safety sake, wear a particulate mask and eye protection as the small steel fibres can get everywhere. Before removing the tape, lightly brush away the remnants with a rag or soft-bristle paintbrush.

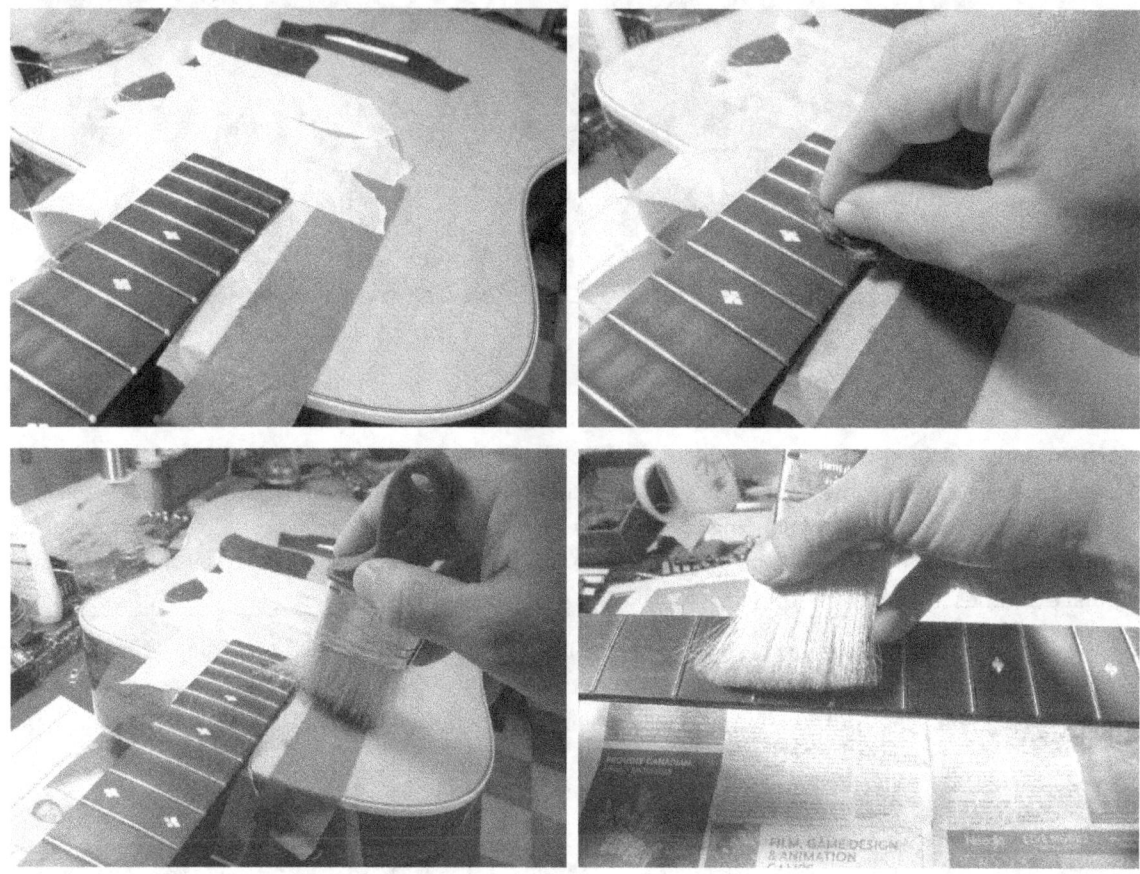

The best way to keep your fretboard in good shape is to clean your strings after playing with a cotton cloth or old t-shirt. Doing so will also give your frets (and strings) a much longer lifespan.

Oil the Fretboard (if applicable)

If the guitar has a rosewood fretboard, and it looks dry, you can apply a fretboard oil to bring it back to its lustre. I say "fretboard oil" to steer you in the right direction, which is to the guitar brand names you know and trust. The truth is, there are a lot of products that will do the job, but those made by Planet Waves, Dunlop, or Fender, for example, are sure to be safe for use on your guitar. Oiling the fretboard doesn't need to be done often- in fact, some people overdo it. It truly depends on the environment you live in (humidity levels) and how often the guitar is played. So, my rule of thumb is- if it looks dry, oil it. If it doesn't, don't. Keep in mind that maple fretboards do not require oil. Ebony, on the other hand, may benefit from it periodically, but it is a tight-grained wood and penetration can be minimal. Look for products that are for all wood types to be the most effective.

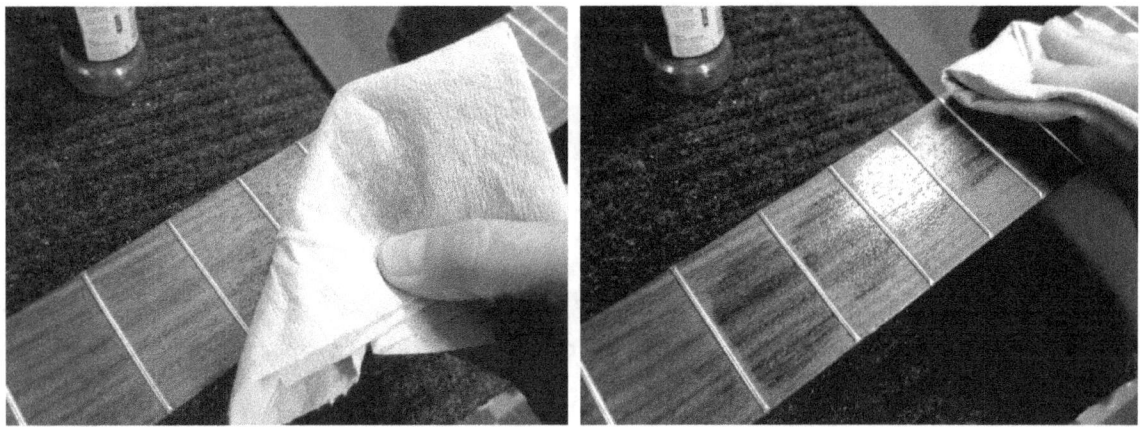

Apply a <u>small</u> amount of oil to a lint-free cloth or old cotton t-shirt and wipe it evenly across the fretboard so that there are no areas missed.

You'll notice a little goes a long way. You can allow the oil a few minutes to penetrate the fretboard if it is severely dry. I wouldn't dowse the fretboard by any means- use a small amount and reapply if needed.

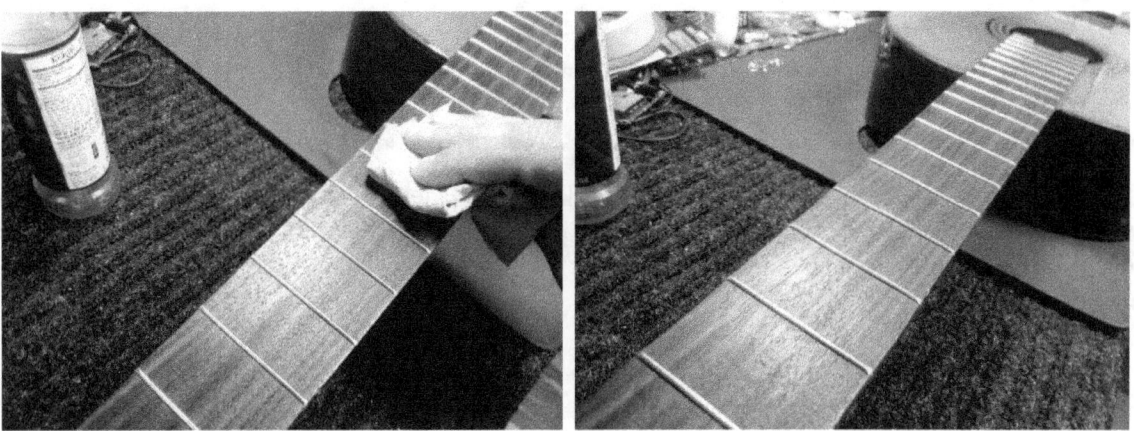

Once applied, take a different cloth (or a dry portion of the oil cloth) and wipe off the excess oil until it is dry to the touch.

Remember that this should not be done too often and only when it appears to be dry. The oils on your fingers will also transfer to the fretboard while playing, so this is not a critical step.

Cleaning the Neck

GLOSS - Fretboards and necks can come in a range of materials and finishes. For certain guitars, the neck may be finished in the same style and finish as the body, in which case you can apply the same cleaning techniques to the neck.

SATIN - Most necks are finished in either a satin or gloss finish. A slightly damp cloth will clean either of these finishes, as would a suitable guitar cleaner. Be sure the cleaner is formulated for satin finishes, or it may turn the finish glossy.

UNFINISHED/ RAW - Unfinished necks, although not as common, are best cleaned with a dry or just slightly damp cloth- being mindful that any moisture from the cloth can be potentially transferred into the wood grain (not recommended) and this can cause the wood to swell. Besides a dry cloth, you can use Naphtha as a cleaner if needed or #0000 ultra-fine steel wool. Ultra-fine steel wool is gentle enough to use on bare wood and abrasive enough to remove dirt and grime buildup.

Cleaning the Strings

Strings often sound their best in the earliest stages of their life. This is when they have the most volume, sustain and the best tone. When strings start to wear, they lose sustain and often sound duller. Also, frets will wear prematurely if regularly played on with old rusty strings. Those old, oxidized, crusty strings act like files against the frets, eventually wearing them down until some notes no longer ring out or sustain.

Once the frets wear out, the only fix is to take the guitar into a professional technician or luthier and have the problem addressed with either a fret dressing or total refret (depending on the severity). A fret dressing is a process carried out when all of the frets are filed down equally (to the lowest wear point), rounded and polished. A refret is a larger job where all or some of the frets are removed, and new fretwire is installed. This is followed by a complete fret level, and then finally, they are all rounded and polished. Those fixes can really add up in the shop, sometimes costing much more than the guitar is worth. Moral of the story here, keep those strings clean!

String wear is caused by sweat and dirt accumulation from your hands after prolonged use. The thicker strings collect dirt between the windings and the thinner strings become prone to tarnishing and rusting. If the strings are corroded (determined by their dark, rusty colour), it's time to change them.

It is easiest to clean the strings directly after playing. All it takes is a few wipes with a cloth to remove excess sweat and dirt. I prefer to clean each string separately by pinching the string with the cloth in one hand and running up and down the length of the fretboard. This way, I am cleaning the entire string and not just the tops.

There are also products available which can help in cleaning your strings.

Planet Waves XLR8 lubricates and cleans your strings for faster playing and longer life. It removes friction for faster playing as well as finger noise.

GHS Fast Fret cleans and lubes strings and fretboards. Fast Fret™ has been a favourite of working guitarists since its introduction back in the 1970s. Glides on, wipes off, with no silicones to interfere with future refinishing.

Natural Oils - Another more natural option is to use some coconut oil from the cupboard, which is an effective natural cleaner (and one I use regularly). It keeps the strings and fretboard ultra-fast without having any petroleum-based products on your guitar or hands. It is also water-soluble, making clean-up a breeze.

Cleaning the Hardware

The metal hardware on the guitar is prone to tarnishing. Sweat and dirt can eventually oxidize and corrode the metal hardware if not cleaned regularly. Corrosion is most commonly seen on the guitar bridge and pickups where your hand has most contact.

You can use a dry or slightly damp cloth to clean these areas whenever changing strings. Most guitar hardware brands can withstand a light rub with guitar cleaner or naphtha if needed.

One of the more difficult places to clean is between the bridge saddles. You can use an old toothbrush to get into those hard to reach places to remove any stubborn dust and grime. Alternatively, you can spray some cleaner into the bridge, give it a scrub and blow it out with compressed air.

If the hardware on your guitar already shows signs of heavy corrosion and rust, you can either replace the parts or use a product like WD-40 (A penetrating oil and water displacement spray) to help clean and remove the rust from the hardware.

Repairing Scratches

Most surface scratches can be removed with a little polish. Polish is an abrasive product that helps to eliminate surface scratches, swirls, oxidation, dirt, and other minor imperfections. The keyword is *abrasive*, not unlike sandpaper- just a whole lot finer. Never use polishes on sensitive finishes.

There are all sorts of polishes available in the marketplace designed specifically for guitar finishes. Some autobody polishes can also be used, although be sure it is safe with the finish on your guitar and not overly aggressive. In autobody supply, they are often sold in abrasive grades or strengths.

CAUTION: A potent polish, if used excessively, can wear right through a guitar finish. Always use a small amount - a little goes a long way.

Put a small amount on the scratched area and apply it in a circular pattern. Some polishes will work right into the finish, leaving a gloss when done. Others may leave a dull haze, which will require buffing out with a second cloth- these are generally heavier polishes for deep scratches.

GENERAL HARDWARE ADJUSTMENTS

With the strings off the guitar, check for loose hardware. You'll often find the hardware coming loose at the tuners, strap buttons, output jack, neck bolts, pickguard mounting hardware screws, etc. Check to see if any screws or nuts can be tightened. Also, check to see that all the controls and switches are firmly tightened. If a volume control is loose, you may need to remove the knob to tighten it. For this step, you'll need a screwdriver, along with a wrench, crescent wrench, or nut driver.

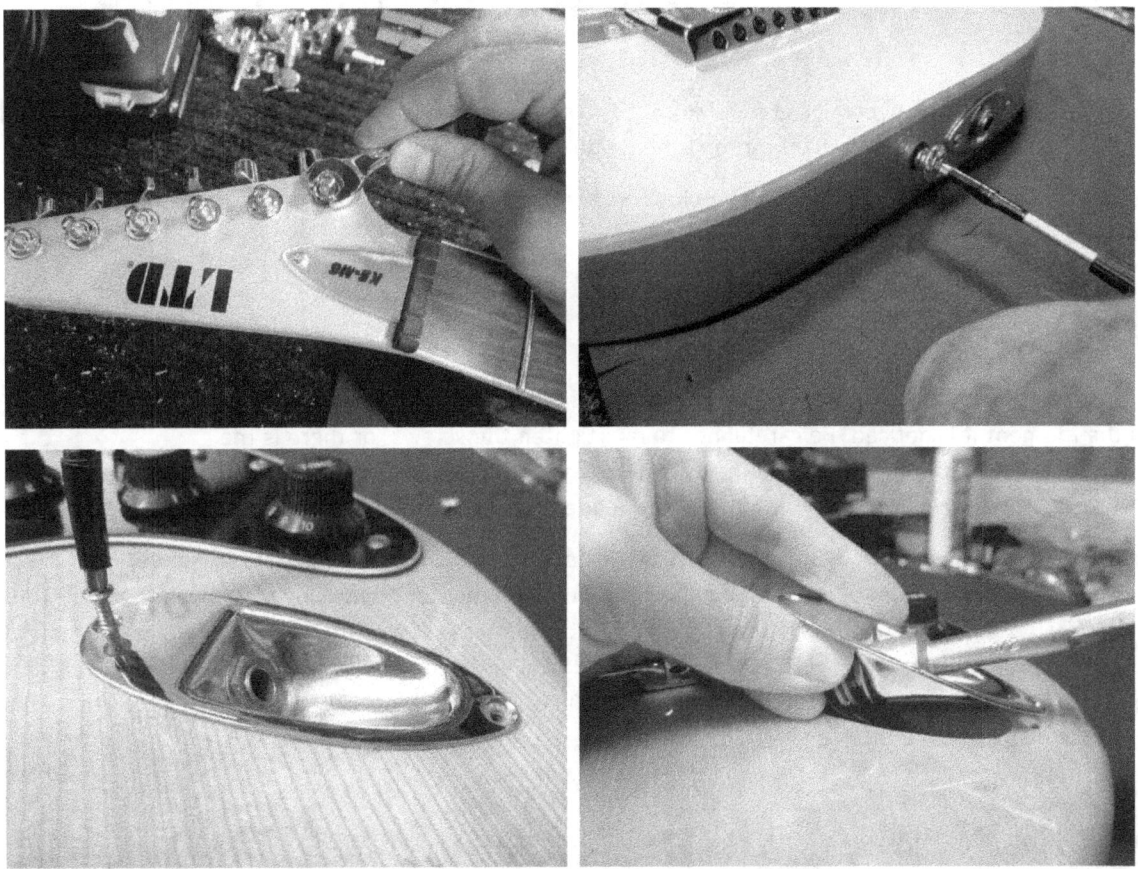

If the output jack is really loose, you may need to remove the jack plate in order to tighten it. If it is spinning freely, there is a good chance the wiring will become loose or severed.

Don't forget to tighten overly loose tuner knobs. The set screw holds the knob as well as sets the tension, so it doesn't need to be really tight (or the tuner knob will be too stiff to turn freely).

Guitars with locking nuts should also be checked for loose nut bolts either under the clamps or at the backside of the neck. If they become loose, the strings will go out of tune while playing.

How to Fix Loose Strap Buttons

Strap buttons can become loose with normal use. It is always best to tighten them back up the moment it is noticed. Be careful not to overtighten the screws, or there is the potential to strip the wood. When they are left loose, they only get worse, until eventually letting go completely, with the guitar headed straight to the floor.

If the wood becomes stripped, the strap buttons will no longer hold the guitar securely. Stripping can happen from overtightening the strap button screws or from using a strap while the buttons are overly loose. To remedy this, you can fill the strap button screw hole with wooden dowel or toothpicks. For extra durability, use wood glue as well. With the dowel inserted, lightly hammer the end until it is fully seated within the screw hole. Cut the end with an Xacto knife or simply break it off. Reinstall the strap button and screw it in until it butts up against the guitar body. Tighten until firm.

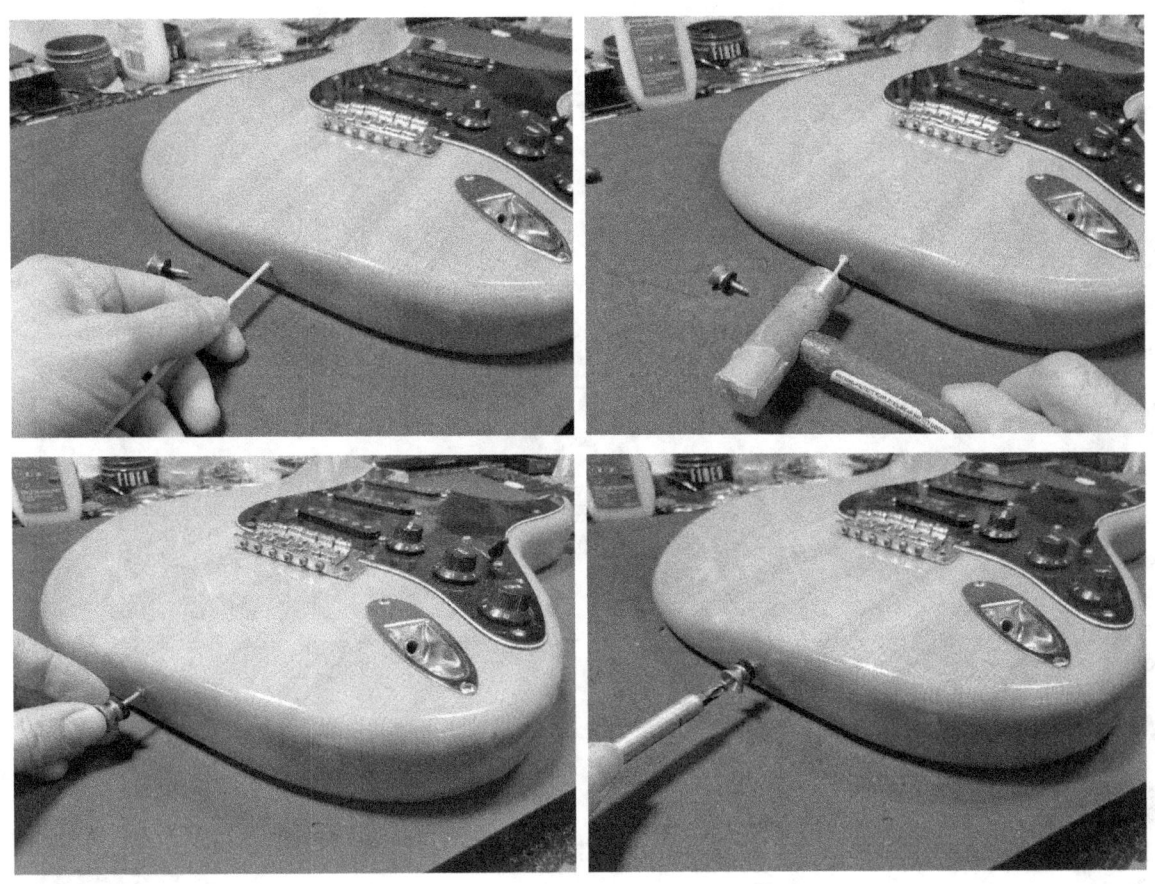

How to Remove the Control Knobs

Often, we can simply pop off the control knobs by grabbing and pulling upwards. Other times, the knobs are too tight, and we need to use a different method. On rare occasion, a person may have glued the knobs right onto the control pot shaft, making them impossible to remove (without destroying the potentiometer)

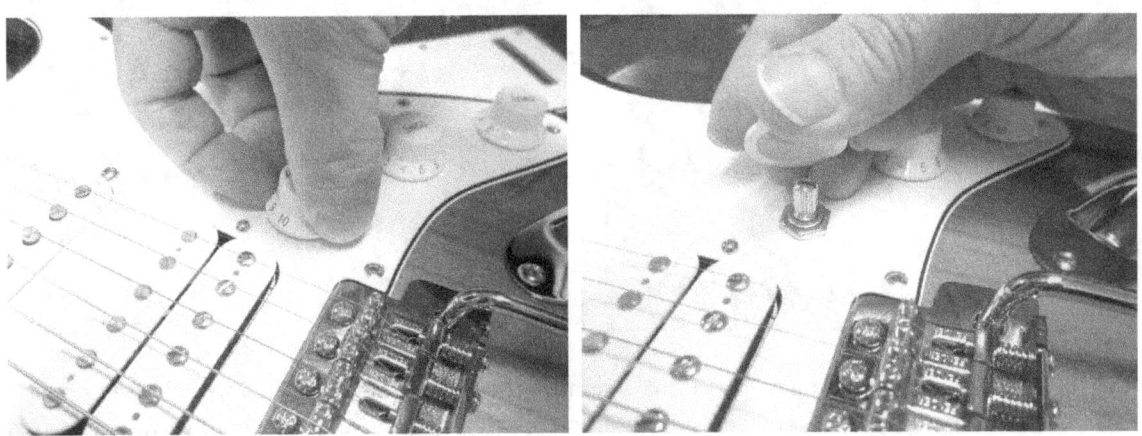

Using a Cloth as a Puller

Slide the edge of the cloth underneath the knob. With one end, wrap it around the base while holding the other end secure. Continue to twist the cloth until it is wrapped around the bottom of the knob.

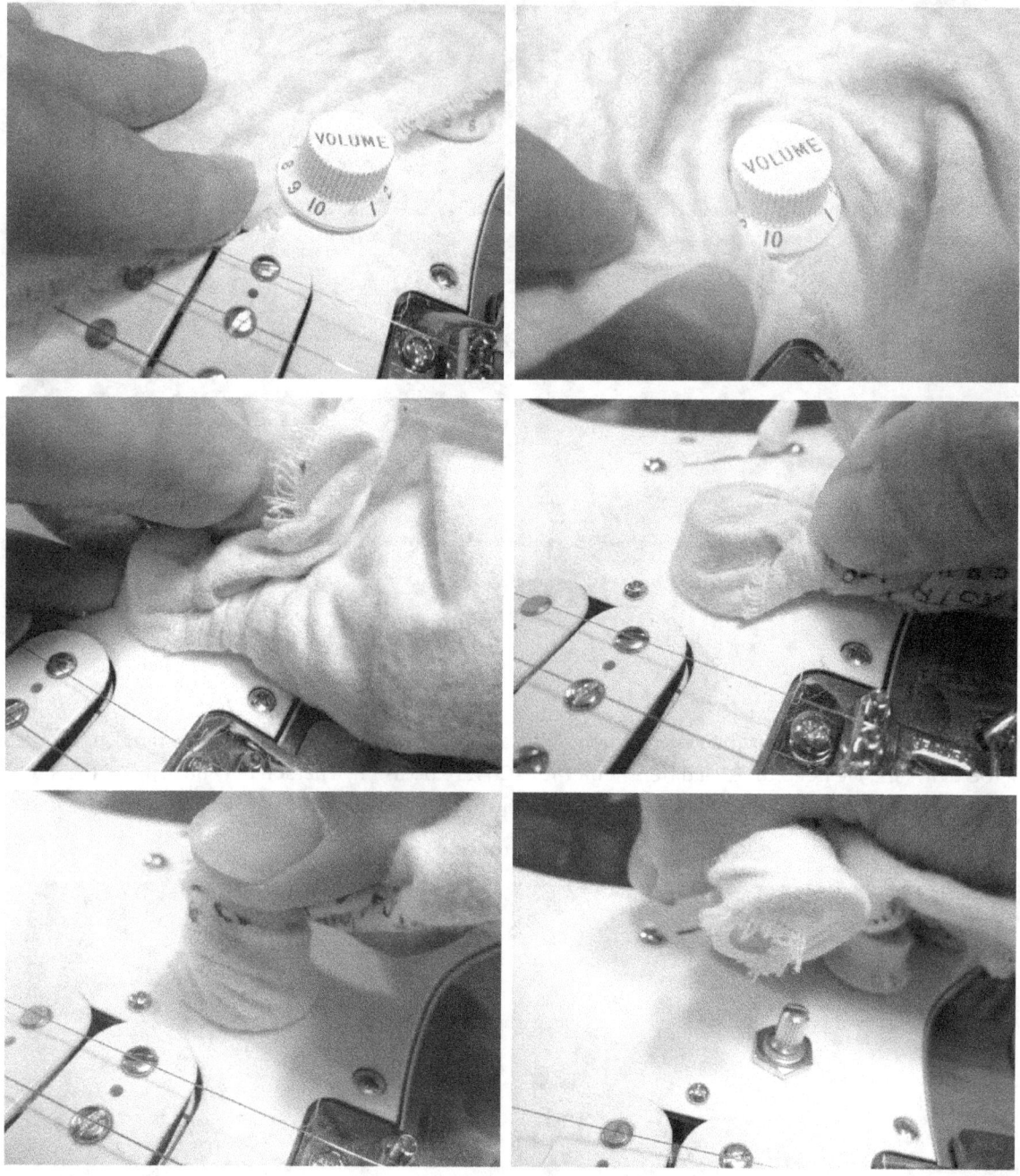

With gentle, slow pressure, pull up on the cloth, to remove the knob. Whatever you do, don't use excessive force- plastic knobs easily break and so do potentiometer shafts. If this doesn't seem to work, let's try another method.

Using a Tool

There's always the right tool for the job. My favourite go-to tool is the ESP multi-use guitar tool pictured below. I recommend not prying up on the knob with a screwdriver as it is almost a guarantee for a new scratch or ding on your guitar (if it doesn't break the knob in the process).

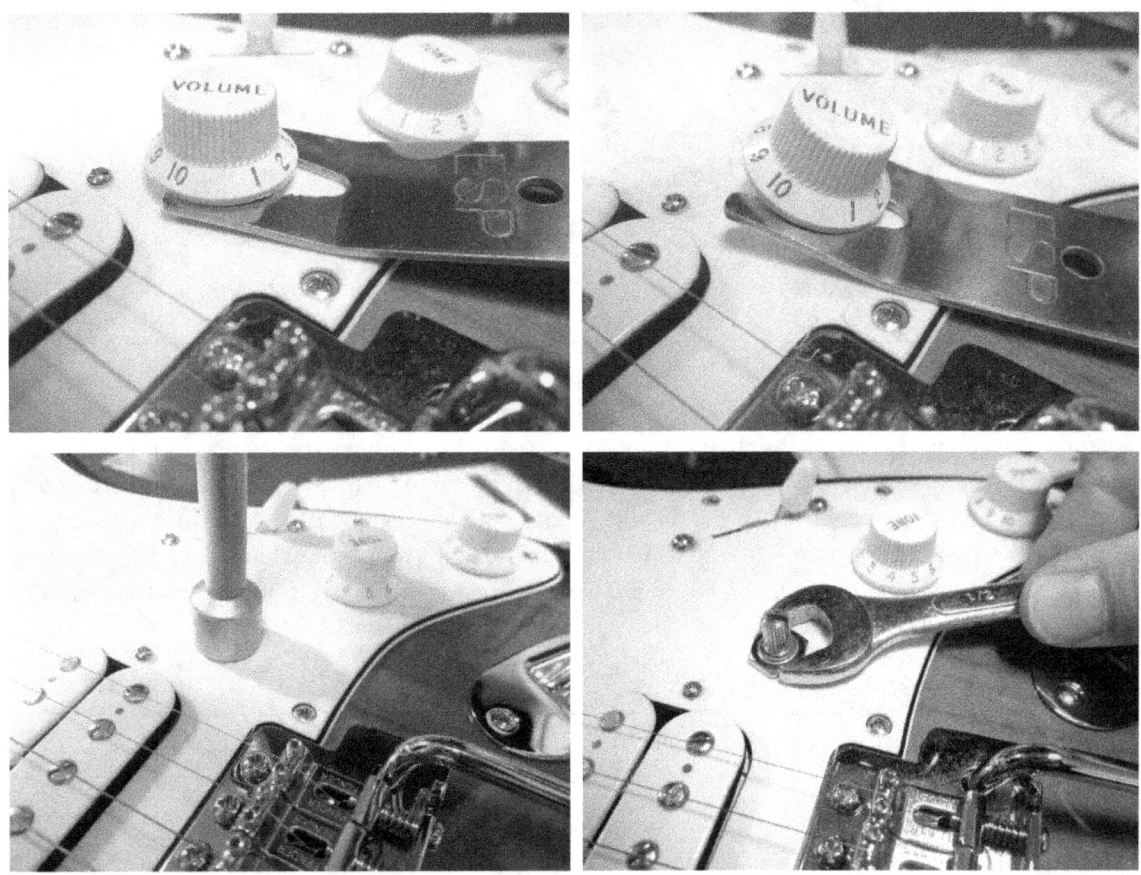

Once the knob is removed, use either a nut driver or wrench to tighten it up. Be careful not to over-do it- too much torque will destroy the potentiometer.

What is a Potentiometer? Often referred to as a volume or tone "pot", the potentiometer is a variable resistor in the guitars' circuit. As the shaft is turned from 0-10, the amount of resistance is altered within the circuit. When wired as a volume control, we hear the sound increase or decrease, depending on how we turn the shaft. A tone control works similarly. A potentiometer can be used to control a variety of functions inside an electric guitar. Besides functioning as standard tone and volume controls, they can also be wired up to blend pickups or attenuate (reduce the value of) one coil of a dual-coil pickup (humbucker), and much more.

How to Clean Dirty Potentiometers and Controls

The electronic controls on the guitar can become dusty or oxidized and can produce noise. If you have a scratchy sounding volume or tone control, take some contact cleaner (<u>with lubrication</u>) and spray the inside of the potentiometer while turning the shaft back and forth. You can use WD-40, Deoxit D5, or other similar products. It will often clear up the issue, but if after a few attempts it hasn't, a new pot may be necessary. If the pickup selector has become noisy, you can spray the contact points while moving the switch through its different positions.

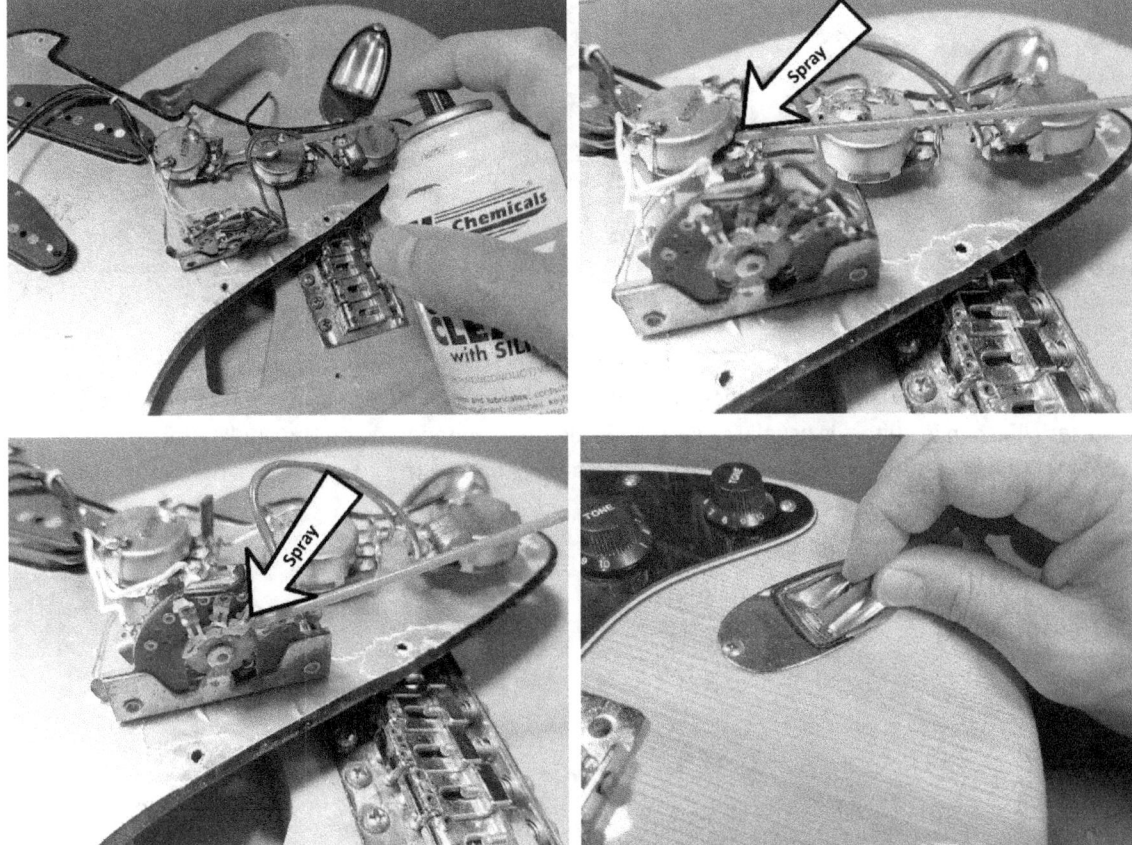

Noisy or intermittent output jacks may improve with a shot of contact cleaner. If that doesn't work, try using some fine abrasive sandpaper (600 grit or higher). Roll it up into a small cylinder so that it fits into the diameter of the jack, and twist it around the inside to clean off any oxidation (it shouldn't require much).

Static Electricity

Just like our clothing, guitars can attract static electricity. The sound comes right through the amplifier and can be quite frustrating. Luckily, the fix is usually quite easy. You can take a dryer sheet and place it right inside the electronics cavity of the guitar. Give the interior and underside of the pickguard a good wipe down with it first. It should help eliminate the problem and also prevent it from returning.

How to Check Battery Voltage

If your guitar has active electronics, you may want to check the voltage of the battery. To do this, you will need a voltmeter or multimeter. Choose the *DC (direct current)* selection on the meter and the appropriate voltage for the battery (9-volt batteries can be checked within similar ranges such as 0-10 or 0-20 volts). Place the positive and negative lead on the appropriate battery terminals to measure the voltage.

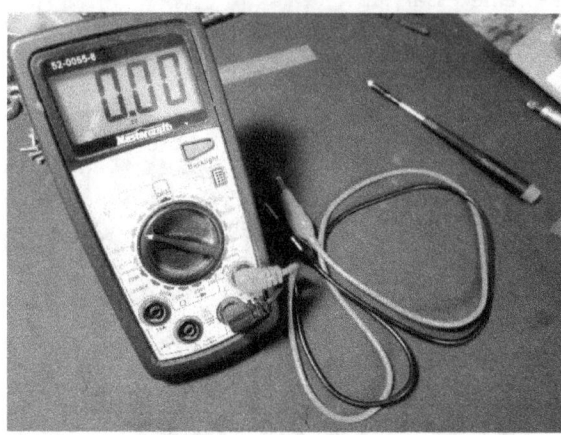 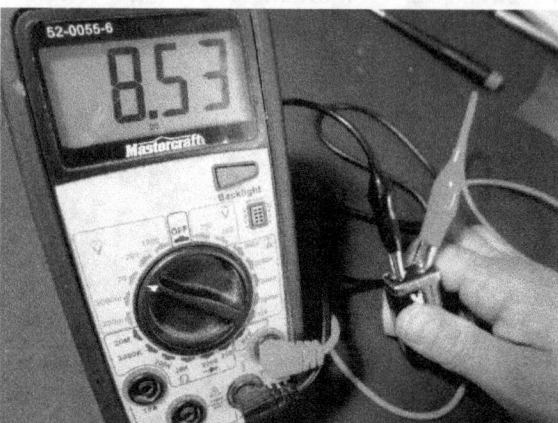

If you don't have a multimeter to test batteries, change them as soon as you hear any noticeable depreciation in sound quality. Guitar electronics will work best with a fresh battery. If in doubt, change it. The battery lifespan in guitars is usually several hundred hours, depending on the application. Use a quality alkaline or lithium battery for maximum lifespan and always unplug the guitar cable when not in use.

SETUPS & ADJUSTMENTS

What Is a Setup?
Guitars require adjustments on a regular basis to maintain proper playability and performance. A guitar setup is a complete adjustment and calibration of the entire instrument to ensure that it is as playable and as responsive as possible. A setup also includes some basic preventative maintenance and a thorough inspection.

Just like you can hot-rod your car or truck, you can fine-tune your guitar to perform its best. A setup includes adjusting, where applicable, the neck relief (neck bow), the saddle and nut slot height, the bridge angle, the neck angle, the pickup height, and the intonation. It is also a good idea to be sure that the hardware is torqued down, the controls are functioning correctly, and that any worn out parts are replaced. Since a guitar is primarily made of wood, which will expand and contract, it will need these adjustments periodically.

What Influences a Great Guitar Setup?
Before getting started, it is essential to note that any guitar can play poorly or exceptional, depending on the setup and what your preferences are. The ideal setup is one made for you, your guitar, and your style (meaning, how you play the guitar, what tunings you use, which string gauge you prefer). All these will factor into how the guitar should be adjusted. This guide will give you the know-how to make these adjustments with measurable results.

LEGEND
Instructions in this book will refer to each guitar string as they are numbered below.

#6 string – commonly the low 'E' string, or the lowest and thickest string

#5 string – commonly the 'A' string

#4 string – commonly the 'D' string

#3 string – commonly the 'G' string

#2 string – commonly the 'B' string

What You'll Need:

The following list of tools will be adequate under most circumstances. See individual chapters for additional tools or supplies that may be required.

- Fresh guitar strings & a capo
- Truss rod wrench
- Steel ruler that measures in 64ths of an inch
- Automotive feeler gauge set that measures in thousandths of an inch (.001")
- Multi-head screwdriver / precision screwdriver set
- Your guitar's saddle height adjustment wrench (if applicable)
- An accurate electronic tuner
- String cutter /side cutters or cutting pliers

These items can be found at your local music and hardware stores or online.

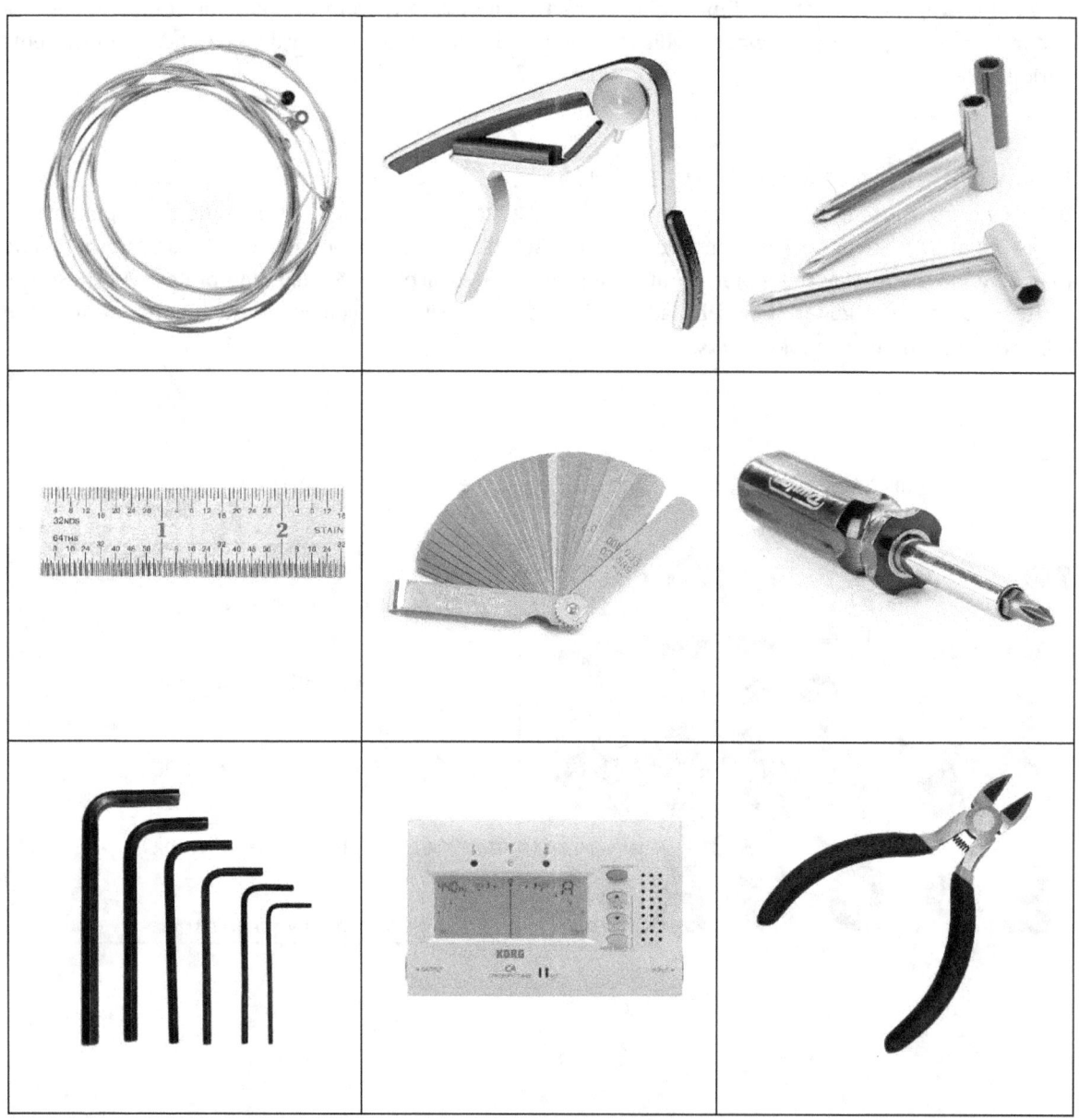

Additional Specialty Tools

Specialty tools mentioned in the book, such as a **"string action ruler"**, **"radius gauge"**, or **"under-saddle radius gauges"** are not required to do a setup, but they are tools that you may have heard of before, and maybe interested in trying.

At the back of this book, in the **FURTHER RESOURCES** section, we have provided cut-out templates for some of these tools, so that you can try them out for yourself, as well as the methods explained. Trying these methods will provide you with all the know-how, for a wide range of circumstances and guitar types. The cut-outs can be traced onto thin cardboard, such as a cereal box, or a thin household plastic for many uses over.

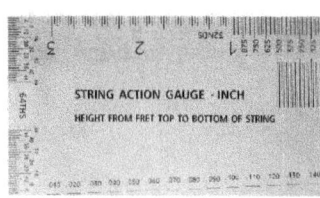 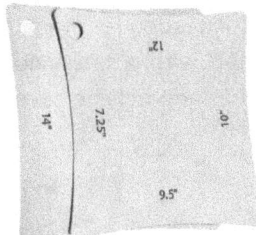 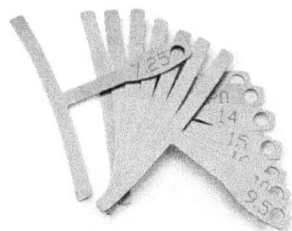

The 8-Step Pro Setup

1. Clean, polish, oil, & lubricate
2. Check the hardware & electronics
3. Restring and tune to pitch
4. Adjust the relief in the neck (via truss rod)
5. Adjust the string height at the bridge
6. Adjust the string height at the nut
7. Adjust the pickup height
8. Adjust the intonation

What is not included in a typical setup: Fretwork (although some shops may include this), electronic repairs, structural repairs, or any other repairs needed for the guitar to be set up appropriately. Meaning, if the guitar is in bad shape and neglect to start with, a setup alone may not take care of its current state and often further repairs or billable time in the shop may be necessary before the guitar *can* be set up.

A note on measuring methods

Throughout this guide, the examples are given in measurements of thousandths of an inch (.000"), and fractions of an inch (1/64"). Thousandths of an inch can be measured by using an automotive feeler gauge set. Fractions of an inch can be measured with a quality steel ruler. There is also a chart at the end of this guide which converts thousandths of an inch to fractions of an inch to millimetres.

Before you get started, please note the following specifications are meant to be a guide. They should not be construed as hard-and-fast rules, as players' subjective requirements often differ.

ADJUST THE NECK RELIEF (BOW)

a) What is a Truss Rod?

A truss rod is a steel rod that runs down the interior of the guitar neck. Its purpose is to counteract the pull of the strings by applying a counterforce within the neck. Furthermore, the truss rod allows adjustment of relief (or bow) in relation to how much tension is being applied to the neck.

Typically, a neck needs adjustment after changing tuning or string gauge. Additionally, the neck may need adjustment any time after the guitar has been subjected to temperature or humidity fluctuations (typical seasonal changes).

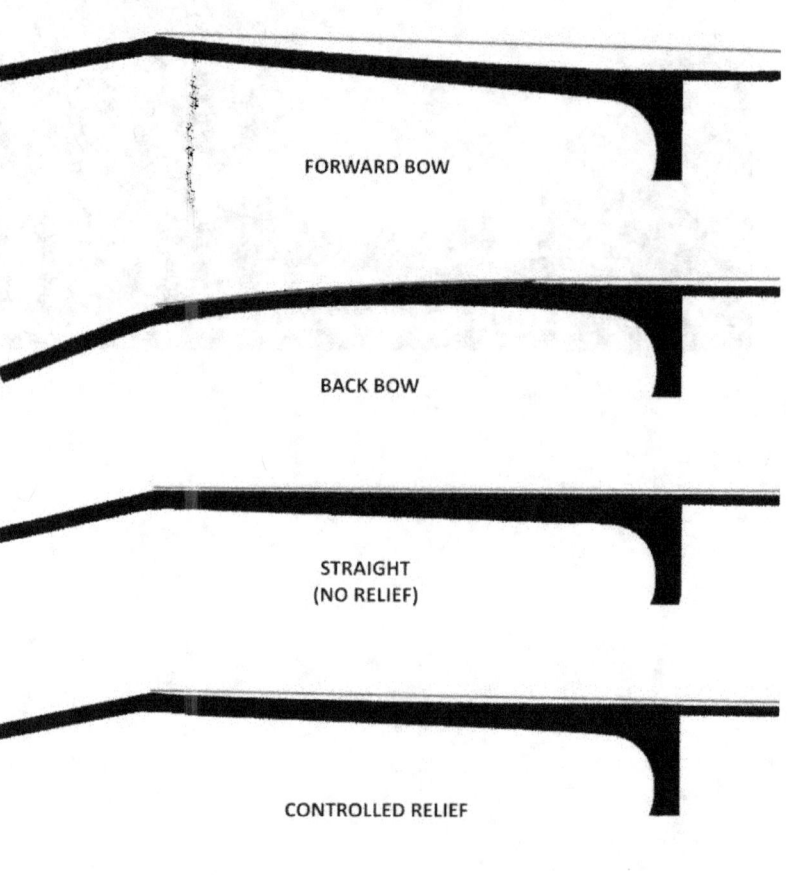

NOTE: Any time the guitar's playability changes after it has been set up for a specific tuning and string gauge, the truss rod likely needs readjustment.

There are two kinds of adjustable truss rods: single action and dual-action. A single-action truss rod, which is the most common, can be tightened to adjust the neck into a back bow (to counteract the pull of the strings). But what if the neck is already back-bowed while under string tension?

A dual-action truss rod works just like the aforementioned but can also be adjusted to create forward bow (relief) in a neck that is too stiff or is stuck in a back bow. There is no way to see the difference between the two truss rod styles, but you will find that when you continue to loosen a dual-action truss rod, it will eventually begin getting tight again, while simultaneously pushing the neck into a forward bow.

These images show a truss rod adjustment nut at the top of the neck. Many guitars share this design, which allows easy access for quick neck relief changes.

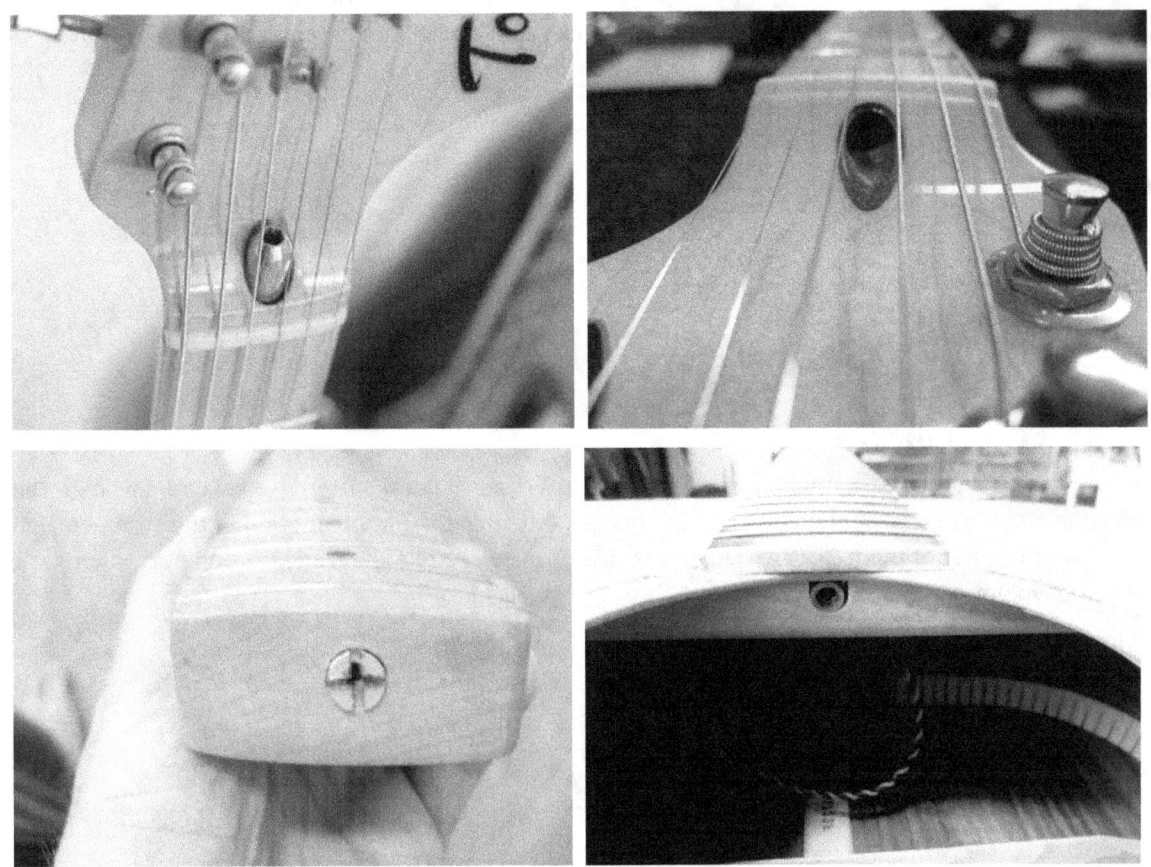

(Image: Tim Patterson)

With heel area truss rod access (image above), you may need to unscrew and remove the neck to access it. *See the next section on **removing bolt-on necks**.* Other times, you may only need to remove the pickguard to access it.

A common location for the truss rod adjustment on an acoustic guitar, besides the top of the neck, is right through the soundhole and under the fretboard.

Many nylon string guitars do not have a truss rod, because they do not withstand the same kind of neck tension as steel-string guitars.

Also worth mentioning is the dual truss rod configuration. You may see this with some basses or 12 string acoustic guitars. It is two individual truss rods sitting side by side. With this configuration, you can adjust each side of the neck independently.

(Image courtesy Roadside Guitars

b) Why Set the Relief?

When a string is plucked, strummed, or picked, it vibrates in an elliptical pattern (see diagram below). This is why the guitar needs a slight bow (relief) in the neck to match the natural motion of the string - mainly in the lower register of the fretboard. Otherwise, the string will strike the frets, causing buzz, poor tone, and loss of volume.

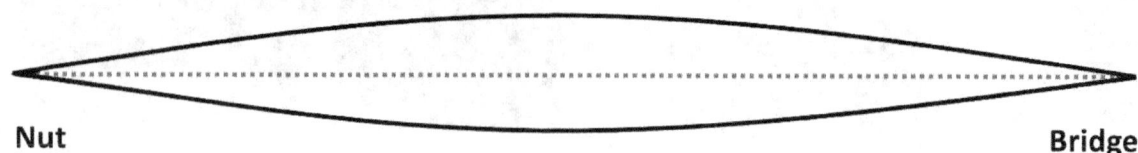

Nut   **Bridge**

If you play hard, you will exaggerate the movement of the string. Depending on your preference, you may need more relief (bow) in the neck and/or a higher string height to compensate. Players with a lighter touch can have straighter necks with lower action. This is why electric guitars often have less relief than acoustics (although not as a rule). When adjusting a bass, you will require more relief than on a guitar because the strings are much larger and vibrate in relativity to their size.

What You'll Need:
- A capo
- The guitar's truss rod adjustment wrench
- Automotive feeler gauges or string action ruler (if you want to measure your results)

c) How to Measure Neck Relief

There are a few golden rules when adjusting a truss rod. First, only use the truss rod to keep the neck as straight as it needs to be. Do not use it to adjust the action! Second, only use the proper tool. If you do not know what that is, check with the manufacturer or your local guitar store. Truss rod nuts are easy to strip, and once they are stripped, they are expensive to fix! Finally, do not force anything- an eighth of a turn can make a significant change.

1. Start by sitting with the guitar in the playing position.

2. Check that it is tuned to pitch.

3. Capo the first fret. If you do not own a capo, you can use your fretting hand to bar the first fret.

4. With your picking hand, bar or press down the string as follows: If you have a bolt-on neck, bar the last fret on the #6 string (lowest string). If you have a set-neck (glued in), bar the fret closest to where the neck and body meet, typically the 17th-19th fret.

Now use these two points as a measuring reference. The string is now acting as a ruler. The neck will bow either away from or against the string. This is one way you can determine the amount of relief in the neck. You can also use a steel ruler placed along the length of the neck (while in playing position).

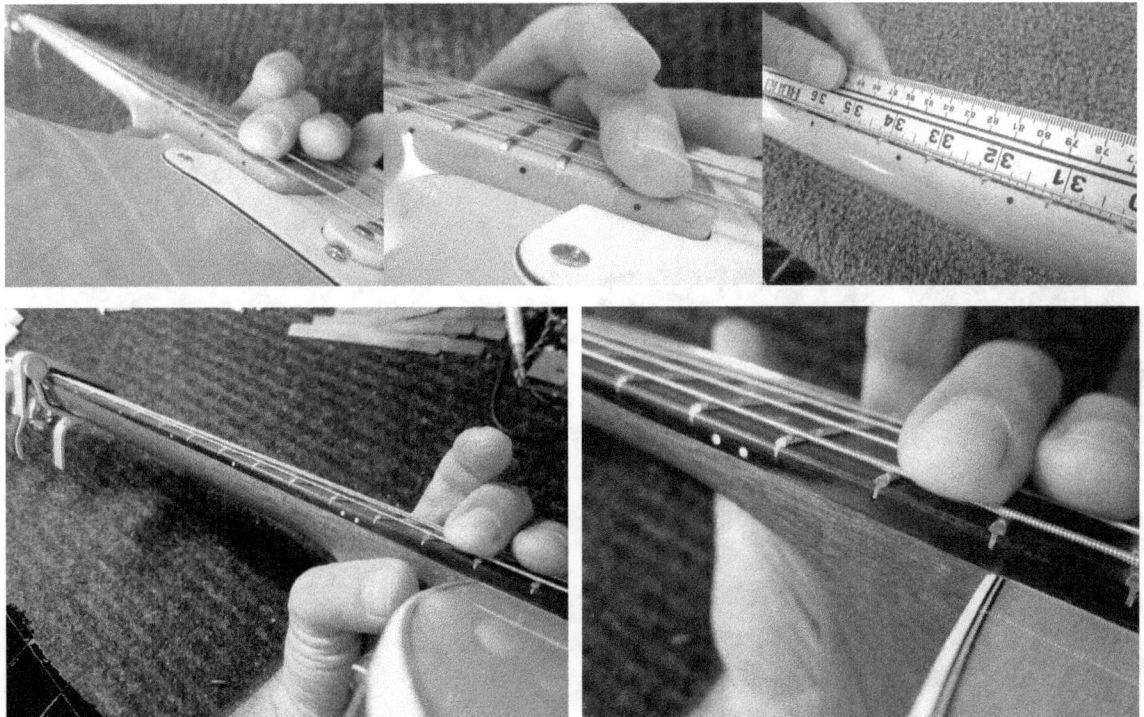

When checking an acoustic guitar, bar the fret closest to where the neck and body meet (often the 14th fret).

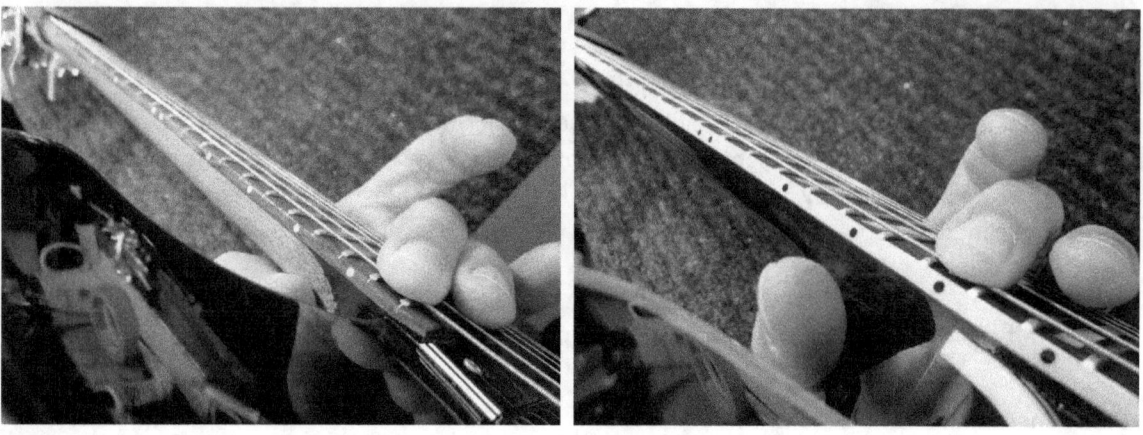

These two set-neck guitars are different in design, but the same rule applies. Bar the fret closest to where the neck and body meet. The Gibson DC Special on the left will be 22nd fret and the Gibson ES-349 on the right will the 19th fret.

"Does it matter exactly which fret I should be using?"

Choosing one fret over the next will not make or break your setup. Just be consistent and follow the suggestions for the process to work.

5. Between the frets barred, find the centre (it is often the 7th or 8th fret on an electric guitar). Measure the distance between the top of the fret and the bottom of the string, as pictured. Notice the gap, if any.

6. If you have a gap, you likely have some bow in the neck. If there is no gap, the neck is likely either dead straight or back-bowed

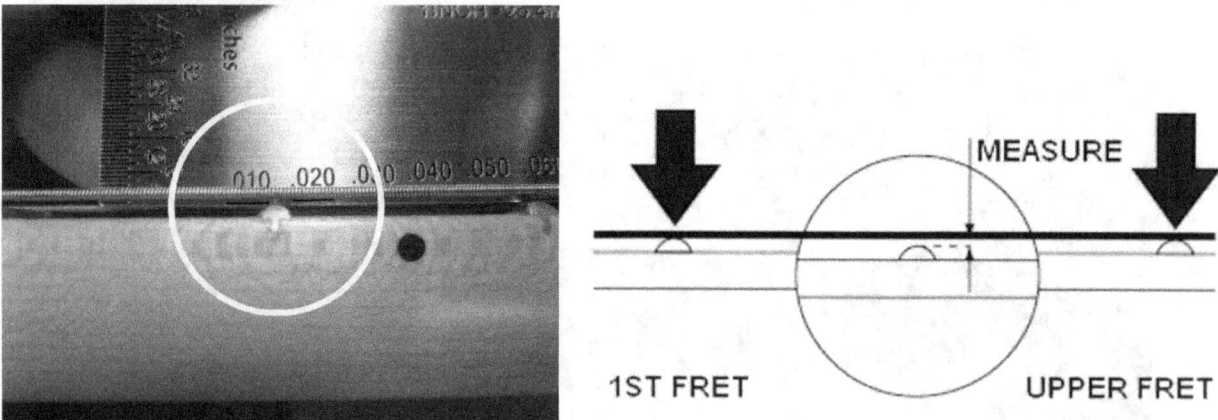

Using a string action ruler above, we can see that there is approximately .020" of relief measured.

This next example is using feeler gauges to precisely measure the gap. This tolerance is measured by placing the correct feeler gauge blade in the gap. When doing so, there should be no lateral play. The gap should be precisely equivalent to the thickness of the feeler gauge. Be sure that you are not pushing the string up when sliding the blade into the gap. It is a tricky procedure to obtain accuracy and master, but with enough practice, you will get it!

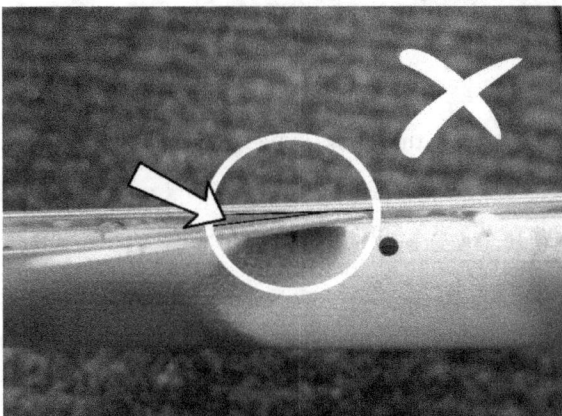 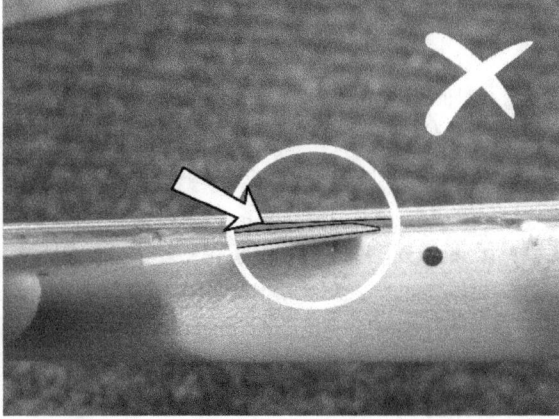

Pictured above left is showing side-to-side play when the feeler gauge is rocked over the fret. The second picture is showing a small gap between the feeler gauge blade and the string. These two examples suggest the feeler gauge is thinner than the gap being measured. In this case, a thicker blade must be tested until the correct size is found.

d) How Much Relief is Enough?

The bigger the gap, the more relief is in the neck. So, how much relief should you have?

Most players feel that a near-straight neck is the most comfortable to play on, but this is subject to personal preference. Usually, there should be a small amount of relief in the neck for optimal playing: about the thickness of a business card or less. For those with feeler gauges, .010" is a good starting point. If there is no gap, you will need to loosen the truss rod counter-clockwise to allow some relief into the neck.

 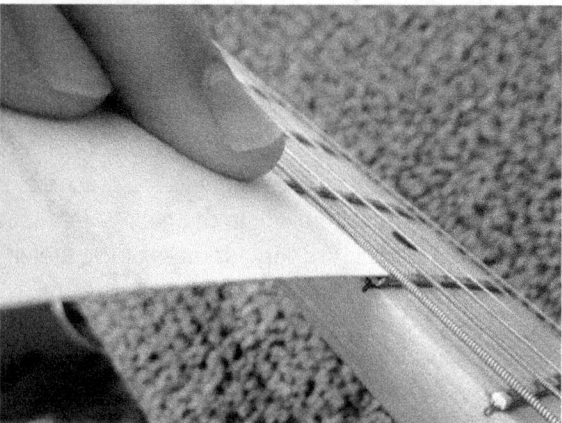

For the technically minded, try setting the relief to .008"-.010" for most electrics, .010"-.012" for acoustics, and .015"-.020" for basses (there are lots of examples in the back of this book, as well as in the **Guitar Setup Calculator**, available at *www.learn-guitarsetups.com*).

Make an incremental adjustment and then measure the results, a ¼ turn or less at a time. Keep doing so until you have the results you want. You will measure this tolerance just as you did previously when first checking the relief, either with a string action ruler or set of feeler gauges. The more experience you get doing this, the quicker and more accurate the process will be. If you are not using a measuring tool, keep in mind that some business cards can range from .010"- .020" thick. You'll want to consider giving the truss rod another slight turn one way or the other to dial in minimal relief.

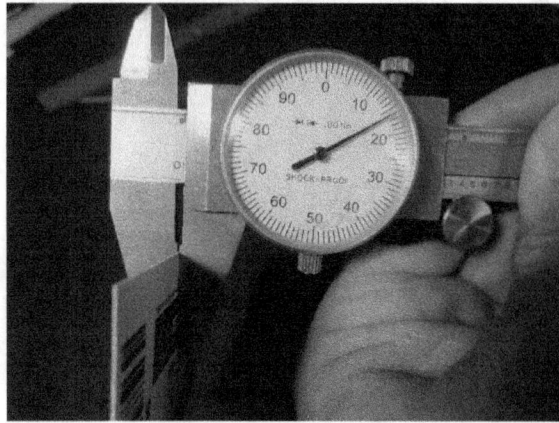 

Note the measured thicknesses between a business card and a string package. A difference of approximately .007" is small, but enough to change the feel and performance of the guitar.

How to Adjust the Truss Rod

No matter where the truss rod nut is located, either at the head of the neck, or the heel- the same rule applies: Righty-tighty, lefty-loosey. To tighten the truss rod and straighten the neck, turn it clockwise. To loosen the truss rod and allow relief or bow into the neck, turn it counter-clockwise.

It may be necessary to move the strings aside to allow access and adjustment to the truss rod nut. Doing so will also help avoid marring up the strings.

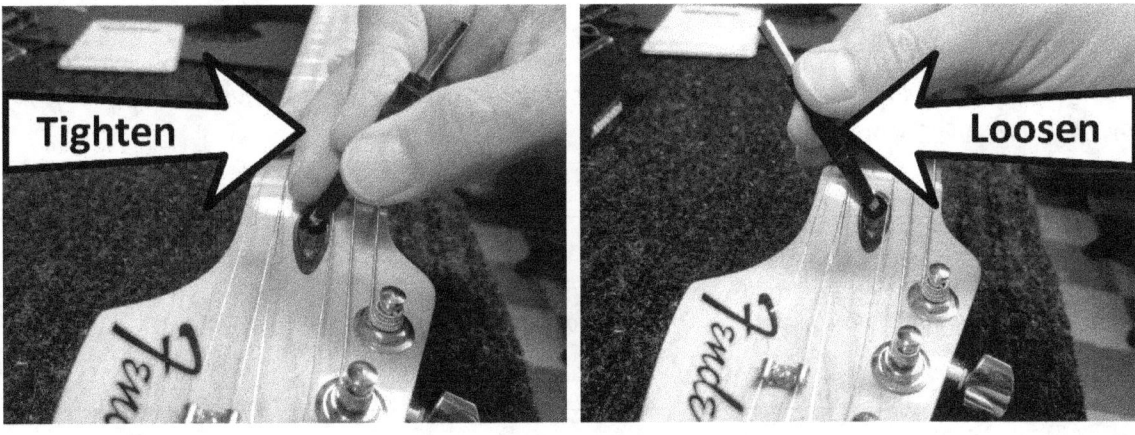

HINT: If the strings are buzzing when playing in the first few frets and open strings, it may be an indication of a back bow.

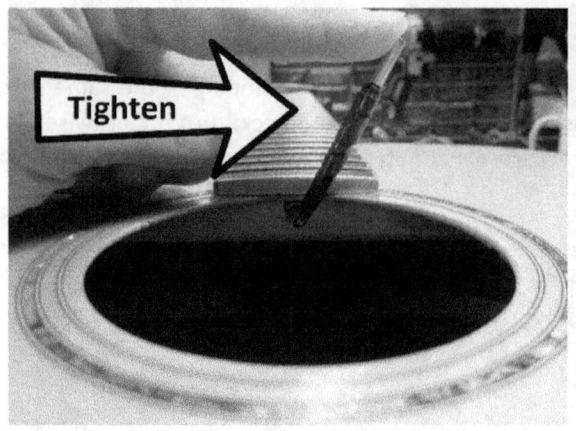 

Dual-Action / Two-Way Truss Rods

With guitars that have dual-action truss rods, you will apply the same adjustment procedure as previously explained. The main difference is that you can exert both a forward bow or back bow into the neck, whereas with single-action truss rods, you can only exert it into a back-bow. These truss rods are most useful when the guitar neck is too stiff, straight or stuck in a back-bow and requires counterforce to create the ideal relief.

NOTE: When adjusting a dual-action truss rod counter-clockwise, it may first loosen off before it starts exerting forward bow into the neck. Keep checking the neck relief throughout the adjustments being made.

Do not force anything to get the results you are after. If the truss rod is hard to adjust or spins freely, you may need professional assistance.

CAUTION: There is no way to visually know if the truss rod in your guitar is single or dual-action. The guitar's owner's manual will specify these details and provide instructions for use.

How to Remove the Neck for a Truss Rod Access

First, loosen all the strings until slack. Turn the guitar over to access the neck bolts, unscrew and remove them completely. If the neck screws are of different size, label them or lay them in order, so they are reinstalled in the same location (and you don't mistakenly drive the wrong one through the fretboard, ouch!!).

Remove the neck to access the truss rod nut. You may be able to tilt it outwards to gain access, or you may need to remove it from the neck pocket altogether. Keep an eye out for any shims that may be present. If loose, they may fall out and will need to be put back. Neck shims change the neck angle and will completely alter the setup if removed.

Make a slight adjustment to the truss rod, ¼ turn at a time, and reassemble the neck. If your neck is majorly back bowed or bowed forward, you can turn it a ½ turn until it gets closer to the range needed. Retune the strings to pitch, and check the relief. Repeat as necessary. As you can imagine, this process can get tedious quickly. Be careful not to overtighten the neck screws as they can become stripped.

PRO TIP: To prevent the strings from tangling when removing the neck, put a capo on the first fret.

How to Adjust the Neck Alignment

After reinstalling the neck, check that the neck is aligned in the neck pocket. Or perhaps you have never removed the neck, and now have just noticed that it isn't quite straight. The strings should spread across the fretboard evenly. If they are falling off to one side, try repositioning the neck. To do so, loosen each neck screw by a ¼ turn, and push the neck into position. You may need to hold it in place when retightening. You can usually keep the strings tuned to pitch when doing this; detuning isn't normally necessary. It usually doesn't take much effort to shift the neck, but all guitars are different. You can eyeball it, or for precision, you can measure the edges of the #6 and #1 strings to the edge of the fret.

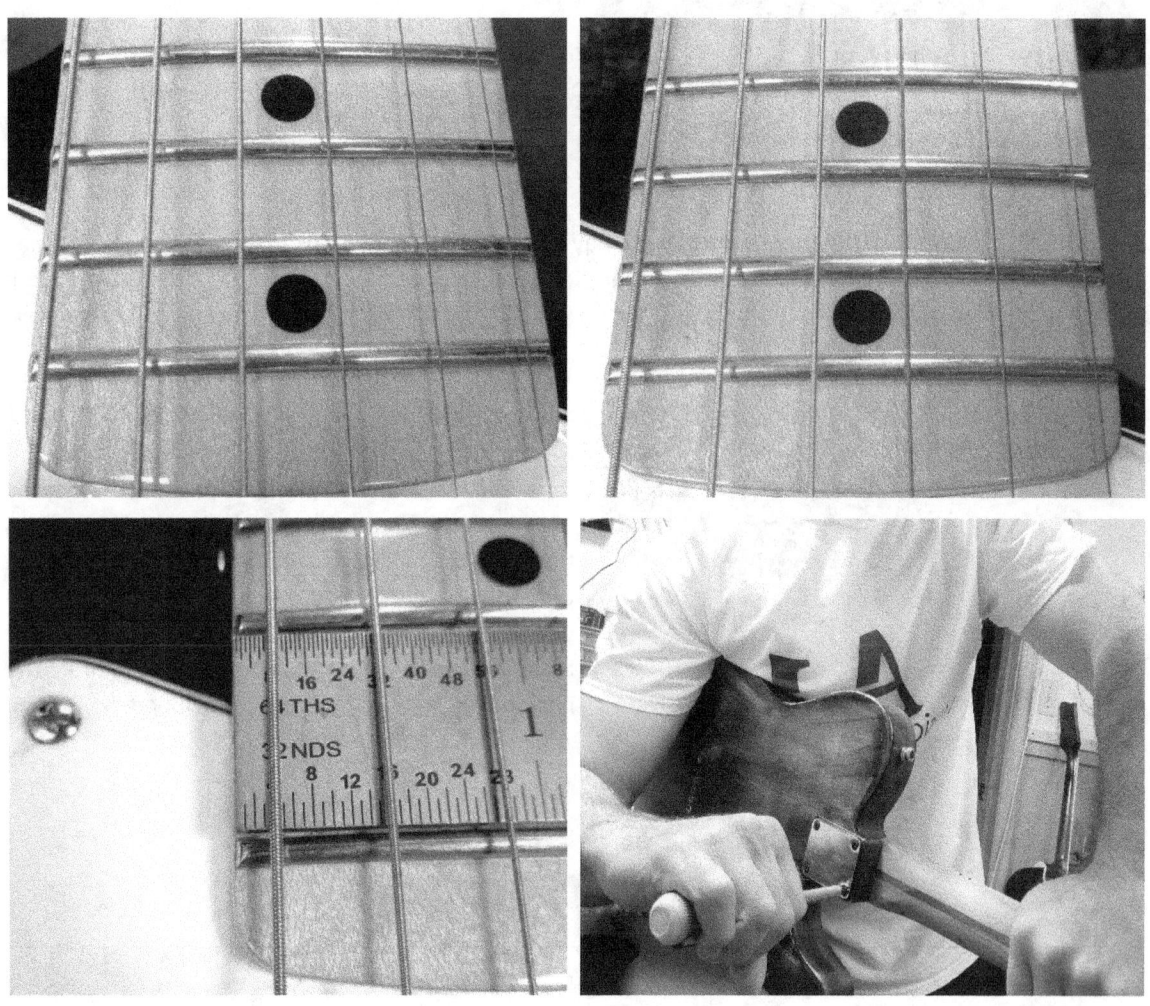

The final step in setting the optimal neck relief is to test the guitar out. Take note though, straightening the neck may make the guitar play worse. When the truss rod is tightened, the height of the strings is lowered, which can create string buzz if the guitar has not been set up correctly in the past. Likewise, it can make a poor fret condition more noticeable. If the guitar plays worse after adjusting the neck, it is either too straight or requiring more work (full setup, fret dressing, etc.). Thankfully, you can easily reverse the changes you have just made or move on to the next step, which is raising the string height at the bridge.

HINT: Some necks may take some time to settle after adjustment. Specifically, maple necks can be stiff and may not settle immediately after an adjustment. It is often best to check periodically after making the initial adjustment for any further changes in relief and readjust as necessary.

Neck Relief Suggestions (Guitar)

Neck Radius	Relief
7.25"	.012" (0.3 mm)
9.5" to 12"	.010" (0.25 mm)
15" to 17"	.008" (0.2 mm)

Neck Relief Suggestions (Bass)

Neck Radius	Relief
7.25"	.014" (0.35 mm)
9.5" to 12"	.012" (0.3 mm)
15" to 17"	.010" (0.25 mm)

Read on to the next chapter to learn more about neck radius.

ADJUST THE STRING HEIGHT AT THE BRIDGE

About Fretboard Radius

Before you adjust the string height, here is a quick overview of the fretboard radius, and how it plays into the setup.

The **fretboard radius** is the measured amount of curve on the playing surface, as pictured below (r = radius). Most guitars have a slightly rounded fretboard, some more noticeable than others. The exception would be classical-style guitars, which are typically flat or near flat.

When doing a guitar setup, the height of the strings generally follows the same arc of the fretboard radius. Common fretboard radii are 7.25", 9.5", 10", 12", 14", 15", 16", & 20". The smaller the number, the rounder the curve of the fretboard and the higher the number, the flatter.

Generally, the flatter it is, the lower you can set the string height while still having full playability of the strings, particularly in bending. When bending the strings, they must clear the highest point of the fretboard, which is in the center. You can test this by bending the #1 (commonly the high 'E') string through several frets up the fretboard. If it chokes out at any area, the string height must be raised until you have the clearance you require.

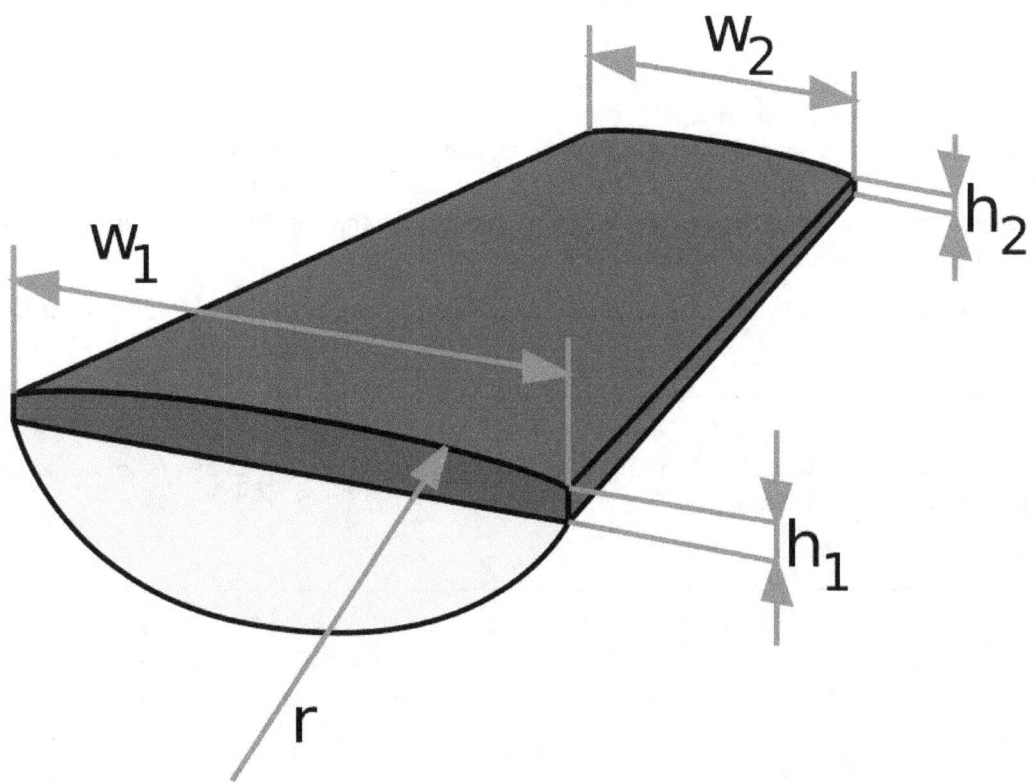

The diagram above showing radius ® alongside widths (w1, w2) and heights (h1, h2) of the fretboard. Image © User: GreyCat / Wikimedia Commons / CC-BY-SA-3.0

Procedure Overview

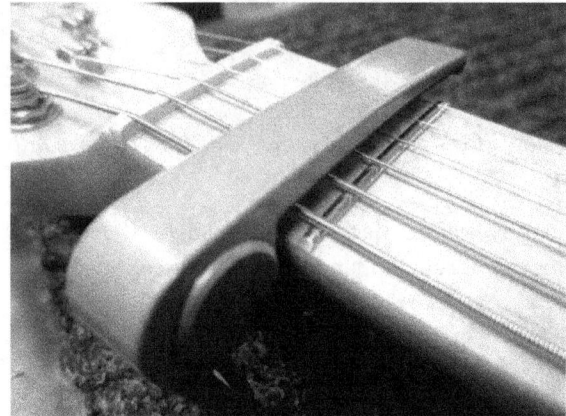

After adjusting the truss rod, leave the capo on at the first fret. As before, we will use some generic settings. You can stray from these later and find your preferences using the setup specification charts at the end of this book or by using the **Guitar Setup Calculator** online at *www.learn-guitarsetups.com*

The following examples given will be measured at the 12th fret using a steel ruler or feeler gauge set. Just like when measuring neck relief, the distance between the top of the fret and bottom of the string is *always* measured while in playing position, *not* when the guitar is lying flat on a bench or table. The reason for this is when a guitar is lying flat, any amount of pressure will affect the neck bow to a degree. Even gravity can affect it if the guitar is heavy enough, and the readings you take will be false. Any change in neck relief, no matter how subtle, will affect the string height and subsequently, the measurements you are taking. We always want to set the guitar up while in playing position.

The Different Guitar Types

Because we are covering several different guitar types, and all requiring slightly different procedures, some methods of string height adjustments, or aspects of, may carry over from one to another. I have arranged the instructions to avoid repetition as much as possible, although this chapter may require some back-and-forth for the correct sequence of procedures.

Read the subsections about your guitar type and any relevant articles as you move throughout this chapter.

> *NOTE: It is usually best to loosen the strings when raising the bridge or the saddles (so as not to strip the threads on the adjustment screws).*

Gibson-style Hard-tail Bridges (Tune-o-matic)

Gibson-style bridges have two height adjustment bolts on each side of the bridge. The saddles are already positioned to match the radius of the fretboard, so this part is done for us.

Take a ruler and place it on the 12th fret next to the #6 string. Adjust the bridge thumbwheels until the bottom of the #6 string measures 4/64". Then, take the ruler and move it over to the #1 string. Adjust the bridge until the bottom of the string measures 3/64". Go back and check that the bass side is still at 4/64", you may need to readjust.

Notice with this example, the string height tapers down lower with the treble strings, as it provides a comfortable, natural feel. It also provides the thicker strings slightly more space to ring out when played, creating more sustain and louder tone. If you want to try this setup using feeler gauges, 4/64" = .063" and 3/64" = .047".

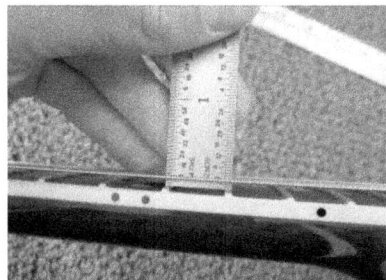 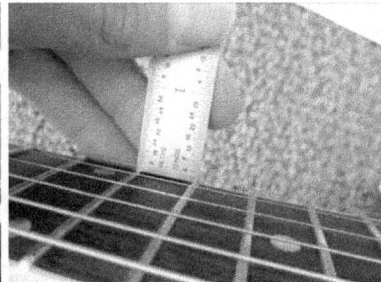 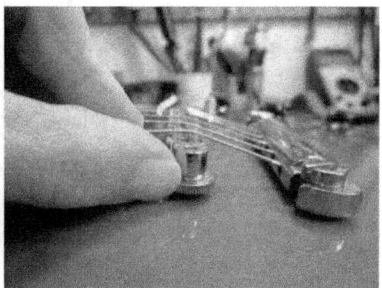

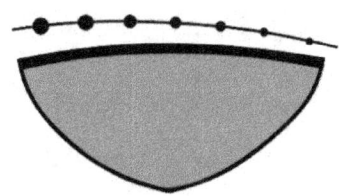

Graphic image courtesy John Staehli http://jmstaehli.com/

Adjusting Stop Tailpieces

People often ask how to adjust the stop tailpiece on a Gibson-styled bridge set. The stop tailpiece is adjusted closer or farther from the body and will affect the tone and feel of the instrument. There are many theories as to what's best, but a good rule of thumb is to have it as low as possible without the strings making any contact with the backside of the bridge. This will depend on how the intonation is set, as well as the rest of the setup adjustments, so leave it until last. Try and find a coin or screwdriver that will fit the wide adjustment slot snuggly; otherwise, you may dent or strip it. *HINT: it's easiest to adjust the tailpiece with the strings detuned.*

Image showing strings making contact with the back of the bridge. The tailpiece should be raised in this example.

The tailpiece has now been raised slightly, showing no string-to-bridge contact.

Fender-style Hard-tail Bridges

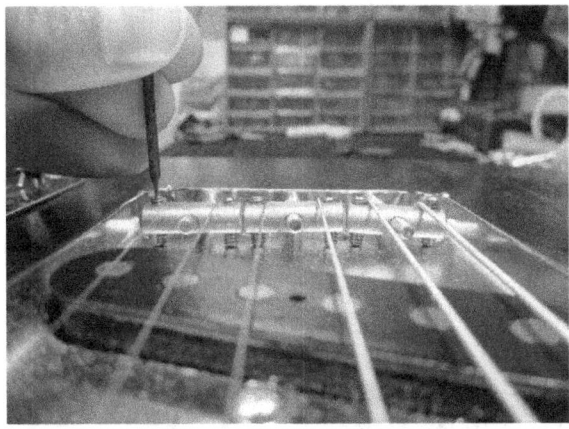
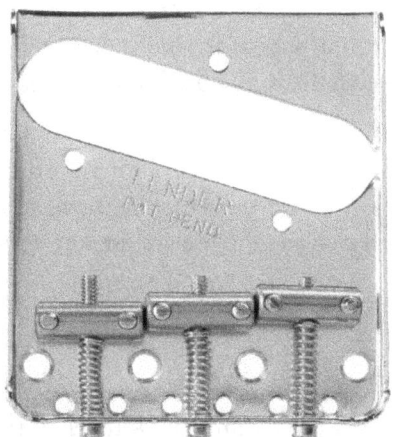

Traditional Fender-style bridges have individual saddle height adjustment, which must be calculated or determined in order to be setup. The adjustment often requires a hex key or a small precision screwdriver. In the guitar pictured above, two strings share one common saddle, and each side of the saddle is adjusted to match the radius.

On guitars that have one saddle per string, each saddle should be adjusted parallel to the bridge plate. This will create solid contact and will improve tone and sustain, as well as help prevent the adjustment screws from backing off (and rattling, etc.).

How to Adjust Individual Saddle Height

With multiple saddles to adjust, we will need to determine the string height for every string. The most accurate tool for measurement is feeler gauges, using thousandths of an inch (.000"). Alternatively, you can forgo measuring each string individually by using an under-string radius gauge in conjunction with a steel ruler, although this method is not as precise- it is close enough for some (more on this later).

To calculate the height of each string, first determine the height for the #6 and #1 strings. Knowing the factory specifications can help with a starting point. For demonstration, use .078" (5/64") for the #6 string and .063" (4/64") for the #1 string. Now, subtract the difference between the two and divide it by 5. This formula will give you the precise amount to incrementally lower each string while matching the fretboard radius.

Example:

#6 string = .078" *(Measurement is taken at the 12th fret with 1st fret barred)*

#1 string = .063" *(Measurement is taken at the 12th fret with 1st fret barred)*

Subtract the difference: .078" - .063" = .015"

Divide the difference by five: 015" ÷ 5 = .003"

After adjusting the #6 string to .078", lower each proceeding saddle by .003," and you will have an even, gradual taper to the treble strings. Since you are taking your readings off the fretboard, the string height will match the radius perfectly.

#6 string	#5 string	#4 string	#3 string	#2 string	#1 string
.078"	.075"	.072"	.069"	.066"	.063"

*Check the Setup Specification Section at the back of the book for many more examples!

If you have not used feeler gauges before, they do take some practice. Stack up enough blades so that when combined they equal .078" and insert them between the top of the 12th fret and bottom of the #6 string. Just like when measuring neck relief, place them perfectly parallel with the string to get accurate results (see the next photos). Adjust the saddle by its height adjustment screws evenly, until the string grazes the blades. Again, there should be no lateral play, and the blades should not be bumping or moving the string. You may need to raise the saddle(s) first before adjusting down to the correct height.

Once you are satisfied with the #6 string, move on to the next. You can place the feeler blades under the previous strings you have already adjusted and work your way across the neck, from #6 to #1.

NOTE: When you make these adjustments, the strings may lose pitch. It is crucial to retune the strings throughout so that the neck relief is not affected by the changes in string tension. A change in neck relief will affect the string height.

 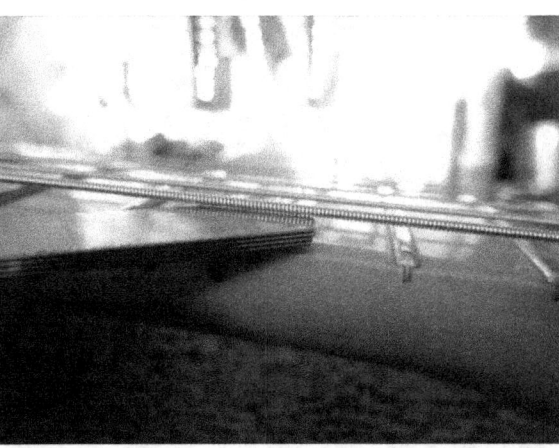

If you prefer to have consistent string height across the fretboard, you can simply measure and adjust each string to the same height at the 12th fret, for example, 4/64", which converts into .063", or 1.6mm.

#6 string	#5 string	#4 string	#3 string	#2 string	#1 string
4/64"	4/64"	4/64"	4/64"	4/64"	4/64"

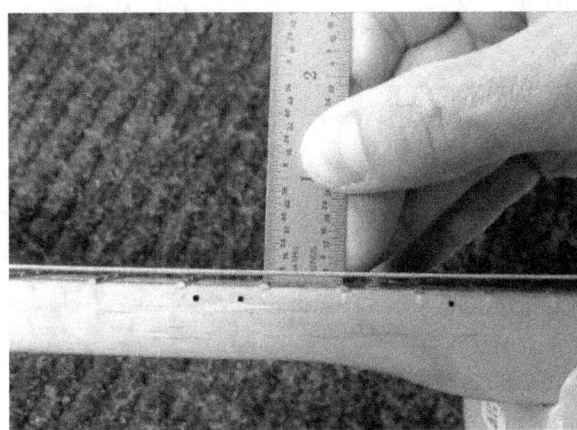 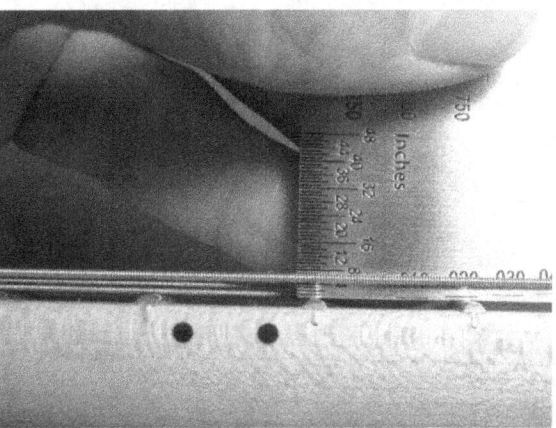

You can measure this with a standard steel ruler or a string action ruler.

How to Use Under-String Radius Gauges

If you prefer to use an under-string radius gauge set with a steel ruler, the method to determine and set the #6 and #1 string heights will be the same as previously mentioned. We can then use the gauge to match the remaining saddle height to the correct radius, bypassing the need to do any calculations.

First, we will have to back up slightly and determine what the fretboard radius is (if we have not yet done so). You can find the radius of the fretboard by measuring it with the correct gauge. You can use an under-string radius gauge or a standard radius gauge for the job (check out **FURTHER RESOURCES** and make your own!). Try several sizes until you find the closest match. Place the gauge on the 1st, 12th and last frets to determine if the radius is uniform. You will have found the correct size when you can't see any gap or visible light under the gauge. A mismatch is most obviously seen directly in the middle or at the edges of the gauge.

 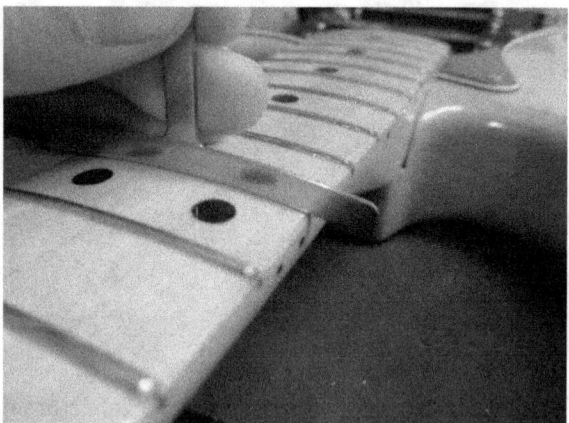

NOTE: Some guitars may have some variances. Meaning, the fretboard radius has become worn in areas and possibly inconsistent, or perhaps it never was consistent to start with. If your guitar is older and has some wear of its own, check the fretboard in multiple places and determine the closest match. You can also check the top of the frets to factor into your results, if in doubt.

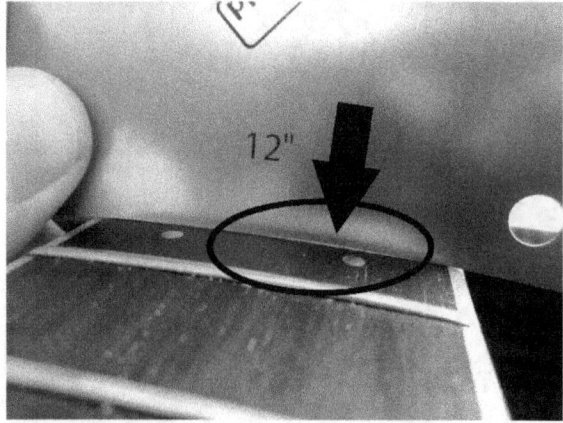 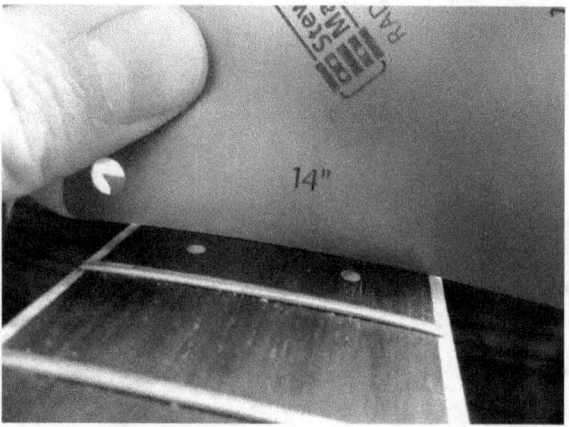

Notice in the first previous image, the gauge is closely matched to the fretboard, but there is light peeping through the middle, suggesting a mismatch. 14" is the proper reading.

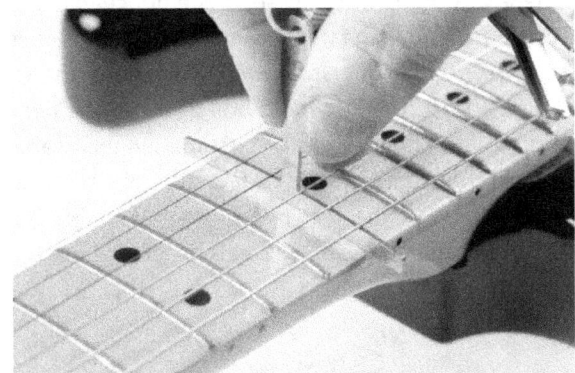

If using under-string radius gauges, as the name implies, most of the fretboard can be measured with the strings on. Slip the gauge under the strings or slightly detune them if it makes it more accessible.

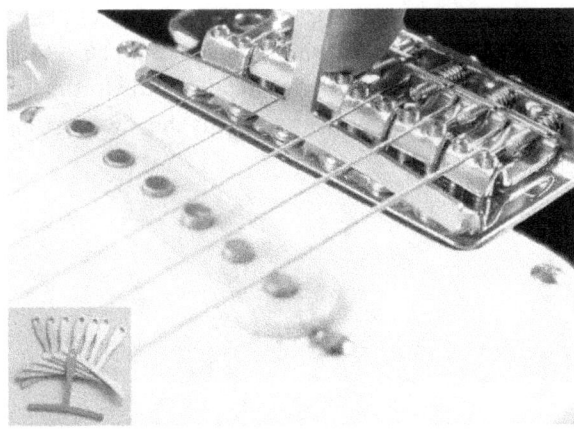

Once you have found the correctly matched radius gauge, we can proceed with the setup. Adjust both #6 & #1 strings to the suggested settings (and retune). Place the gauge under the strings, near the saddles, as pictured. *Lightly* pull upwards (*do not pull the strings with it*) to determine the placement of the other strings. You will see if they need to be adjusted either higher or lower to match the gauge. You may need to raise them first if any are too low to start with. Adjust the saddles for strings #5, #4, #3, and #2 so that they graze the gauge equally, making a uniform radius.

Compound Radius Necks

Some guitars may have a compound radius fretboard which is designed to gradually change from a rounder radius at the nut end to a flatter radius at the heel end. For example, you may find 10" at the 1st fret, and 16" at the last fret, or 9.5" at the first fret, and 14" at the last. Whatever the case, it is a noticeable and drastic change throughout the length of the fretboard. If you do find that you have a compound radius fretboard, I'd suggest using the ruler or feeler gauge method of adjusting string height for best results, because as you can probably guess, the radius gauge to use is uncertain. It would boil down to the neck length, radius profile and a little theory in guitar design- which, can easily become unnecessarily complicated and long-winded. If you still want to give it a shot, experiment with a few different sizes, so you know what works best on that guitar. Start with the radius of the last fret measured, make the adjustments, then give it a play-test throughout the entire fretboard and see how it feels. After that, try the next couple sizes up (going higher in radius).

Conclusion

After trying these methods, experiment and find what string height you like the best on your guitar. Keep in mind that the lower you set the strings, the more chance you will end up with string buzz. If you set the #1 and #2 strings too low, they will choke out when you bend them up towards the middle of the fretboard. Lower them just enough so that they clear through a full bend, and you will know that is the lowest string height setting for that guitar.

Vintage-Style Tremolo Bridges

Vintage-style tremolo bridges, which are often seen on reissue Strat-style guitars, are typically mounted to the body with six screws. The bridge is designed to pivot off these screws, and the tremolo can be set several ways; either hard-tail (bridge-to-body), one-way tremolo (downwards), or two-way tremolo (both up and downwards).

The bridge angle must be set first, as any changes made will affect string height (learn how to in the next section, **Bridge Angle Adjustments**). Once the bridge angle is set, adjust the string height as explained previously in **Individual Saddle Height Adjustment**

A factory-style setup will usually angle the bridge for two-way tremolo, for both up and downward use. The bridge is often set at around a 1/8" off of the body. This setting is entirely up to you and what you hope to achieve with the tremolo. You can set it higher off the body for a more upward pull (and less downward), or set it lower to the body for less upward pull (and more downward).

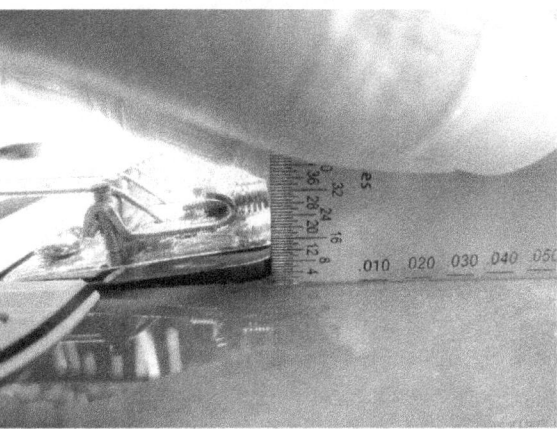

Players that do not use tremolo may set the bridge right to the body for quick tuning and better tuning stability. This can further be dialled in to allow downward tremolo, or virtually none- for more of a hard-tail setup – or anywhere in between! These adjustments are made by changing the tremolo spring tension in the back of the guitar.

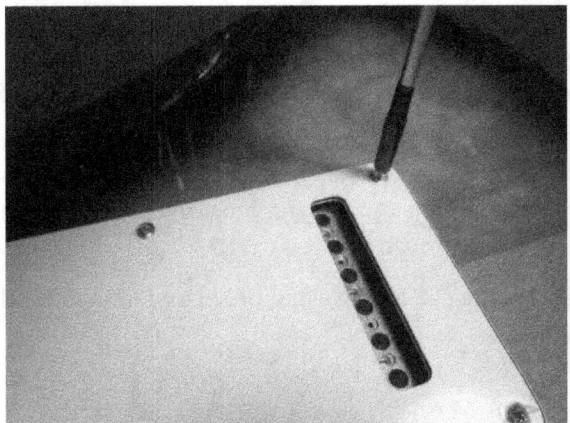
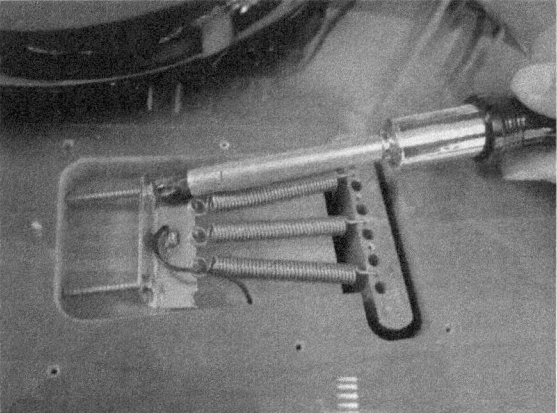

Modern Tremolo Bridges

Modern tremolo bridges will require a slightly different approach to adjusting the string height. These bridges rest on two bridge posts. The bridge is balanced between the tension of the tremolo springs and the guitar strings, similar to vintage-style bridges. This balance then affects the bridge angle, either higher off of the body or lower to the body. When it is perfectly balanced, the bridge sits parallel.

When setting up a tremolo bridge, we must first set the bridge height *and* angle, because these adjustments will affect the string height, as will any changes made after the fact.

Image left showing bridge parallel with the body, set approx. — 1/8" high. Image right showing the bridge angle set slightly higher for more upward pull

The bridge height is generally set at the factory to allow full use of the tremolo. Although the bridge can be set higher or lower to varying effect, it will generally influence the string height and overall setup the most. As with most tremolo bridge guitar setups, it may be a matter of experimentation to determine the best configuration.

Procedure

The bridge height is adjusted by tightening or loosening the two bridge bolts (see the next image). On most guitars, it is best to adjust without string tension to avoid any potential damage. If there is no bridge height specification available for your guitar, you can leave it as it is, or adjust it to measure 1/8" off of the guitar body (equally on both sides), as a generic setting. You may need to have it higher or lower in some cases. *NOTE: Fender American Standard Strats are set to 3/32" above the body.*

Once the height is correct, adjust the bridge <u>angle</u> (if required). The bridge angle is set by adjusting the spring tension in the back of the guitar (see the next section **Adjusting Bridge Angle**). Loosening the spring tension will set the bridge angle higher to favour more upward tremolo play while tightening the springs will do the opposite by pulling the bridge down towards the body. It is common for modern bridges to have individual saddle height adjustments as well as bridge height, like those pictured next.

Once the bridge height and angle are set, adjust the string height as explained previously in **Individual Saddle Height Adjustment**.

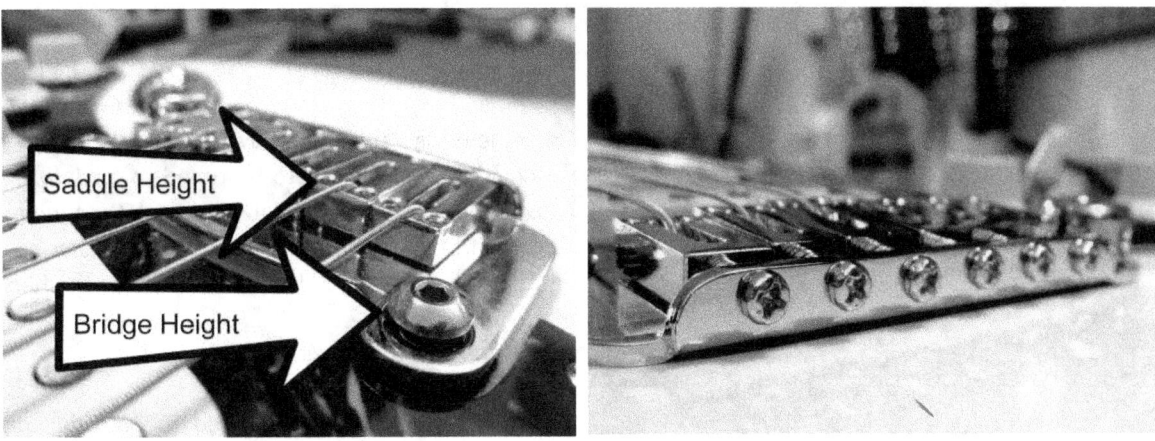

Image left showing individual saddle and bridge height adjustments. Image right showing the bridge set to the body for no upward play.

NOTE: When making adjustments to bridge posts, be sure to loosen the string tension. The sharp knife edge on the bridge can cut into the bridge posts and create divots and ditches that can hamper the tremolo's range and travel. Often, this is one of the causes of tuning problems with tremolo equipped guitars.

How to Adjust Tremolo Bridge Angle

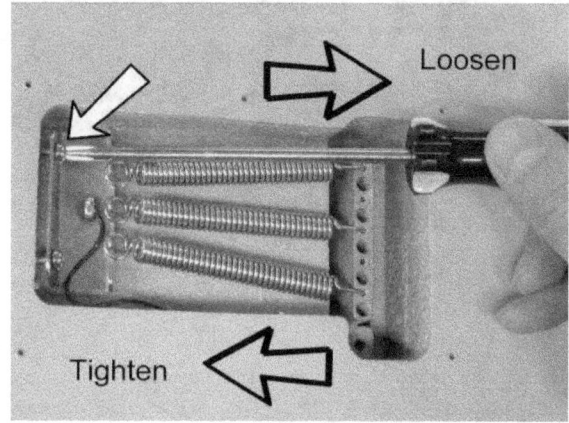

Since the bridge angle is set by changing the tremolo spring tension, we want to be tuned to pitch when making these adjustments (always check the tuning). We can increase or decrease this tension by tightening or loosening the tremolo claw in the back of the guitar.

NOTE: Sometimes, you will need to painstakingly reset the saddle height to the bridge height and vice versa, like a balancing act over and over before the setup is right.

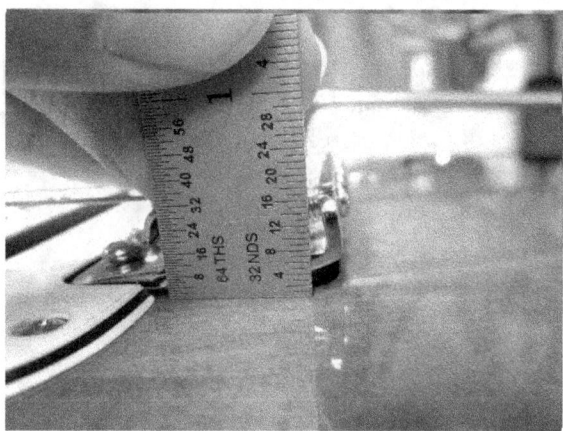

Standard 2-way tremolo: Set the backend of the bridge to be approximately 1/8" off of the body. This will give you 1 to 1.5 steps (the equivalent to 1-3 notes) in upward pitch when pulling on the tremolo bar to its maximum. Adjust the tremolo spring tension, then retune the guitar, and then check to see if the bridge angle is correctly set. Repeat this process until done. This setting will give you adequate upward and downward tremolo action. Fine-tune it to your preferences from here.

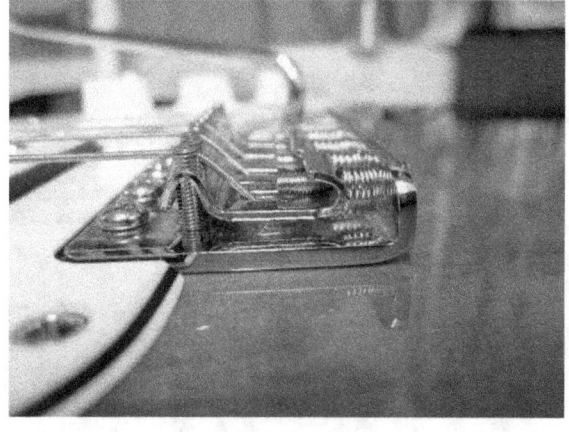

1-way tremolo (downward tremolo use only): Tighten the tremolo spring tension until the bridge sits flat on the body. Be sure to check that both sides are sitting even. Retune the guitar and check again. You will need to tighten the tremolo springs a few extra turns to ensure the bridge remains seated while bending strings, etc. You can fine-tune the tremolo bar action (making it easier or harder to use) by further adjusting the spring tension one way or the other. The more spring tension that you have, the harder the tremolo bar action will be, and vice versa. After making your adjustments, give it a play-test and try bending a treble string up a full step (with your fretting hand) and watch how much the bridge raises off of the guitar body. If you require more stability, tighten the spring tension as needed.

Hard-tail (no tremolo use): Follow the instructions for 1-way tremolo, but tighten the tremolo spring claw until it hits the back wall of the tremolo cavity. This will create the most tension and hold the bridge down to the body under most playing circumstances. If you notice that the bridge still isn't as stable as you prefer, try adding more tremolo springs.

If you need more spring tension, you can add more springs or replace them with a higher tension. You can use a small flat head screwdriver to guide the loop-end of the spring onto the tremolo spring claw.

Remember that the string tension is a combination of the string gauge and the tuning on the guitar, so anytime you are changing the string gauge, your bridge angle setting will require a re-adjustment. Is this a good excuse to have more than one guitar? Well, yeah, you bet it is!

Additional Tremolo Bridge Notes

I should mention the importance of lubrication. One of the best ways to reduce string breakage is to lubricate the saddles. Apply a light machine oil (like 3-in-1 oil) where the string makes contact with the saddle. The oil will insulate against moisture (and oxidization) and reduce metal on metal friction as well. For guitars that have string trees, you can apply some Chapstick or Vaseline where the string meets the underside of the string tree. This will help with tuning stability and lessen those annoying 'pings'.

Floyd Rose Bridges

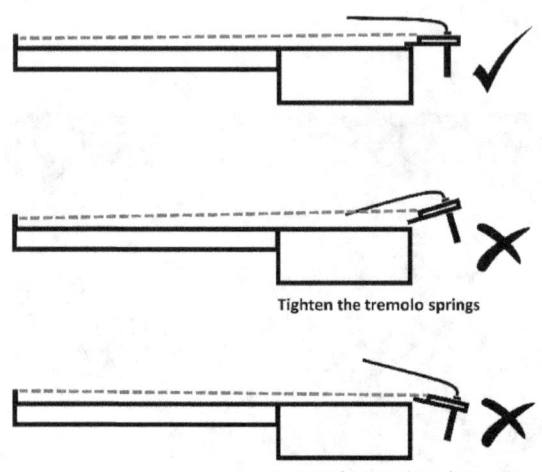

Floyd Rose-style double-locking tremolo bridges are usually designed to sit parallel with the body. One of the reasons for this is that the tremolo can be equally utilized when diving up or down.

With the nut clamps still removed, and the guitar tuned to pitch, check the **bridge angle**. If the bridge is tilted forward (away from the body), tighten the tremolo claw screws a ¼ turn each, then retune and check again. Repeat this process until the guitar is in tune and the bridge angle is correct. If the bridge is tilted backwards (into the body), you will need to carry out this process by loosening the tremolo claw screws.

Like Gibson-style bridges, the saddles on a double-locking bridge are already preset into the correct radius, so the only adjustment needed is at the bridge posts.

Procedure

When tuning is complete, and the bridge angle is correctly set, check the string height at the 12th fret (with a capo barring the first fret). If it is too high or low, adjust the two bridge studs using the correct adjustment wrench or screwdriver. Tighten to lower and loosen to raise. For example, set the #6 string to 4/64" and the #1 string to 3/64". Go back and check the #6 string for any fine adjustment, as needed. *NOTE: You may need to retune after making a bridge height adjustment.*

It cannot be overstated that adjusting these posts under full string tension can cause damage to the bridge posts. The exception is on some modern redesigned bridges, such as the Ibanez Edge. Besides detuning the strings when adjusting the bridge height, you can also manually pull the bridge away from the bridge posts temporarily while making the adjustments. You can use a wooden dowel as a wedge or a specialty tool designed for the job.

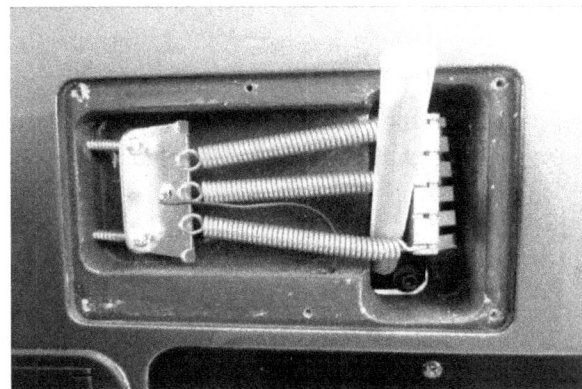

If you have enough space between the tremolo cavity and bridge block, you can use a dowel to produce some leverage. Take a dowel and situate it between the bridge block and guitar body, inside the guitar's tremolo cavity. Point it towards one of the bridge posts.

With the dowel acting like a wedge, you can move the bridge away from the post by using the tremolo arm. Slowly pull upward until the bridge moves away from the bridge post, and then hold it there to make the adjustment.

Move the bridge only enough to make the adjustment, and be careful while doing so. It is easy to pop the entire bridge right off the bridge posts (and mar them up in the process). Adjust the height incrementally, then remove the dowel and manually guide the bridge back onto its post. You may have to go back and forth a couple of times to get it right.

Finally, check the tuning and make adjustments as necessary. Repeat each step until the tuning, bridge angle and string height are all correct.

PRO TIP: Apply some 3-in-1 oil on the bridge posts to help avoid any scratches or dings when making these adjustments

Acoustic Guitars

Adjusting the string height on an acoustic guitar can be a little more involved than on an electric. In most cases, if you want to lower the string height, you must sand down the saddle. Other times there will be shims that can be removed. Alternatively, when raising the string height, shims are usually used for the job, unless a new saddle is required.

Tools Needed:
- Steel ruler and/or feeler gauges
- Pencil
- Sandpaper
- Callipers (for marking out measurements)

NOTE: Acoustic guitars can develop much bigger problems where shimming will not be a reasonable or effective method of string height adjustment. If in doubt, take it to a professional for an assessment.

The Procedure

Only adjust the string height once the relief is correctly set. With the capo on the 1st fret, take a steel ruler (or feeler gauges) and place it on the 12th fret, next to the #6 string as pictured below. Write down the measurements. Now do the same for the #1 string.

A common preference for the string height on an acoustic guitar is anywhere between 7/64" - 4/64" at the #6 string, relatively tapering down to 5/64" – 4/64" at the #1 string. You will develop a taste for how you like the action on an acoustic guitar. Higher action produces a clearer tone and louder volume. Lower action facilitates ease of play. For this example, set it to 5/64" at the #6 string, and 4/64" at the #1 string, which is a medium/low action.

The Calculation

Acoustic Guitar String Height	#6 string	#1 string
The current string height (example)	6/64"	5/64"
The target string height (suggestion)	5/64"	4/64"
The difference between them	1/64"	1/64"

To lower the action by 1/64", remove exactly TWICE that equally from the base of the saddle, which is 2/64".

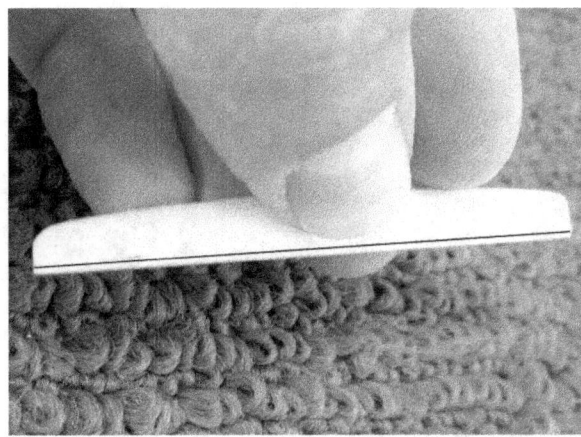 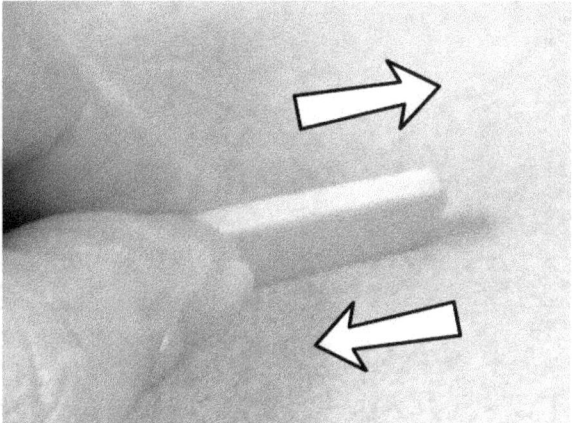

Having a calliper will come in handy for marking precise measurements. Take a pencil and mark off 2/64" from the bottom of the saddle, as pictured. Lay a piece of coarse-grit sandpaper on a flat surface and sand the bottom of the saddle down to the pencil marks. Move the saddle back and forth along the sandpaper, using gentle, even pressure. Be careful to keep the saddle upright while doing so or one side will become lower than the other. An uneven saddle will not sit in the slot properly and may produce poor tone. Also, if you have an under-the-saddle pickup, it must make firm contact with the entire base of the saddle, or it may produce uneven string balance when amplified.

Once the appropriate amount of material has been removed, reinstall the saddle and strings to test the guitar. If you've been precise, the resulting string height will have changed to the specifications intended. If it is not, repeat the process carefully until correct.

TIP: Start high and work your way down – checking your work throughout, so that you do not take too much material off.

Raising the Action

If you need to raise the string height, use the same method of calculation to get the desired result. For example, to raise the string height by 1/64", raise the saddle twice that by 2/64". You can use cardstock, veneer, or flat toothpicks as shim material and lay it freely into the saddle slot (underneath the saddle). The shim should match the thickness needed, as well as the footprint of the saddle as closely as possible. Because this can be tricky, an alternative method is to glue some wood veneer to the base of the saddle (with cyanoacrylate/crazy glue) and then sand it down incrementally until perfect.

NOTE: If you have an under-saddle pickup, always place any loose shims underneath the pickup for the best performance.

ADJUST THE STRING HEIGHT AT THE NUT

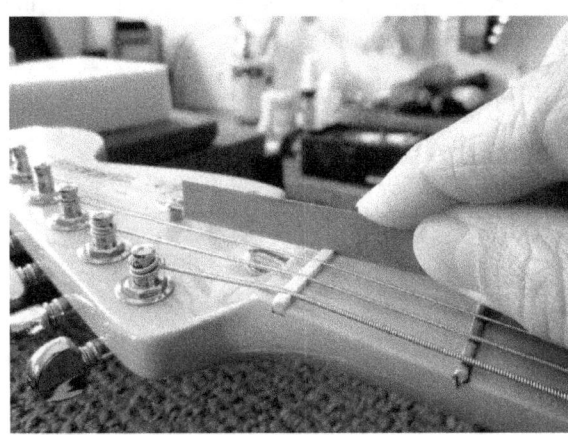

If the first couple of frets are uncomfortable to play, the nut slot depth may be too high. This section will show you how to fine-tune the string height at the nut.

Every manufacturer has their own specifications to follow, so we'll use common specs based on a medium height fret wire. The goal is to file the nut slot depth to allow enough clearance for the string above the 1st fret.

For this work, you will need specialty nut slotting files — there are a couple of different styles to choose from.

The double edge nut file is a favourite for durability and efficiency. Each file cuts two different width slots. The blade is tapered, and designed for nut work only. Single gauged nut slotting files, on the other hand, can be used for more than one job, such as saddle slot cutting. These files are not as durable but are preferred by many professionals as the tool of choice.

Determine the Fret Height

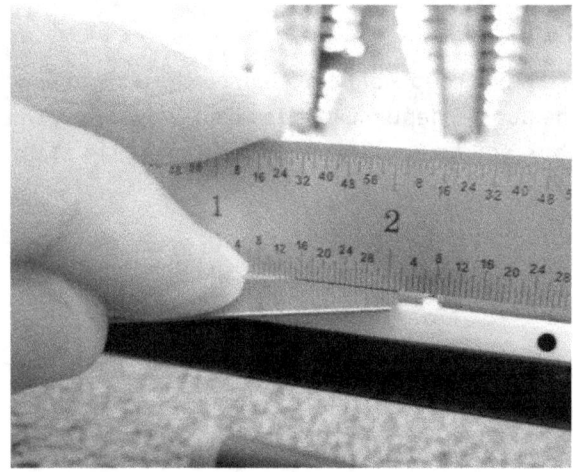

Before getting started, we need to determine a measurable clearance above the 1st fret. Knowing the size of the fret wire will help.

In this example, the fretwire used is .040" high.

Measure the height of the first two frets by laying a straightedge across them and sliding the correct combination of feeler gauge blades underneath.

How to File Nut Slots

Start at the #1 string and add .025"-.030" to the measured fret height. If the fret height is .040", start at .070". It is much better to work down than to miscalculate and over cut.

Place the feeler gauges next to the nut, under the strings and against the fretboard (see the next photos). Be sure the feeler gauges are held down firmly on the fretboard when cutting. Be careful not to use excessive pressure when holding them down, as you may overbend them into an arch and affect the depth of your cut.

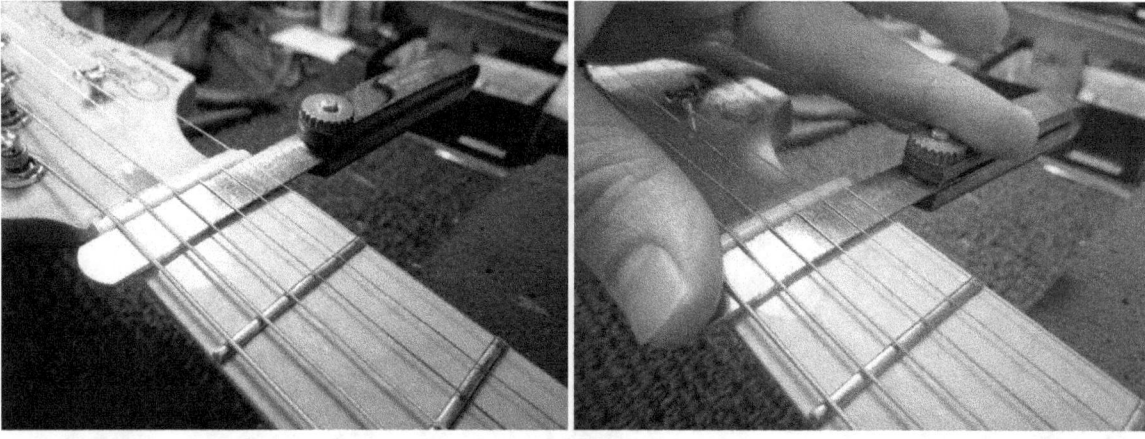

NOTE: If the fretboard is warped, or you have unseated frets, this method may produce poor results and is not recommended.

When using nut slotting files, choose the file size that matches the string gauge (as closely as possible). If the file is a little narrower, you can rock it slightly side-to-side to widen the slot. But when the nut slot is too wide, the string can vibrate and buzz when played open. If you ever find this problem, it is a common issue that requires fixing (see the next section on **the crazy glue and baking soda trick**). Generally, we can get away with a little wider, but even a few thousandths of an inch can be too much sometimes.

Procedure

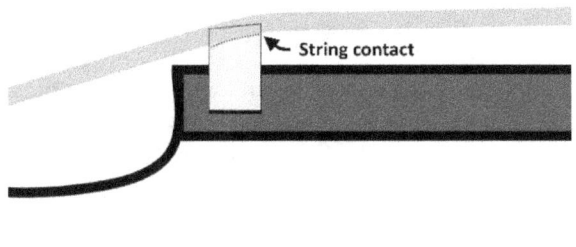

File at an angle to the nut's front edge. In other words, follow the string path toward the tuners and match the same angle. Doing so ensures that the string will be seated in the nut slot properly and will have sufficient downward pressure. The string's contact point should be at the front of the nut to properly intonate and play in tune.

On guitars with angled headstocks, such as Gibson's, Gretsch's or Jacksons, follow the angle of the headstock itself. On Fender-style guitars, file the appropriate angle for each string.

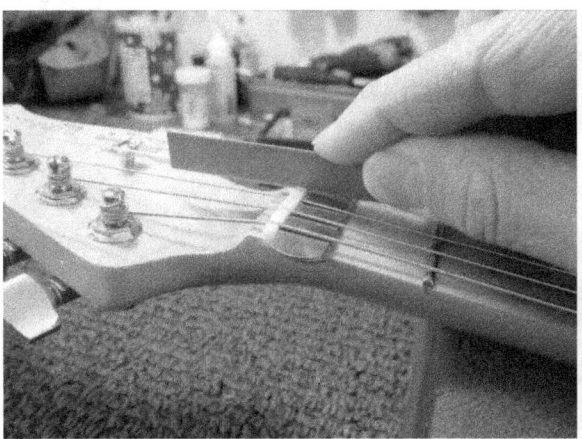 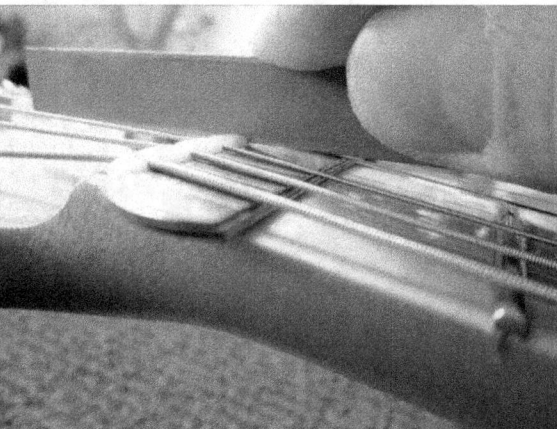

Notice the varying string angles in the next example. The #6 string has the steepest string angle due to the location of the tuner, which is closest to the nut. Follow the pitch of each string as closely as possible.

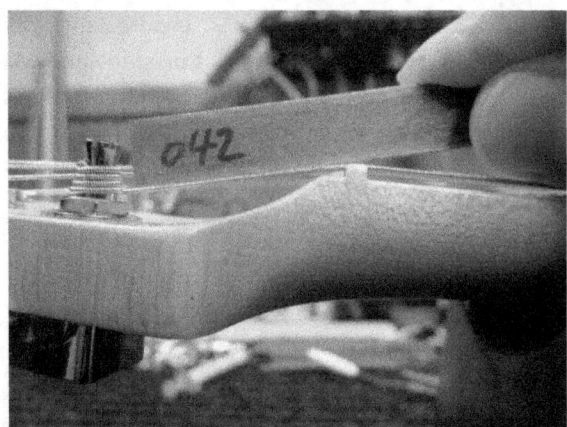

Hold the file straight and cut one pass at a time. Continue filing until the file grazes the feeler gauges.

Once the file makes contact with the feeler gauge blades, pull the gauges away from the fretboard and check your work. See how it feels when playing at the 1st fret. Play the open string and listen for any excessive buzzing or rattle.

Hold down the string at the 3rd fret while tapping it at the 1st fret with your other hand. If the string height is getting low, you will hear a high-pitched "pinging". The sound is produced by the string bouncing off the fret at a minimal distance.

To gauge your work, you can measure the string height at the 1st fret. Bar the 3rd fret while measuring the gap between the top of the 1st fret and the bottom of the string. An acceptable tolerance here is 006" at the #1 string and .010" at the #6 string.

If you have more filing to do, lessen the number of feeler gauges you started with by .002" or .003" at a time until you are closer to this spec.

When ready to move on to the next string(s), incrementally add a few thousandths of an inch (.002" to .003") to each pairing of strings as you go across the fingerboard toward the bass side. This is because, as each string gets thicker, it requires slightly higher action at the nut for a clean tone. For example, shoot for .006" for the #1 & #2 strings, .009" for #3 & #4 strings, and .012" for #5 & #6 strings. Remember to start higher than planned and work your way down until you have this process mastered. Tolerances can be even lower than this for more effortless playing, but do so at your own risk! Low nut slots can produce a lot of string rattle.

Finish things off by adding some string lube, Vaseline, or graphite in the nut slots for better tuning stability.

NOTE: You will know you've filed too much if you hear a lot of string rattle when playing the open string(s). To correct this, you can try and fill it and recut – or – you'll have to carefully remove the nut, shim it with cardstock or veneer, and then recut the slots again to proper depth- or take it into a professional technician.

Filling Nut Slots with Crazy Glue and Baking Soda

Maybe you've heard of it, and maybe you haven't. Well, this little trick is a godsend, a little hack for overcut nut slots – although, it only works effectively on *bone* nuts.

So, you cut too far on one string, and the last thing you want to do is to start over completely. Good news for you, we've got this covered!

Take some paper or a business card and fold it in half. Pour some baking soda onto it and tap it into the nut slot. Pack it in there the best that you can and brush away the excess powder (so there is none on the fretboard or surrounding areas). Apply some thin viscosity cyanoacrylate glue (crazy glue) to the baking soda and wait until it hardens. Make sure there is enough to saturate the baking soda, but don't allow so much as to drip onto the fretboard, etc. It's always a good idea to have a paper towel nearby, so you are ready to catch any excess. Put a little lighter fluid on it beforehand for quick cleanup standby.

> *TIP: Further protect the fretboard and headstock by applying some low-tack masking tape to the area before gluing. Always pull the tape off of lacquered surfaces carefully and slowly.*

The baking soda and glue will dry into a super hard, bone-like material for a fresh start. Now you can recut that slot properly. Finish things off with some string lube.

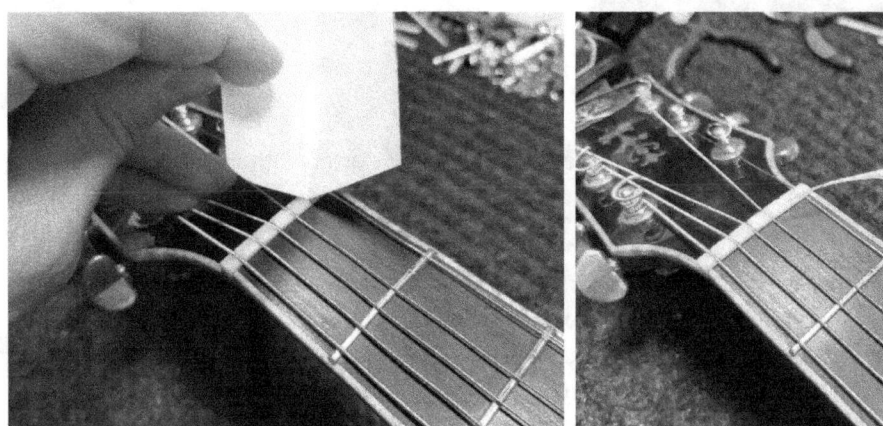

Nut Removal & Replacement

Nut removal and replacement are delicate, intermediate-level repair work and is best left in the hands of an experienced technician. For the amateur repair person, there is some potential to damage the guitar irrevocably. Due to the multitude of guitar design, the instruction below is a general reference that can be followed with caution.

What You'll Need:
- X-Acto precision knife or razor blade (new)
- Wood block
- Flathead screwdriver
- Light-duty hammer

Overview

Nuts are often glued in place. It is usually necessary to gently break the nut free. They can be easy to remove in some cases, yet difficult in others. Some models will have lacquer sprayed over top of the nut, making it much more difficult to remove. Other times, the nut will not budge and may need to be destroyed in order to remove it.

Some guitar nuts sit on top of the headstock, whereas others sit within a precisely cut slot. Guitars with a nut slot or groove require additional care to avoid any damage.

Procedure

1. Remove the strings if not already. Take an X-Acto knife with a new blade and trace around every edge of the nut to cut away any lacquer from sticking to it. Be sure to cut through the lacquer completely to avoid chipping the finish. Avoid cutting deeply as this can also chip the finish. Lightly cut away at the finish using repetitive strokes until complete. *TIP: If there is heavy lacquer buildup around the nut, you can use a hobby saw to cut it through it.*
2. If the nut is **not** sitting in a slot or groove, place a small wood block on the fretboard and lightly tap it to break the glues' bond and set it free. Sometimes you may need to tap it from both angles, going back and forth a few times until it's free.
3. If it **is** sitting in a slot or groove, you will gently tap it out sideways using the edge of the block (recommended), or a screwdriver.
4. Once it has started to move out sideways, pull on it in the same direction with a pair of pliers to remove it completely. *TIP: Nuts that are difficult to remove, may come out easier being pulled out from the top.*

NOTE: Sometimes, the nut will not budge when being hammered sideways. Due to the nut slot shrinking over time, or a strong glue bond, the nut becomes fixed in place and will not come loose no matter what you do. This often results in the nut being destroyed or broken during the process.

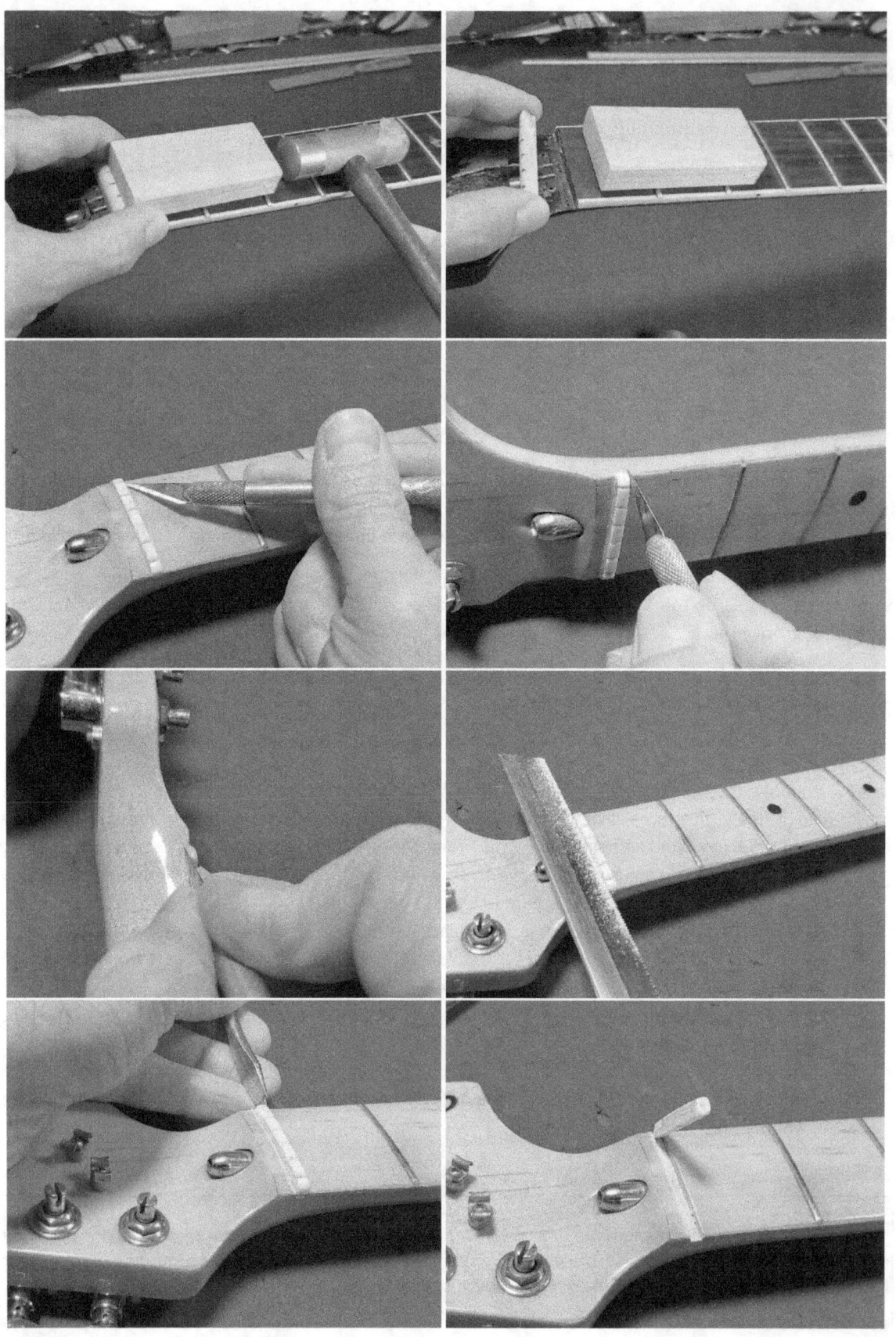

Nut Replacement Procedure

Scrape away any old glue or debris from the nut slot. It should be flat and square.

Check to see that the replacement nut and the original nut have the same string-to-string placement.

Check to see if the new nut fits into the slot without requiring excessive pressure or force. It should fit snugly, yet easy to remove, and with no side-to-side play. If it's too thick, you can sand down the walls by placing medium-grit sandpaper (400 - 600 grit) face-up on a flat surface and sanding down the walls until it fits.

At this point, the nut should fit in the slot. If necessary, trim the ends of the nut so that they are flush with the guitar neck. If they are poking out, your hand will continually braise over them with discomfort. You can use a pencil or an X-Acto knife to mark the ends of the nut. Remove it from the neck and sand it to the marks. *TIP: String up the guitar and ensure the strings are evenly spread across the fretboard before doing the final shaping of the nut. Sight up the low and high E strings and check that they are both equal distances away from the edge of the fretboard. You can use a ruler or simply eye-ball it.*

The final step is cutting the nut slot depth, which is covered previously in the section for **nut slot filing**.

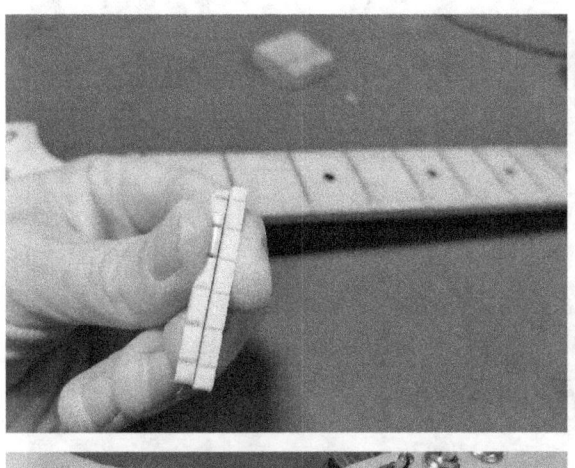

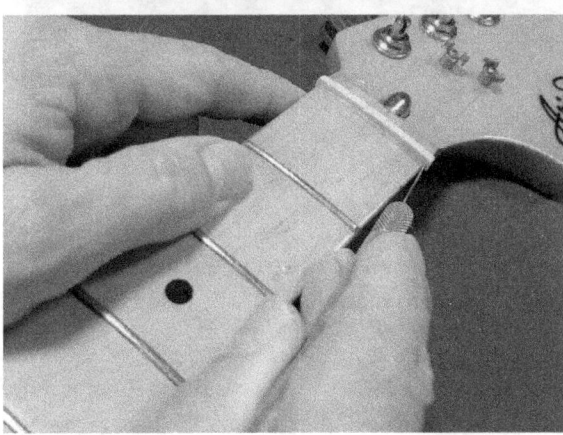

Locking Nuts / Roller Nuts

If there is a locking or roller nut on the guitar, it will require removing or adding of shims to change the string height at the nut. Often metal shims are included with the guitar, but if these aren't available, you can use wood veneer, paper, or cardstock.

Loosen the strings first, then the nut bolts. Remove or add the shim(s) under the nut. You can usually do so without removing the strings completely. Reinstall the nut, retune the guitar and check your work.

To gauge your work, measure the string height at the 1st fret. As previously mentioned, bar the 3rd fret while measuring the gap between the top of the 1st fret and the bottom of the string. An acceptable tolerance here is 006" at the #1 string and .010" at the #6 string.

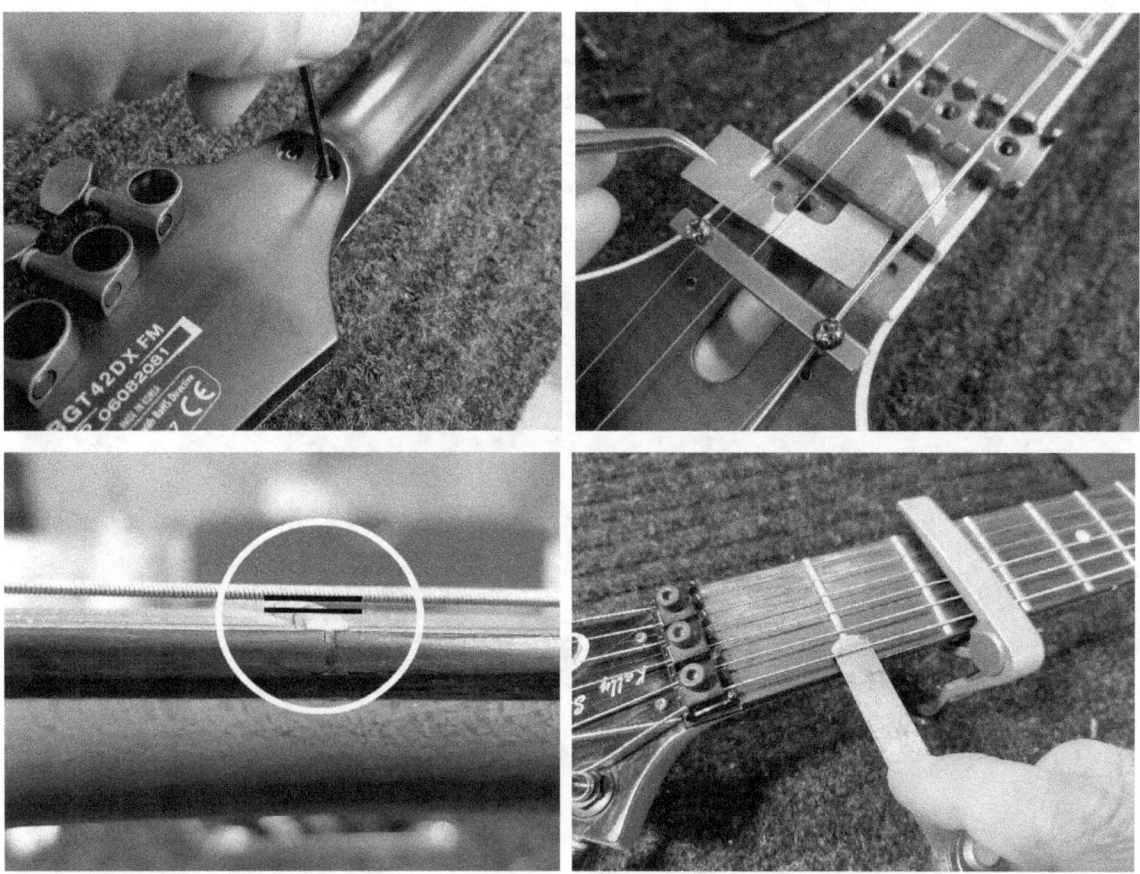

If you need to raise the string height at the nut, because of excessive open string buzzing (and you've double-checked your work up to this point), try adding .005" of shim material until it's resolved. You can double up on your shim if needed or use thicker material.

If you need to lower the string height, simply remove the shims present and test the results. If there is more than one, they could be of different thicknesses. Experiment with what works best- lower the nut incrementally until the string height is just right. Reinstall the nut and tune to pitch. Essentially you will discover what configuration works best. You may need to replace the shim currently present with a thinner or thicker shim to get the results you want.

ADJUST THE PICKUP HEIGHT

Now that the action is set, adjust the pickup height to the strings accordingly. With the strings tuned to pitch, bar and hold down the #6 string at the last fret and place a ruler on the pickup pole as shown below. On covered humbuckers such as those first pictured, place the ruler on the exposed pole, as opposed to the cover. There is some room to experiment with, but a reasonable distance away from the strings is 6/64" on the #6 string side. Now do the same on the treble side for the #1 string and adjust it to 4/64". These specs can be used similarly for each pickup on the guitar and later modified for volume balance by ear if needed.

Follow the method pictured below. The low wound strings (#6, #5, #4) have a wider range of motion, so adjust the pickup height a little lower to accommodate this. Doing so will produce a more even sound across all the strings.

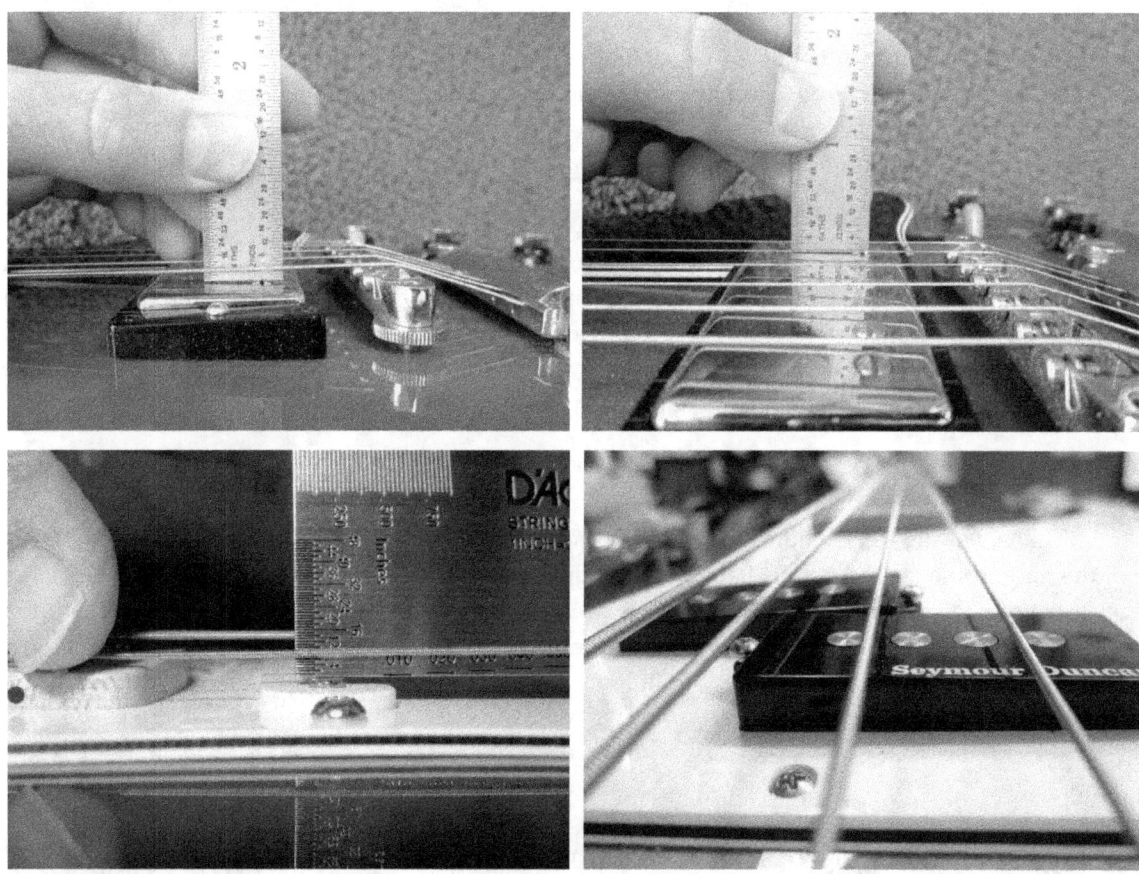

For bass guitars, you will want to allow more space for the strings to travel. Try setting the pickups to 8/64" at the lowest string and 6/64" at the highest. Notice in the picture how the pickup height matches the radius of the strings.

You may notice that changing the pickup height affects the volume output of the guitar- but be aware: if the pickup is set too close to the strings, it may produce poor intonation and off-sounding notes. This happens when the magnetic field of the pickup interferes with the strings' harmonics. If you ever come across some random intonation issues, try lowering the pickups, especially with single coils. Also, if you have a Floyd Rose-style equipped guitar, check that the pickup height doesn't interfere with the rest of your setup. Pull the whammy bar all the way up to make sure the strings don't bottom out on the pickups.

ADJUST THE INTONATION

About Intonation
Intonation is the degree to which notes sound in tune. Since each string on the guitar is a different diameter and pitch, as well as a different tension, they require scaling. If you've ever tuned the guitar with an electronic tuner, and then played some notes or chords only to find they were slightly out of tune, you may need to adjust the intonation. Let's start by saying that no guitar plays "perfect" all up and down the fretboard. Some people can hear the imperfection and others cannot.

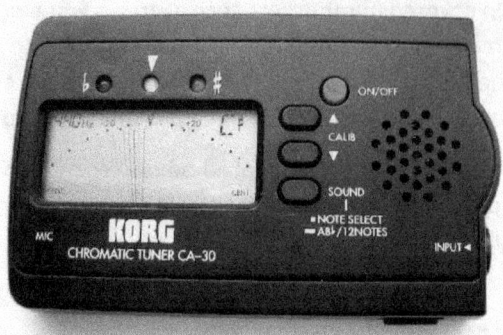

Several factors affect guitar intonation. Besides the setup adjustments, these would include fret condition, saddle & nut slot wear, string gauge, tuning, and string quality. Although nothing can substitute for a well-serviced guitar, we can easily correct intonation if the bridge saddles are out of adjustment. Intonation is the last step of the setup because every other aspect of the setup will affect it.

How to Check Intonation
With the guitar tuned to pitch (and in playing position) play a harmonic note at the 12th fret on the #1 string. Check that the note is perfectly in tune and retune if needed. Now press down and play the same note naturally at the 12th fret. Keep in mind that excessive finger pressure will cause the note to sound sharp. Compare the harmonic note to the natural fretted note on the tuner. Listen to them both- they should sound the same. If they are not, the intonation requires adjustment.

Adjusting Intonation
The goal is to make the harmonic note at the 12th fret the same pitch as the fretted note. If the harmonic note is in tune, yet the fretted note is sharp, "lengthen" the string by adjusting the saddle <u>further</u> away from the neck. If the fretted note is flat, "shorten" the string by adjusting the saddle <u>closer</u> towards the neck. Make the adjustments in small increments while checking your progress with a tuner. Repeat the procedure until the harmonic and natural fretted notes are identical, as verified by the tuner and your ear.

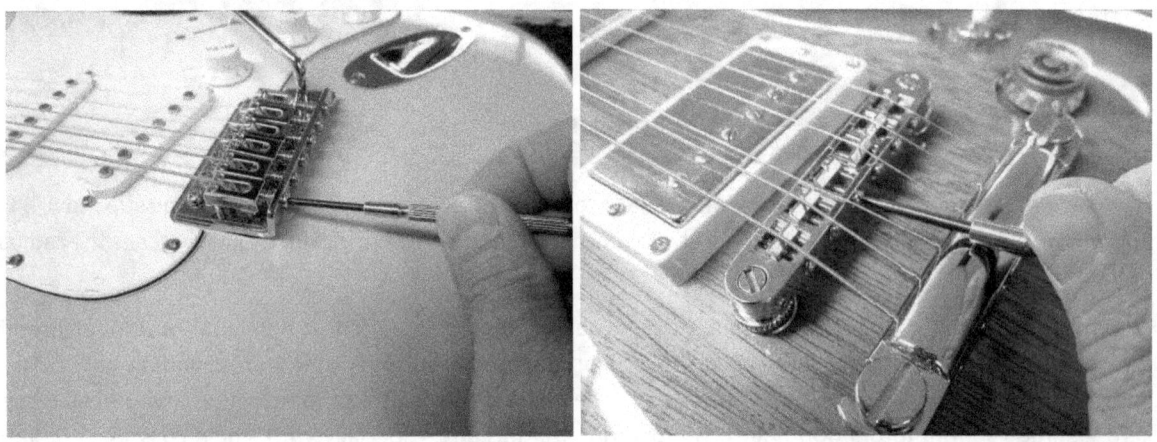

WIRING & ELECTRONICS

Guitar Electronics 101

Let's take a look at a typical guitar circuit. It commonly consists of the pickup(s), which produces the sound, potentiometers to adjust volume and tone, a switch to select between different pickups (if the instrument has more than one), and the output jack. There may be additional controls for specific functions; the most common of these are described below.

Guitar Pickups

Pickups are the heart of your guitar. An electric guitar pickup is an inductive sensor that consists of a coil wrapped around a magnetic pole piece(s). When the string vibrates, a signal is generated in the coil. That signal is then amplified to create the sound you hear.

There are countless pickup models in the marketplace, and they vary greatly in design. There is a countless combination of materials used which contribute to the properties in the tone produced. For the most part, electric guitar pickups can be thrown into one of two categories: **single coil** or **dual coil** (better known as **humbuckers)**.

Single coil pickups have a single bar magnet wrapped in copper wire. They are generally bright and articulate sounding, and most commonly found on Strat- and Tele- styled guitars. This design can be prone to picking up hum and RF interference from electrical power cables, power transformers, and fluorescent light ballasts in the area.

Humbucking pickups are composed of two coils side by side, which makes the signal approximately doubled when wired in series (which is usually the case). Humbuckers also have a fuller (fatter) tone, and are generally less bright sounding than a single-coil, but are hum-cancelling and preferred by those seeking a fuller sound from their guitar.

Potentiometers

Potentiometers (often abbreviated as "pots") are variable resistors and are used to control the volume and tone of the pickups. Depending on the design, there may be one or more on the guitar. Besides functioning as tone and volume controls, they can also be wired to blend two pickups together or attenuate one coil of a humbucker, among other things.

Potentiometers can be categorized into resistor **value** and **taper**.

- **The resistor value** is the actual resistance of the pot measured between the two outer lugs. The most common values are 250 kΩ (kilo-ohm), which is well-matched to single-coil pickups, and 500 kΩ (kilo-ohm), which is well-matched to humbuckers. Values ranging from 50 kΩ to as high as 1 MΩ can be used, although the choice is subjective to the players' preference. A volume pot with a higher resistance value will allow more treble to pass through to your output, resulting in a brighter sound. Alternatively, a volume pot with a lower resistance value will bleed off high frequencies, resulting in a warmer tone. 25 kΩ pots are generally used with active pickups or electronics exclusively.

- **Taper** can be likened to the sweep of the pot. In guitars, there are linear pots (designated by the letter B) and audio pots (designated by the letter A). Linear pots work much like they are named, in a linear fashion. As you roll the shaft in the pot, you get an even, graduated sweep. An audio pot is slightly different and has a pronounced dip in the taper. These are generally used for volume controls, although not as a rule. Linear pots can be used as volume pots as well, offering a slightly different sweep that may appeal to those wanting that type of control.

Besides Volume and Tone controls, there are specialty pots available for other switching and blending functions.

- **Push-pull pots** incorporate an on-off DPDT switch on the underside of the pot that's engaged by pulling the shaft upwards and disengaged by pushing it back in (hence the name). The switch is electrically independent of the pot and can be used for many switching options, like coil splitting, in/out of phase switching, series/parallel switching, and pickup selection.

- **Push-push pots** are a variation of those as mentioned earlier but incorporate a spring mechanism into the switch, which is activated and deactivated by pushing in.
- **No-load pots** have the clockwise lug disconnected from the resistive strip within, resulting in infinite resistance between the wiper and the other outer lug when turned fully clockwise (10 on the dial). These are sometimes used as tone controls to remove the load on the pickup(s) by the pot and the tone cap, resulting in a circuit with less resistance (which may translate into a 'truer' direct pickup tone.
- **Dual-gang pots** are simply two pots stacked together, either with concentric shafts, allowing the independent control of two different parameters, or with a common shaft. The latter type can be used for blending the signals of two pickups and may feature an indent in the centre position.

Capacitors

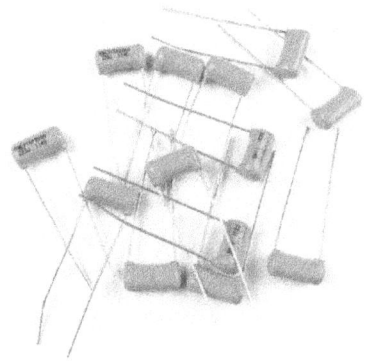

A capacitor (better known as a "cap") is a passive two-terminal electrical component used to store energy in an electric field temporarily. Caps are like a filter which let the highest frequencies pass, but resist lower frequencies. When connected to a lug on a potentiometer, this will, in turn, become a low-pass filter shorting high frequencies to ground. As the shaft is turned from the 10 to the 1 position, the cap is introduced into the signal. This cuts the treble, the more the control is turned down.

Caps can also be wired in such a way as to prevent the loss of high frequencies as the volume pot is turned down, specifically called a *treble bleed mod* (see below).

There are not only different value caps available to use, but many different brands and styles to choose from. Traditionally, a .047μ capacitor matches well with single coils, and .022μ matches well with humbuckers - although completely subjective, you may find either value with either pickup style. Many different values can be utilized, producing completely different results, most notably the frequency of treble roll-off (how dark or bassy you want the tone to be). Caps consisting of different materials may again provide a change in the subtleness in quality of frequency when rolled off, which again may be obvious to a discerning ear only.

Switches

There are many types of switches used on guitars. Typically, there are lever, toggle, slide, and rotary switches used for various pickup selections, and within these styles, they can vary greatly depending on the circuit involved.

Mini toggle switches are commonly found for pickup selection and custom wired configurations (coil splitting, etc.) and can be found in several styles of switching, such as: on/on, on/off, on/on/on, on/off/on, etc.

Jacks

The output jack is the end of the line. It is where you plug the guitar cable in and push that signal to the amplifier. Like the other components, these can vary in design as well, depending on the intricacy of the circuit.

HOW TO SOLDER

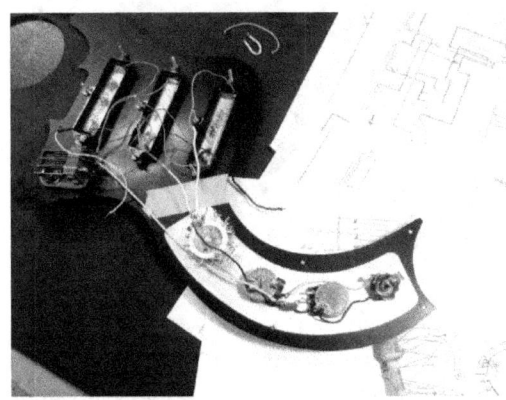

With a little instruction and some practice, repairing guitar electronics isn't difficult. I have found that when people get frustrated in the process, it is often because they are using inadequate solder equipment or just lacking technique.

The guitar circuit itself can be simple or complicated, depending on your needs. There is seemingly an infinite number of ways to wire a guitar, depending on the configuration. Thankfully, the internet is a great source for wiring diagrams for many popular configurations. If you haven't done much soldering before, please read ahead.

Soldering 101

Soldering is a process in which two or more items are joined together by melting and putting a filler metal into the joint, the filler metal having a lower melting point than the adjoining metal.

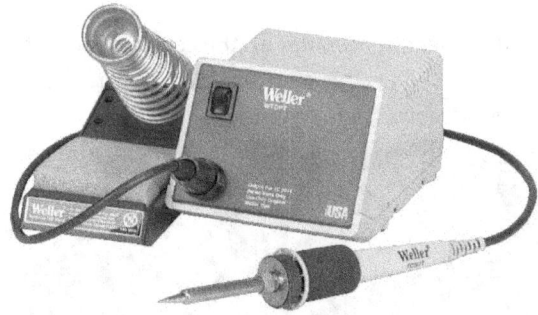

If you haven't soldered before, keep in mind that it does take some practice to do good work. A few key points before starting: Start with a good workspace. Organize your parts and have tools within reach. If you have a strat, you can assemble most of your components onto the pickguard and solder them in place. The same goes for the control plate on a tele-style guitar. Otherwise, I'd suggest making a cardboard template to hold the components like the pots and switches so that it's easy to work on, and you're not fumbling around with a hot solder iron.

Producing a solid solder joint comes down to using good technique and a good iron (35-40 watts is sufficient for guitar electronics). Using a low-powered solder iron or one with a bad/old tip will not get you very good results. I have read some people are suggesting a 25-watt solder iron works well for guitar electronics, and they do, but they don't work well for every job on the guitar. I have found that with heavier-duty jobs such as when soldering potentiometer housings or tremolo claws (for ground wires), that the lower-powered soldering irons just can't get the job done very well.

When purchasing one, try to find one with a variable temperature adjustment. This way, you can control exactly how much heat is needed for the job. Some components, such as potentiometers, may require more heat than a switch or jack. *NOTE: Avoid using a soldering gun as they can alter the magnetic properties of the pickups.*

No matter what configuration you are wiring, there are a few golden rules to follow:

"Tin" the wire and connecting terminal first.

Tinning is a term used to describe the process of applying a thin precoat of solder on the connections before connecting them. There are situations where it is preferable to bypass this step and tie the wiring to the terminal first. But whenever possible, tinning will ensure a good, solid solder connection.

Apply heat to the component/connecting terminal first.

Many make the mistake of trying to heat the solder and force the parts together. This is incorrect. Heat the connection, such as a terminal or lug, and allow the solder to melt and flow over it. You can actually watch the solder meld onto the connection when it is hot enough. Notice in the first picture below that the solder isn't touching the iron - it is right beside it touching the lug. In the next picture, the lug heats up, and the solder melts in place.

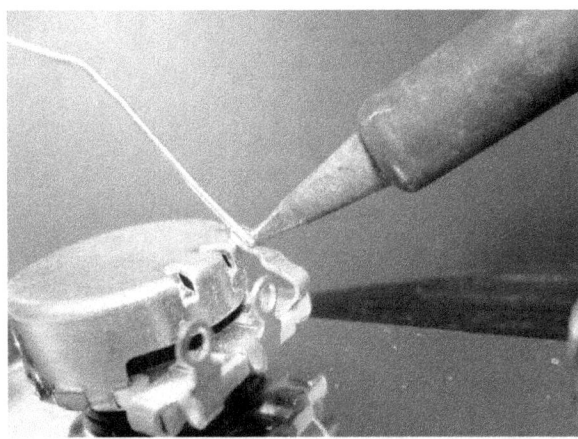

Always "tin" the tip when using a new tip.

Tinning should be done right away when using a new tip. Let the solder flow all over the tip and allow it to sit for 10 seconds or more before cleaning on a tip cleaner or damp sponge. Reapply more solder, clean and repeat. After a few repetitions, the tip should be properly tinned. To get the most life out of a tip, remember to clean it constantly throughout your job and leave the iron on only while using it. Allowing the iron to remain on for any length of time without use will burn the tip out prematurely.

Don't expose a lot of wire when stripping the insulation.

Try and strip back only enough insulation to expose a small amount of wire (approx. 1/16"); otherwise, you may risk having some of the exposed wire grounding out on other connections. If you are crimping the wire around the terminal beforehand, use only the amount necessary.

REPAIRING GUITAR ELECTRONICS

Tools & Supplies You Will Need:
- 35-40-watt soldering iron (pen style)
- 60/40 rosin core solder
- A damp sponge for cleaning the soldering iron tip
- An old rag or t-shirt to protect the guitar while working (recommended)
- Tweezers or a hemostat for holding the wire while working (optional)
- Solder sucker or desoldering bulb for removing excess solder (optional)
- A third-hand for holding the components while working (optional)
- Electrical tape or heat-shrink tubing to insulate any exposed connections (recommended)

Output Jacks:

Intermittent Output Jacks

Output jacks are notorious for becoming loose and going intermittent or dead altogether. What often happens is once they become loose, the internal wiring gets twisted and becomes weak or damaged as a result. This can be remedied quite easily by re-soldering the connections and tightening up the jack. For a good connection, you may need to first remove the old wire completely, strip the end(s) and then solder it back on. If the jack is housed in a metal jack plate, such as a Stratocaster, keep in mind the jack plate will act as a heat-sink and draw the heat away from the jack while soldering. If it is taking too long, remove the jack from the jack plate and try it again.

Jacks can also become worn out- some are not made to last. If the wiring looks good, but the jack is still intermittently cutting out, a replacement may be necessary. Take a picture of the old jack, or cut the wires off just at the insulation, so you can easily do the replacement without any second-guessing.

Other times the terminals of the jack itself have worn or bent away from making contact with the plug. The guitar cable's plug should make firm contact inside the jack, with minimal side-to-side play. If you suspect the terminals are bent, remove the cable and manually bend the contact if possible (barrel-style jacks are generally not serviceable like this).

Static Noise from Output Jack

If you hear static noise and have checked the wiring, the interior of the jack itself may be dirty. As mentioned in the **general adjustments** section, you can often clean a dirty jack by rolling up super-fine grit sandpaper and twisting it into the jack for a few seconds. Alternatively, you can spray a contact cleaner into it and push the cable end in and out a few times.

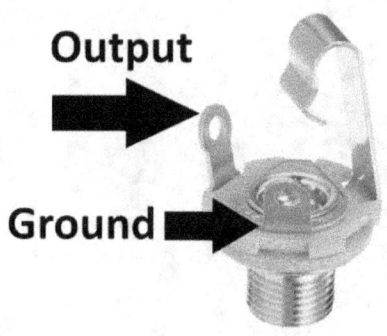

How to Solder Wires to an Output Jack

When soldering a wire to a jack or switch, you can approach it one of two ways. You can pre-tin all the connections as mentioned previously, or pre-wire them.

Pre-wire

It's generally a good rule of thumb to ensure a good physical connection between the wire and terminal before soldering. You can loop the wire through the lug and crimp or twist it in place- or use a tool to hold it, such as a set of tweezers or a hemostat. Fender Guitars will often twist the wire around each terminal, followed by soldering. This is an effective way to ensure the wires stay put while soldering, especially on an assembly line, but it is challenging to remove if ever needing a repair.

Procedure

Heat the terminal with the soldering iron for a few seconds. Put the tip of the soldering iron next to the wire. Bring in the solder and melt it over the terminal and wire- <u>not</u> on the soldering iron. For clarity's sake, it is important to understand the solder is melted by the heat of the terminal, not the iron. If the solder doesn't melt, the terminal isn't hot enough. Continue heating it a few more seconds and be sure the iron is firmly making contact with the terminal. A good iron with a new tip will heat a component in seconds, so the soldering process shouldn't take much longer than that. Using too much heat over too long of time runs the risk of destroying the component.

If the component you're wiring isn't properly supported in either the guitar cavity, pickguard, holding a tool or cardboard template, then it will move around every time the iron is placed on it. The heat will not transfer well, and it will take extra time to do so. Hold and support the components firmly when soldering to ensure a successful job. You can use a tool such as a "third hand" for this (pictured). Once the solder liquefies over the terminal and wire, you can remove both the iron and solder. You only need enough solder to cover the connection, nothing more. Don't glob it on. If you use too much solder, try removing some of it with a solder sucker. When finished, allow the solder to cool and give the wire a little tug to ensure it is solid.

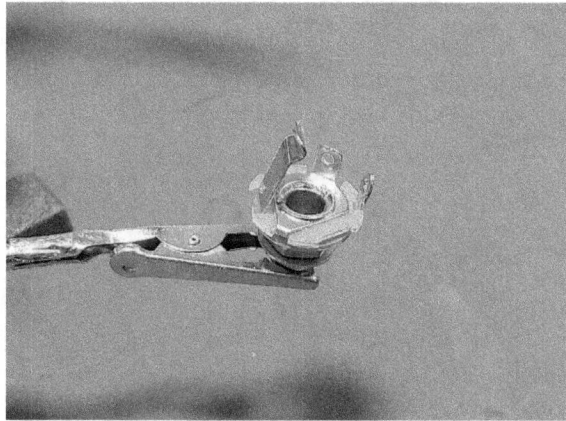

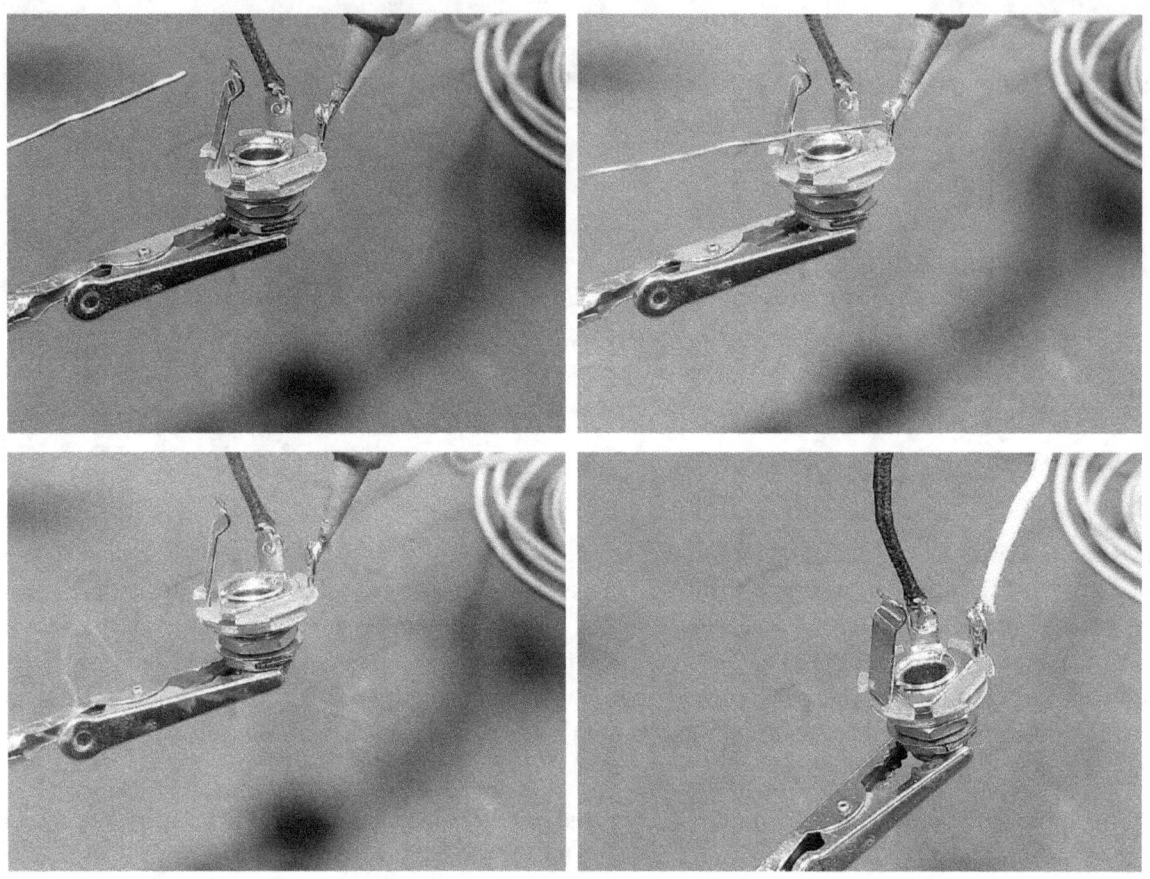

TIP: Solder irons can get extremely hot. Keep in mind that every component, whether a jack, or switch, and all connecting wires will each tolerate different amounts of heat. Robust heavy-gauge wiring, as in the previous pictures, will tolerate much more heat than a lighter gauge wire. Lugs on a jack will tolerate more heat than some switches. It is possible to destroy a switch or pot by applying too much heat. If the insulation around the wire begins burning away, turn down the soldering iron or lighten up on your application.

How to De-Solder

Sometimes, there isn't a clean connection to work with, especially when resoldering or repairing a bad connection, such as with a broken wire. A previously soldered lug will be covered in the old solder. If you have a solder sucker or desoldering bulb, you can remove some of the excesses by heating the lug and sucking off the liquid solder from the connection.

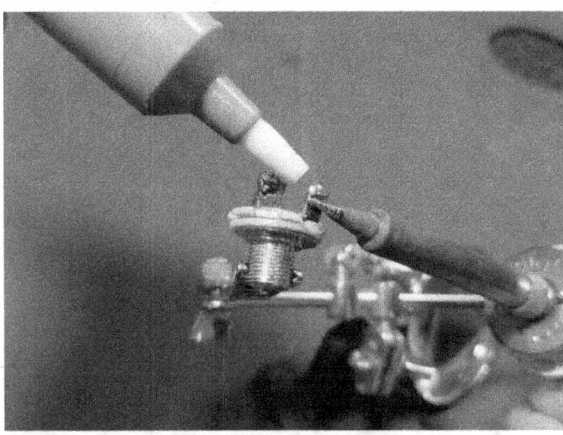
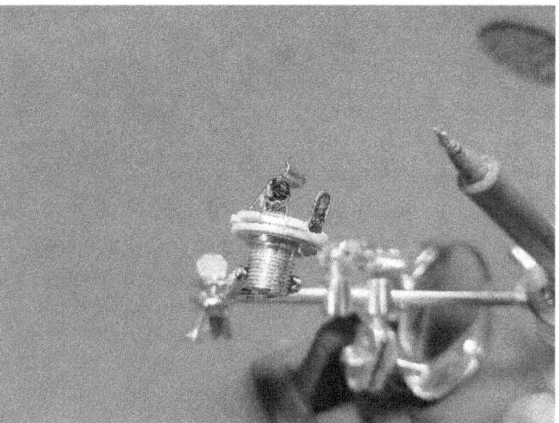

If you do not have these tools, you can still do the repair by using the old solder. Heat the lug until the solder melts and insert the wire immediately, and reposition the iron's tip towards the wire. Hold the wire still and keep it in place long enough for the heat to transfer and solder to bond. In most cases, the heat from the melted solder alone will transfer over to the wire, and that will be enough. Otherwise, be sure to position the iron to heat both terminal and wire to ensure a strong weld. You can tell the weld has "taken" once you see solder "wick" up in the wire.

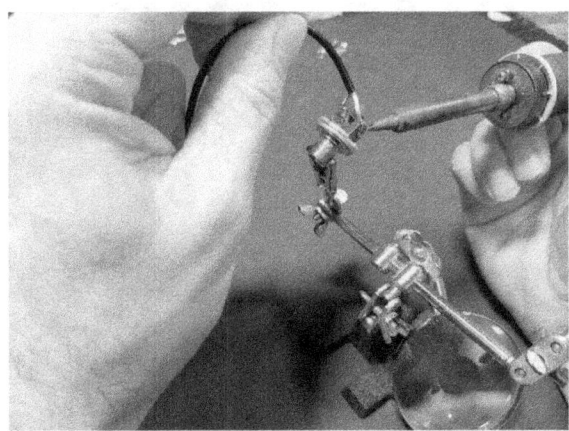

Pickup Selector Switches

Pickup selector switches can also become scratchy or intermittently cut in and out. If you have inspected the wiring and it appears to be ok, the switch may need to be cleaned with contact cleaner, as mentioned previously in **cleaning**. If cleaning doesn't improve anything, it has probably become worn-out, and you may need to replace it. When doing so, follow the wiring from the previous switch or lookup a wiring diagram, such as those in the **FURTHER RESOURCES** section. There are different styles of blade switches available, and they all will work, but there can be sizing differences between them. Find a replacement that is made for the guitar for the best results.

Wiring Pickup Switches

As when wiring output jacks, the process with pickup selector switches is the same. You can tie or crimp the wires around the terminal and apply the soldering iron. These components are generally light-duty and heat up fast, so try not to overdo it. Apply the solder immediately and allow it to cool. Give the wire a good tug to make sure it is solid. Switches especially are easiest to work on while in the guitar (if possible).

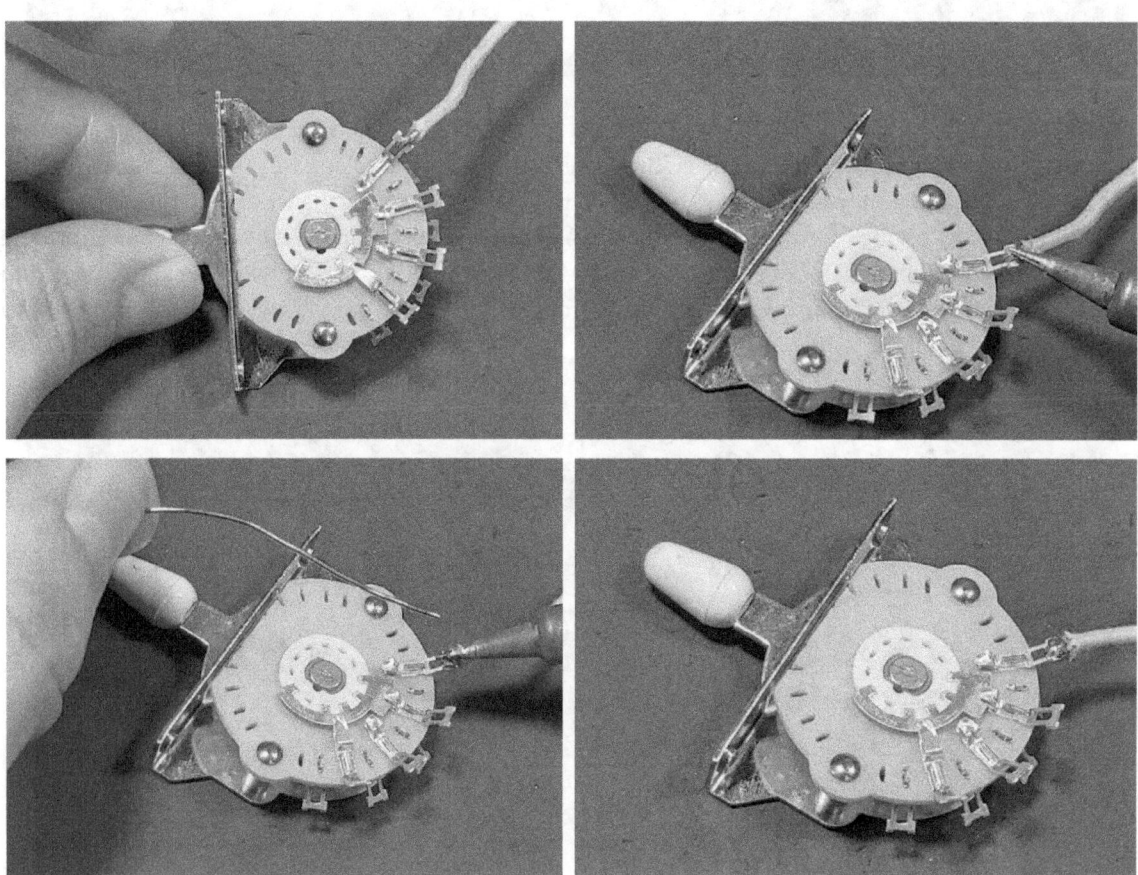

Changing Pickups

Changing pickups is a common modification. In just about every case, you can follow the existing wiring from the old pickup and rewire the new one in its place. When doing anything complex, it's always a good idea to label the wiring. You can use masking tape or use a sharpie and write on the wire itself. Another thing you could do is to take a picture with your smartphone or camera so that you always have a reference for the correct wiring that you can fall back on.

Strat-Style Guitars

Remove the strings to have uninhibited access to the electronics. Remove the pickguard screws and carefully flip over the pickguard to expose the electronics. The pickguard will be attached by one or two wires that lead to the output jack and, if applicable, the tremolo cavity. Place a rag or cloth between the guitar body and pickguard to protect the finish.

When removing a pickup, you can clip the old wires at the terminal, just above the insulation, so that you have a reference to where the new wires will go. Also, the ground wires from multiple pickups are often wrapped together, but it is not necessary to remove them all – just cut the appropriate wire and solder a new ground from the new pickup to the same area. Alternatively, heat the soldered connections with your soldering iron and remove the wiring at each terminal.

Remove the pickup from the pickguard and install the replacement. Follow the original wiring to the switch, ground and output path.

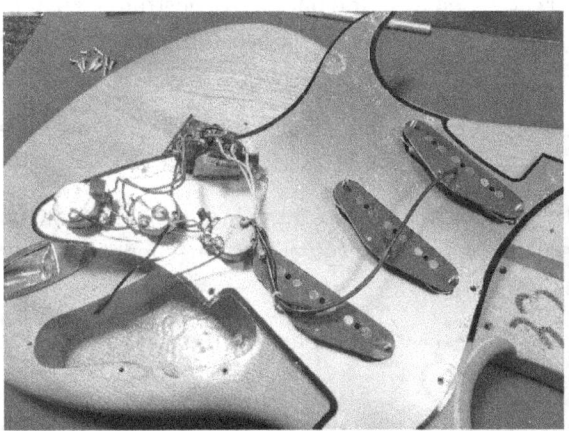

Tele-Style Guitars

Remove the strings to have uninhibited access to the electronics. Remove the control plate screws and carefully flip it over to expose the electronics. If you are replacing the bridge pickup, the bridge will also need to be removed. Be careful not to move the bridge ground wire as it is needed to ground the strings of the guitar. It will be placed loosely under the bridge or attached with a grommet to a pickup height adjustment screw. Place a rag or cloth over the guitar body to protect the finish.

The neck pickup is often screwed into the guitar body itself. When replacing the neck pickup, use the original screws if possible, to avoid any threading issues. Like on Strat-Style guitars, you can clip the old wires at the terminal, just above the insulation, so that you have a reference to where the new wires will go.

Alternatively, heat the soldered connections with your soldering iron and remove the wiring at each terminal.

Remove the pickup and install the replacement. Follow the original wiring to the switch, ground and output path.

Above left: Telecaster control plate / Above right: Gibson control cavity.

Gibson-Style Guitars

For Les Paul-style guitars, the electronics cavity is usually accessed from the back of the instrument. Other models, such as SG's, may have top-mounted electronics. If necessary, remove the strings to have uninhibited access to the electronics.

Remove the electronics cavity cover or pickguard to expose the electronics. Place a rag or cloth over the guitar body to protect the finish.

As mentioned previously, you can clip the old wires at the terminal, just above the insulation, so that you have a reference to where the new wires will go. Alternatively, heat the soldered connections with your soldering iron and remove the wiring at each terminal.

Remove the pickup and install the replacement. Follow the original wiring to the switch, ground and output path.

When changing authentic Gibson-style pickups, the leads may covered in a wire mesh. The wire mesh is the actual ground for the pickup, with the interior being the "hot" wire. The trick with removing these ground wires is to heat the connecting terminal and the wire simultaneously until the wire becomes free. When soldering the replacement, the method is similar, although emphasizing on the terminal if requiring more heat.

> *HINT: Pre-tin both the ground wire and terminal. Tape off or heat-shrink any excessive ground wire to avoiding grounding out on nearby components.*

Pig-Tailing Wires

Pig-tailing is a method to connect two wires, such as in an instance when needing to make one longer. Sometimes during a repair, it may be more favourable to lengthen a wire then completely replace it. Start with fresh wire and strip the end off, so there is enough to twist onto the other. Twist them together and solder. You can finish up by using some electrical tape or heat shrink tubing around the exposed connection. Any exposed wires can potentially cause signal degradation, loss, or other problems. Always keep your wiring tidy and clean for a rocksteady performance.

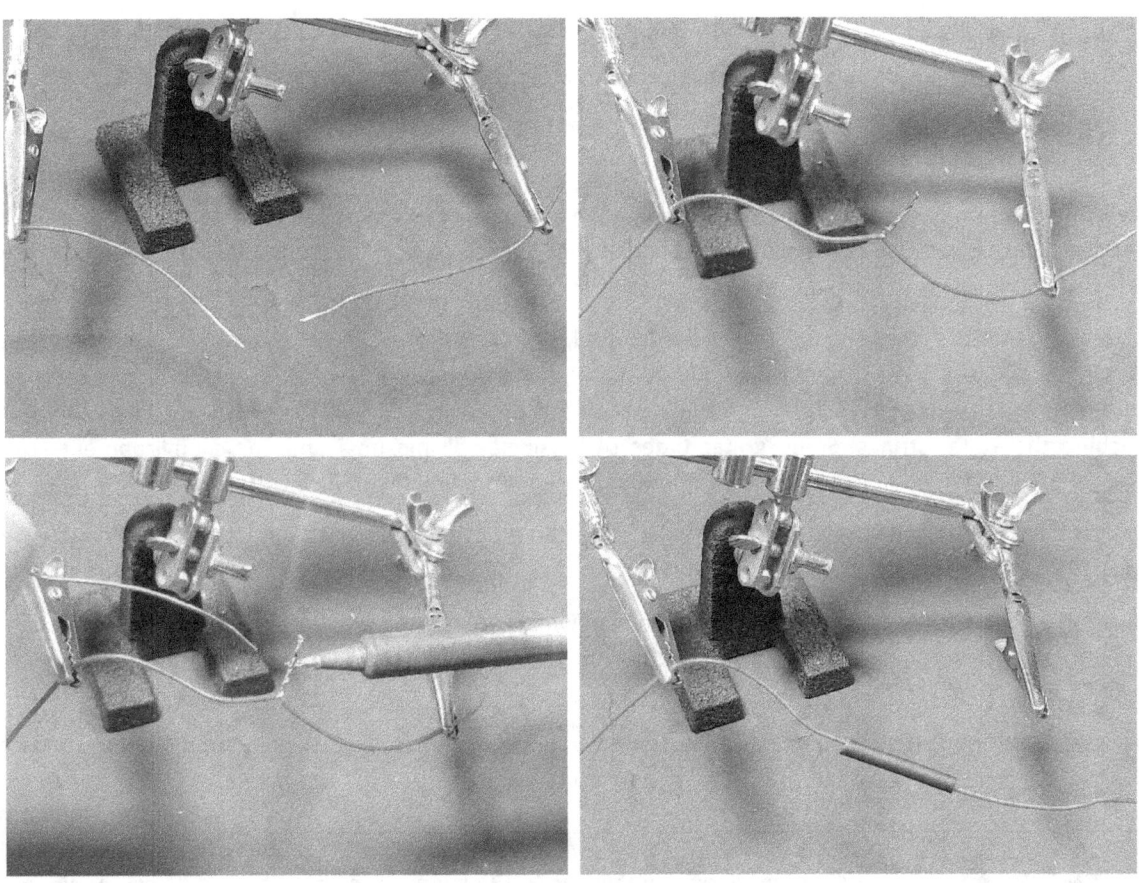

WIRING TIPS

There are multiple ways to wire a guitar, so when starting out, stick with the original wiring for the best results. Common wiring diagrams are available in the **FURTHER RESOURCES** section of this book.

Protect the guitars' finish by placing a rag or old shirt over the top of it. Hot solder spits and splatters and will leave deep marks on guitar finishes.

Every pickup manufacturer uses different colours on their pickup wires. See the chart in the **FURTHER RESOURCES** section for popular pickup brand colour codes.

Small components such as mini switches do not tolerate a lot of heat. Master the soldering process and work quickly to avoid damaging them.

Reversing the pickup wires won't change the sound on a single pickup guitar. But with two or more pickups, it will be out of phase (reverse polarity) and sound thin. When replacing pickups, check to see if they are standard polarity or reverse wired, before installing them.

Always check that all components are wired to ground, as well as the bridge. Bridge grounding ensures that the strings are grounded. Otherwise, a loud audible ground hum from the amplifier will be present. Any loud hums are usually the result of a grounding problem. Some ground hum is normal- when you are *not* touching the guitar strings. Some guitar types (with single-coil pickups) and some environments can produce a lot of ground noise, but this is dependant on environments with RF interference.

Don't leave any exposed wiring that may make contact with other parts of the guitar circuit. Trim all the leads and tape off anything exposed.

Once the solder is applied, a wire must not be moved while cooling, or it will run the risk of creating a "cold solder joint," which can become intermittent or completely fail with little warning. If anything gets moved, reapply the heat and try again.

See the **FURTHER RESOURCES** section of this book for **common wiring diagrams** and **modifications**.

TESTING: You can test the guitar before reassembling it. With an amplifier, you can audibly test the signal by tapping on the top of the pickup magnet with a screwdriver- you will hear a distinct knocking sound if wired correctly (remember to turn the volume control up). Roll the tone knob (if applicable) while tapping to hear it attenuate.

Wiring Diagrams

For a library of wiring diagrams, including those listed below, please see the **FURTHER RESOURCES** section at the end of this book.

Popular Mods

Besides the traditional wiring configurations, there are a plethora of modifications you can try. Here's a list of a few of the most popular.

Coil splitting

Disengage one coil on a humbucking pickup to produce a single-coil sound, most commonly with a push-pull pot, mini switch or super switch.

In phase / out of phase

Flip the phase (ground and hot wires) on a pickup in a two-pickup configuration and the common frequencies of both pickups will cancel each other out, creating a thin and often nasally tone. Most commonly configured with a push-pull pot, mini switch or super switch.

Parallel/series wiring

This mod can be applied to two coils within a humbucking pickup or two pickup wiring. For example, humbucker coils are usually wired in series. For a change in tone, you can wire them into parallel, for a more articulate tone with a higher frequency, not unlike coil splitting. This mod can be engaged by a switch or push-pull pot and requires four-conductor pickup wiring. On the other hand, most two-pickup guitar wiring configurations are parallel wiring- so when both pickups are engaged, they are in parallel with each other. If wired in series, the pickups will have a higher output and a fuller tone when used together. This may be especially noticeable on single-coil equipped guitars and is a popular mod for tele-style guitars.

Pickup blending

Besides switching pickups on or off, you can use a potentiometer to blend two pickups for a more custom-tuned mix. Alternatively, humbuckers with four-conductor wiring can also be wired to blend the output of the individual coils.

Treble bleed mod

A common problem is losing high frequency when turning down the guitar's volume control. The high frequencies are bled to the ground first and can be heard as the volume is rolled down. A common solution is to employ a treble bleed mod, which is a capacitor (and sometimes coupled with a resistor) wired from the outer lug to the centre lug that redirects the high frequency from the ground back into the signal.

GUITAR CARE

HUMIDITY & ENVIRONMENT

What Is Humidity?
Humidity refers to the amount of water vapour in the air. The **term** "relative **humidity**" is used to note the amount of **humidity** as a percent, from 0-100%. The more moisture in the air, the higher the humidity. The lesser the moisture, the lower the humidity.

How Humidity Affects Guitars
Guitars are primarily made out of wood, and wood reacts to humidity. When there is less humidity in the air, wood can become dry and brittle. When there is a lot of humidity, wood can uptake excess moisture from the air and even expand in weight and size. This can have a very noticeable and negative effect on guitars (most notably on hollow body acoustic guitars) and many other wooden musical instruments.

Guitars are produced in climate-controlled environments. The tonewoods used in production are treated, dried and seasoned for optimal stability throughout the manufacturing process.

Have you ever noticed that your guitar plays great one day, and then another day, completely different? Perhaps the strings have become high, or low and buzzing all over the place. Maybe the tone changed, or the ends of the frets have become sharp? Or maybe you opened up the case to discover a crack along the entire top of your prized Taylor guitar. Ouch... been there.

Drastic changes in humidity can occur in as little as a day. Depending on the time of year, humidity, or lack of, can wreak havoc on musical instruments if not monitored and managed. It is worth mentioning that all wooden instruments are affected by humidity levels, but acoustic guitars are especially susceptible. Preventive measures are the key to keeping your guitar in top condition.

Humidity & Guitar Preventative Maintenance
Humidity monitoring is an important consideration as a guitar owner, but most importantly, with acoustic guitars. If not properly humidified, an acoustic guitar can develop cracks. Cracks can occur on the guitar body, binding, and fretboard predominately. When left beyond the initial surface cracks, the guitar has the potential to get much worse, affecting its structural integrity. Alternatively, if over humidified, an instrument can swell up, distort, become discoloured and even grow mould- not without first affecting its volume and tone.

To avoid these problems, you can take some preventative steps to maintain a consistent humidity level, as suggested by the manufacturer of your instrument.

Brand name guitar companies such as Taylor Guitars, Martin Guitars, Takamine' Guitars, D'Addario Strings and many other guitar companies recommend a relative humidity level of 40-55% as being safe for guitars with a temperature range of 21-25 degrees Celsius or 70-75 degrees Fahrenheit. If your guitar is left outside of these ranges, it can develop playability and structural problems. Consult with the manufacturer of your guitar for the specific humidity needs relating to your model.

Low Humidity (Dry) Symptoms

One of the most common signs of a dry guitar is one that develops sharp fret ends. When a guitar dries out, the fretboard shrinks slightly, and the metal frets will poke out along the edges of the fretboard. Protruding fret-ends can be corrected by re-humidification, fretboard conditioning, or fret filing.

Low humidity can cause wood shrinkage as it dries out, and eventually, this can lead to cracks. If you leave a guitar in a low humidity environment for an extended period of time, it can start to show symptoms such as:

- Low action/ string height
- String buzz
- Sharp fret ends
- Rippled (raised) wood grain and/or finish
- Cracks in the finish
- Cracks in the wood
- A hump in the fretboard where the neck meets the body (often at the 14th fret)
- Sunken guitar top (between the bridge and fingerboard)
- Failing glue joints

How to Correct Overly Dry Conditions

The single most effective method in protecting your guitar from low humidity is by using a guitar case humidifier. Generally, these are low cost (under $20) and can be found online or in any guitar store. There are several styles available, some being more effective than others, depending on your local climate (check which is best for your area). By having your guitar in a closed space such as a case, the humidifier can maintain the ideal ambient humidity needed for your guitar.

TIP: You can make your own using a Ziplock bag and cellulose (natural) sponge. Punch holes through the bag, dampen the sponge and place it in your case or soundhole.

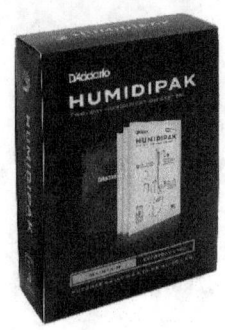

2-way Guitar Humidity Control Systems

Systems such as **D'Addario's Humidipak Automatic Humidity Control System** automatically adds or depletes moisture to maintain the ideal humidity level of 45%-55% RH inside your instrument case. A system such as this is a great option that eliminates the guesswork and anxiety of maintaining your instrument's ideal humidity levels.

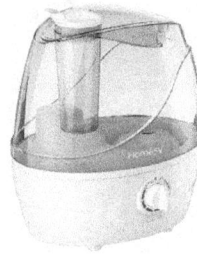

Room Humidifier

If you keep your guitar in one room primarily, a standard room humidifier will keep adequate humidity levels while allowing the instrument to be left out in the open and ready for playing. I'd suggest buying a stand-alone digital hygrometer to monitor humidity levels closely and to be sure your humidifier is keeping up when heating or air conditioning systems are operating, both of which dry out the air considerably.

Which Kind of Room Humidifier Is Best?

There are typically 3 kinds of humidifiers available: Cool mist (ultra-sonic), warm mist (steam vaporizer), and evaporative (cool mist/fan). Every one of these types of humidifiers will get the job done, but there are pros and cons of each.

Cool Mist Humidifiers

Cool mist humidifiers work by using ultrasonic vibration to break water into tiny particles and disperses them into the air. They are very quiet and do not raise the temperature of the room.

Pros: Quiet, filterless (no reoccurring costs), doesn't raise the temperature of the room, low-cost.
Cons: Requires regular cleaning, can produce white-dust (minerals).

What is White Dust?

White dust is caused by mineral content in the water that goes into the humidifier. As the water vapour is dispersed into the air, it eventually lands on furniture and other surfaces (like guitars). The vapour dries and leaves its mineral content behind in the form of white dust. For most people, the white dust is nothing to be concerned about; however, it could be problematic for some people with allergy, asthma or other sinus health conditions. The quality of water will dictate how much "white dust" is produced in the room. Many will use distilled (best) or reverse osmosis water without any problems. Other times, there are water demineralization cartridge products designed for humidifiers to minimize this problem.

Warm Mist Humidifiers
Warm mist humidifiers work similar to a kettle- by boiling water into steam. These are relatively quiet as well but have the additional benefit of creating warmer, cleaner air in the room.

Pros: Quiet, filterless (no reoccurring costs), produces clean, bacteria-free vapour, low-cost, low maintenance.
Cons: Can be dangerous if left unattended (hot-steam), can be difficult to regulate output.

Evaporative Humidifiers
Evaporative humidifiers rely on fans to blow air through their wick filters. The water wicks through the filter as the fan blows, which disperses the water vapour. They are not typically as quiet as the others, but they can produce better results for larger rooms/homes.

Pros: Great for larger rooms, doesn't raise the temperature of the room.
Cons: Fan noise, higher cost, maintenance costs (filter replacements).

Guitar Re-Humidification - What to Expect
Depending on how dehydrated it is, a guitar will generally respond well to a properly humidified environment (45%-55% RH) and can show signs of improvement within a week or two. Extremely dry guitars may require longer. In some special cases, you may want to double up on your humidification media. If needed, you can insert two humidifiers in the soundhole with an additional one at the headstock. This can expedite recovery in critical cases when needed, and in extremely dry environments, the additional media will help bolster adequate humidity levels.

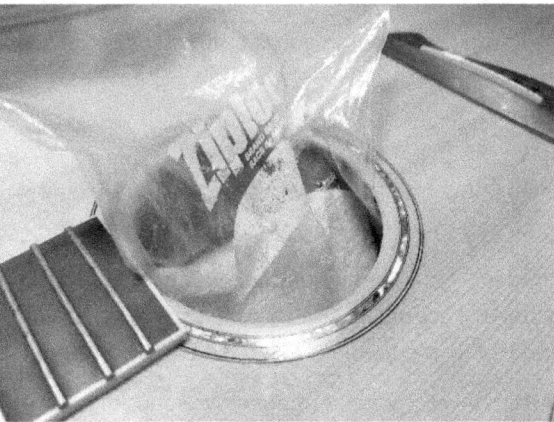

As the guitar improves, you will notice cracks getting smaller and beginning to close, ripples in the wood grain or finish relaxing and improving, sharp fret ends becoming less prevalent, and string height returning to normal. With ongoing monitoring and humidification, cracks may completely close (and seal), structural warping may return to normal (such as humps at the 14th fret and sunken soundboards), and playability can be restored. *Keep in mind, there is an entire spectrum of dehydration accompanied by corresponding symptoms or damages. Extreme cases should be approached with caution and only after the advice of a seasoned luthier/ technician.*

High Humidity (Wet) Symptoms

High moisture levels can be absorbed by the wood of the guitar, causing swelling, warping, and structural distortion. Here are a few signs to watch out for:

- High action- strings that are unusually high off the fretboard, making it difficult to play
- Frets popping 'up' from the fretboard
- Warping of the neck
- Finish peeling, bubbling, or discolouring
- Guitar sounding dull due to high water content in the wood
- Body bulging
- (Acoustic) Guitar top and back bulging out

How to Correct Overly Humid Conditions

Although overly damp conditions are not as common as dry, there are areas where it is an issue. If you live in a damp place, Taylor Guitars suggests prevention as the first line of defence.

If your climate does not have high humidity year-round, consider using the **Two-Way Humidification System from D'Addario®**. Featuring two-way humidity control technology, the breathable membrane packets will automatically maintain a relative humidity level of 48 percent by absorbing excess moisture in humid environments.

In areas with extreme or year-round high humidity, place several silica gel or bamboo charcoal packs in the guitar case and change them every few months.

Use a room de-humidifier where you store your guitar. It's also wise to monitor the humidity levels with a digital hygrometer. You can find a good digital hygrometer through your local music stores, TaylorWare®, at taylorguitars.com, Amazon.com, or other online retailers.

Periodically remove the guitar and blow-dry the interior of the case with a hairdryer for 10-15 minutes.

Tips for Seasonal Humidity Changes

We all know humidity changes as the year progresses, and this can be minimal or extreme, depending on your location and where your guitar is stored.

Summer - In general, summer weather brings higher temperatures and higher relative humidity. The instrument's wood swells as it absorbs moisture. If you use an air conditioning unit in your home, keep in mind that these systems will make the air drier, and indoor humidity levels can fall as a result.

Winter - Winter weather generally means dry air- it is the worst time for guitars. The relative humidity can fall to the extremes when heating systems are in use.

Hot and Cold Temperatures

Heat exposure can also have a destructive effect on wooden instruments. For example, when a guitar is left in a trunk of a car on a hot sunny day, the heat exposure can soften the glue joints so much that they literally fall apart.

On the other hand, in cold climates such as where I live (in Alberta, Canada), the freezing temperatures can be quite destructive in their own way. Some instruments may have delicate finishes, such as with nitrocellulose lacquer. A guitar brought in from the cold into a warm home or bar should be left to acclimatize before it is removed from the case. I have witnessed hairline cracks, otherwise known as "checking," instantly appear in a finish from the contrasting temperatures. A sad day indeed... or cool, if you're into the relic look. Other times, this same contrast in temperatures can literally split acoustic guitar tops in an instant.

Conclusion

Get yourself a digital hygrometer. A hygrometer measures the humidity of the air relative to temperature. These are available at most guitar stores as well as amazon.com and many other outlets. Know the relative humidity of the space you keep the instrument stored in. If it's comfortable for you, it's probably comfortable for your guitar.

HUMIDITY SYMPTOMS CHART

Extremely Humid Humidity levels this high will affect the guitar quickly. • It may not play properly or play in tune. • The tone will sound dark and deadened. • The top and back will belly outward. • The strings will become high off the fretboard as the neck guitar top bows. • Fingerboards may twist or warp. • Certain finishes can develop a haze, whereas some lacquer finishes may bubble or peel. • Frets may lift and glue joints may become unstable and release. • Guitar bridges may lift or release entirely. • Mould may appear inside the guitar.	75%-100%
Too Humid If left in this environment, the wood of the guitar will swell and expand. • The strings will often get higher off the fretboard as the neck guitar top bows, making it difficult to fret and play in tune. • The tone of the instrument will sound dead and flubby. • If left for long periods, bubbles or discolouration can occur in the finish. • Binding and glue joints can become loosened and unstable. • The top and back will likely belly more than usual.	55%-65%
Safe Zone The ideal environment for your guitar. Storing your guitar in its case while using a hygrometer and humidifier system will keep your guitar in the safe-zone.	40%-55%
Too Dry If left in this environment, the wood of the guitar can shrink. • The neck may straighten or back-bow, strings may lower to the fretboard, causing more buzz while playing. • Fret-ends can poke out the sides of the neck, feeling sharp. • Hardware may become loose. • A hump or rise may develop in the neck where it mates with the body causing the strings to buzz-out or deaden. • The guitar top may shrink and fall flat or concave, also pulling down the strings further, producing more string buzz.	25%-35%
Extremely Dry Humidity levels this low will affect your guitar quickly. The wood will release its moisture content and shrink rapidly, causing playability issues and structural concerns. • The fretboard may twist or warp. • Cracks may develop in the fretboard, bridge, guitar top, back and or sides. • The neck angle of the instrument may be affected, rendering the guitar impossible to set up for playing. • Glue joints and binding may become unstable and release. • Fret ends will be pronounced and sharp across the fretboard. • Acoustic bridges may lift or separate altogether. • There may be drastic changes in the playability. • Seams and joints may separate. • There may be a slight separation between the bridge and the top. • The finish may sink into the wood grain. • Cracks may appear in the top, body, bridge and/or fretboard. • The glue joints in the neck, bridge, and braces may separate.	0%-20%

INSTRUMENT STORAGE

Short-Term Guitar Storage

The best place to keep your guitar is in its case. A quality case will help protect the instrument from humidity and temperature fluctuations, as well as any accidental knocks, dents, or falls.

Acoustic guitars are much more sensitive to humidity and temperature fluctuations than a solid-body electric. A hard-shell case is the best storage for your acoustic guitars and provides a reliable, closed environment to monitor and regulate humidity levels.

Granted, when an instrument is in its case, it is not as often picked up and played. This is a bit of a catch-22 and, therefore, a personal decision when deciding what is best for you and your storage needs. If it is not kept in its case, it should be left on a stand.

NOTE: Any storage, either in the short or long-term, should be within a climate-controlled environment. Any extreme temperatures or moisture levels can destroy a guitar when left in these conditions **(refer to the section on Humidity)**.

Choosing a Stand

Guitar stands come in all shapes and sizes, and there are plenty of choices available to accommodate most situations.

Single floor stands – As the name implies, single floor stands are designed to hold and display one instrument. They are generally low cost (under $20) and one of the most common stands available. There are many styles available, some more space-saving or aesthetically pleasing than others. When shopping for one, keep an eye on how secure the guitar is in the stand. For example, can it be tipped over easily? Some models that cradle the neck also lock, which can also help prevent accidental falls.

Wall hooks – Wall hooks help save space and beautifully display your instrument simultaneously. They get the instrument off the floor and away from high-traffic environments — a favourite to those who have multiple instruments.

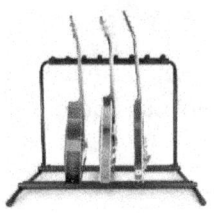

Guitar racks – For those with a growing collection of guitars, a guitar rack may be a good choice. Many affordable racks allow you to store between 5 and 10 guitars in a sideways orientation. This style of stand is generally more functional than aesthetical and will allow a large collection of guitars in small space. Perfect for stage, studio and home.

> CAUTION: Certain types of rubber and plastics used on common guitar stands and other guitar accessories can actually eat away a **nitrocellulose lacquer** finish! These components aren't the only agents that will affect a lacquer finish chemically. Bug spray is notorious, as are some colognes. To prevent wrecking the finish on your guitar, you can cover the points of contact on your stand with a cotton cloth or similar.

Long-Term Guitar Storage

If you aren't using your guitar for an extended period of time, consider some long-term storage precautions to help prevent any potential damage occurring.

Get a Hard Case

The best way to store your guitar for longer periods is to keep it in a hard case. This creates a controlled environment for your instrument and helps in long-term protection. Besides environmental concerns, a hard case also protects the guitar from any accidental physical damage that may occur.

Release string tension: Before storing your steel-stringed guitar for the long-term, consider detuning the strings down a full step to alleviate the tension on the neck and body (especially on acoustic guitars). A full step down is about the same as a full twist of the tuner knob.

Detuning is more a safeguard to protect the instrument through any uncontrollable environmental fluctuations that may adversely affect it. For example, a guitar left in an old basement for several years under no supervision may develop an irreparable warp or twist in the neck. Or perhaps an old acoustic guitar left sitting through the years may develop a bulged top or separating bridge that could rip right off the body due to the high tension. These horror stories are not necessarily going to happen, but because of the many environmental diversities in the world, and how they can affect musical instruments, it is merely a suggestion as a countermeasure. Keep in mind when doing so, the truss rod is applying tension in the neck to offset the string tension. So, if you lessen the string tension, be sure to check the neck relief and loosen the truss rod if necessary (see the section on **HOW TO ADJUST THE NECK RELIEF**).

Environment and humidity: Humidity is a real concern when storing guitars, even if you use a hard case. Depending on where you live and the ambient conditions of the storage facilities, humidity levels may not be optimal. Avoid storing your guitar in a place where it will face extreme temperature or humidity changes. Exposure to extreme heat from a radiator or other similar sources can result in irreparable damage.

A humidifier system will help to maintain an adequate humidity level while in storage and may help prevent any humidity-related damage. Keep your guitar safe and remember to hydrate!

Inspect the guitar occasionally: If possible, check up on your guitar every couple of weeks to a month to make sure there are no problems developing. Doing so, you can intervene before any issues become a serious problem.

SHIPPING GUITARS

We've all heard the horror stories. Guitars getting broken in transit, arriving at their destination with a broken headstock, dents in the body, or a dislodged neck. You might be shipping a guitar or receiving one, or perhaps you're taking a trip on a plane.

The first thing to do is to package it well. When sending a guitar over long distances, make sure you've got a suitable case. If you are sending the guitar in a hard case, it is a good idea to add some additional padding around the headstock area as well as around any loose fittings within the case. Bubble wrap or packing foam will help pad this area out to reduce any potential impact. Don't leave room in the case for the guitar to knock around. Add extra support under the headstock, around it and on top of it. Headstocks, especially ones that are angled, are a weak point and should be protected well.

If you are shipping the guitar case inside of a larger box, outline the interior and fill the spaces in the box with packing foam, bubble wrap and packing paper. The additional packaging will prevent the item from moving inside the box and will also act as a shock absorber.

When regularly flying with a guitar, a flight case is your best option and will keep the guitar supported and protected under most conditions. A flight case is built and custom fit with dense foam, which suspends the guitar and prevents any shock-related damage.

It is always a safe bet to loosen the string tension from the neck. Doing so will help prevent any potential shock-damage to the neck and headstock areas (which is a common impact breakpoint).

Choosing a Case

The case you choose will not only suit your storage needs, but it will also serve as a layer of protection for your prized guitar every time you take it out of the house. There are three main types of cases available for guitars.

Gig bag – A gig bag offers the least amount of protection, but the most ease for transport and portability. Many companies offer padded gig bags with hand and shoulder straps and often will feature backpack-style strapping for hands-free transportation. Perfect for those on the go, they are lightweight & easy to store.

Hard case – A fitted hard case will offer a level of protection suitable for most situations. Generally, hard cases are made with either a plywood or a moulded ABS plastic. These types of cases will contain a foam padding inside to secure the instrument and also to insulate it from the elements. The outer shell is knock-resistant and can provide suitable protection.

Flight case – Flight cases are usually more costly, as well as much larger and heavier than a regular hard case. These cases are often made with a reinforced steel housing with hard moulded plastics, while the interior moulds fully suspend the instrument, completely insulating it from any potential impact. Flight cases offer the most protection available and will keep your instrument the safest when flying regularly.

BUYERS GUIDE

What to Look for When Buying a Guitar

When buying a new or used guitar, there area few things to keep in mind. Brands and aesthetics aside, pick a guitar that plays well. First and foremost, a guitar should be comfortable to play! In a perfect world, the guitars on the wall at your favourite guitar store have all been set up and checked over. Unfortunately, that's not always the case.

Big brand guitars commonly have a quality control system in place, which includes having one or multiple personal checking over every aspect of the instrument. One of the aspects we are talking about is the factory setup. Meaning, it is checked over to ensure no issues are surrounding its playability or musicality. This does not mean it is set up to be the dreamiest guitar around, with buttery smooth action and the slickest tone... not as the norm anyways. Here`s why.

Consider this, after a guitar is shipped out the doors, that box may end up anywhere around the world. It may sit in a warehouse for months (or years), it may get shipped off across the ocean, or it may just go down the street. Since we've already discussed how environmental influences can affect wood, we can deduce that this logistical journey from the guitar manufacturer to wholesaler and then to the retailer, will potentially net some negative effect on those boxed guitars. This is primarily why guitars are only "roughed in" at the factory. This "roughed-in" factory setup is adequate for functionality, and allows some give and take should the guitar be affected by any environmental or shipping factors. When unboxed at the store-level, it would then benefit from some further adjustments to improve their playability and sell-ability. Sometimes this happens and other times it does not. If they aren't set up at the store, it's usually an issue of insufficient labour or lack of initiative.

The other reason a guitar is only "roughed-in" at the factory is that everyone has their own setup preferences. The guitar should be custom set up for the player, with their preferred string gauge, tuning and action. This is where a great guitar store can really shine and offer this with the sale.

OK, back to it.

OK, if it doesn't play great- it probably just needs a setup. Even if it doesn't hold its tune, the chances are good that it simply needs a good setup. Some people are completely amazed by what a setup can do for a guitar. I have picked up a $5000 guitar that played and felt worse than a $300 guitar, and perhaps you have as well. Once you become familiar with a basic setup, you will be able to spot whether any guitar is setup or not, and that is a major game-changer (**refer to the Guitar Setups section**)!

So, what should you look for when buying a guitar? Does the neck fit in your hands comfortably? Is the string-to-string spread across the fretboard easy to navigate? For example, those with larger hands may find wider necks easier to play but they may not be as common or available on certain models. A narrower neck may be more difficult to play, and chording may be challenging. Make sure it fits your hands well.

Next, the sound. Does it produce the sound that you want or the sound as your favourite guitar player(s)? If they play a Les Paul, look at similarly-styled guitars. If they play a Strat, check those out. If you want to play rock n roll, an acoustic guitar is not going to inspire you. This is especially true for the young beginner- inspiration equals motivation.

Used Guitars

When buying a used instrument, there are a few things you want to check over besides playability.

Check the Overall Condition

You can give the guitar a once over by eye. Look at the overall condition of the finish; does it have many chips and dents? Does it appear to have been well cared for? Is any of the hardware loose? Does the neck appear to be free from any twists or warps? Are there any cracks in the wood or finish? Are the frets worn or dented?

Common problems to watch for:

- Worn or dented frets – Frets can become overly worn over time, causing dead areas on the fretboard or a low-fret profile, and would require costly fret repair to rectify.
- Frets replaced poorly – Was it refretted professionally? Is there any damage around the frets? Are the frets seated and levelled?
- Worn/ intermittent/ scratchy electronics – Electronics may need to be cleaned or could require replacement altogether.
- Poor set up – It doesn't play well. Can it be set up any better? Can the saddles be raised or lowered? Can the bridge be adjusted? Check the relief in the neck and check for any side-to-side twists or warps.
- Rusty bridge hardware – Quite common on used guitars and may impede adjustment ranges or could be seized altogether. It may be correctable, although complete tear-down will be required.
- Seized/ stripped truss rod nut- Accidents happen, and sometimes that truss rod was stripped either from too much force or the wrong sized tool. Guitars with embedded truss rod nuts will require major surgery to repair an otherwise useless truss rod. Try and check before purchasing it.
- Replaced parts – Are they upgrades? Do they fit and function properly? Do they increase or decrease the instruments' value? Are the parts counterfeit?

Check the condition of the electronics. When plugged in, does it work? Is there sound? Check the volume and tone pots and all switches to see if they all operate as expected. Do you hear any static noise? Are the controls operating intermittently?

Have any parts been replaced? It isn't a deal-breaker, but if you are looking for a guitar with original parts, then this certainly should be on your list of things to check. Replacement parts can lower or raise the value of the guitar, depending on the quality of the parts and the installation.

Parts that are commonly changed or swapped out:

- Complete necks and/or bodies (be sure that they aren't counterfeit copies)
- Pickups
- Electronics- switches, pots
- Bridge, saddles, and/or nut
- Tuners

Has the guitar been previously damaged? Check along the edges of the fretboard for any signs of cracking or repair. Check around the headstock for any signs of refinishing or hairline cracks. Check the neck joint for any cracks.

> *NOTE: Small cracks may develop over time due to the pressure at the neck joint, but these are often more superficial and not necessarily a cause for concern.*

Common damages to watch for:

- Cracks along the headstock, fretboard, and/or neck
- Cracks at the neck joint
- Cracks in the top, back, and/or sides (hollow body acoustics)
- Dents and chips along the neck and/or body (dents in the neck may become uncomfortable)
- Signs of impact, dents, (e.g., the strap button is pushed into the body)
- Finish damage – "checking" may be present and normal, but stains or discolorations are a sign of neglect
- Refinishing/ spot touch-ups may cover previous repairs
- Look for ridges or hairline indentations, which are a common sign of a previous repair

Conclusion

When buying used, give the guitar a thorough inspection before deciding if it's right for you. If it requires a setup, or any repairs or new parts, factor in these additional costs to determine if the final price is worth it.

Amplification and How It Colours the Sound

A great sounding amplifier will inspire you to play and is the key to great tone. When starting out, knowing which amp to buy can be confusing as there are so many brands available, each having their own sound and features. The best place to start looking is at the amplifiers your favourite guitar players use.

With amplifiers, you will often hear the terms of "British" and "American" sounding. It is typically used to describe the mid-range tonal characteristics of classic amps made in Britain and the USA. British amps are often more forward in the midrange and better suited for classic rock and warmer guitar tones. Popular brands include Marshall, Orange and Vox.

American sounding amps can have a slightly lower-midrange or "mid-scooped" sounding than the British variety. Popular brands include Fender, Mesa-Boogie and Soldano. American amps tend to provide more sparkling cleans over their British counterparts, although not as a rule.

Let's look at some examples of a few amp brands and the artists that play them. It will give you an example of the sounds you can expect:

Marshall: Jimi Hendrix, Deep Purple, Eric Clapton (1965 to 1969 Bluesbreakers/Cream era), Led Zeppelin, Iron Maiden, AC/DC

Fender: Eric Clapton (1970 to present), Neil Young, BB King, Stevie Ray Vaughan, Kenny Wayne Shepherd, Keith Richards

Vox: Brian May, The Edge (U2), The Yardbirds, The Beatles

Orange: Oasis, Jim Root (Slipknot), Mastodon, Scott Holiday (Rival Sons)

Mesa Boogie: Metallica, Foo Fighters, Prince, Linkin Park, Tool

Soldano: Mark Knopfler, Vivian Campbell, Gary Moore

Each of these amplifier companies boasts a wide range of players from many different genres. Check out the gear used on your favourite guitar records and head down to your local guitar store to test some of it out. Find the brand with the sound you're after first, then look for additional features, such as effects and channel switching, etc. When you find the right sound, you'll know it.

Guitar Cables and How They Colour the Sound

You might not think that it's a big deal, but a good quality guitar cable can make a difference to your guitar tone. Not only will a quality cable last much longer, but it will often be quieter and retain treble frequencies better. When buying a guitar cable, find the best quality cable that your budget can allow. A quality cable will ensure you get the truest possible sound from your guitar and amp with minimal interference.

Capacitance and Cable Length

Every guitar cable has what is known as capacitance. A capacitor is formed whenever two electrical conductors are put close together. The larger the surface area of the conductors, the larger the capacitance. So, the longer the cable, the more capacitance you are introducing to the output of your guitar. When capacitance is applied to an audio circuit, it creates a low-pass filter, which in simple terms, means that low frequencies come through first, while high frequencies find the ground (and bleed off or out of the signal).

> TIP: Longer cables introduce higher capacitance while shorter cables introduce less. The more capacitance that is introduced in your signal, the more treble will bleed out. With any unbalanced audio cables, such as guitar cables, the shorter the run, the truer the signal (tone). It's generally recommended to stay under 20 feet for the least amount of signal loss and degradation.

Quality

Many guitar cable companies will offer a selection of connector types. These come in a wide range of materials, with each having their audible benefits. For example, a premium cable plug is often gold-plated for its superior electrical conductivity and cleaner, truer signal. Common standard jacks are made from nickel and will suit most players, under many different conditions.

Shielding

Shielding plays an important role in a cable; the shielding surrounds the core of the cable, protecting it from rf (radio) interference. A cable is similar to one long radio antennae. Guitar cables with inadequate shielding can often pick up radio signals and other interference from lights or power outlets. The better the shielding, the clearer the tone transfers from your guitar to your amp.

Picks

Picks come in all shapes, sizes and materials. How do you know which pick is right for you? Aren't they all the same?

The easiest way to answer that question is to try several different sizes, materials and thicknesses and see what feels right for your playing style and skill level. You may find one pick that works best for you, or you may find that you use a range of picks across different applications in your playing.

Let's look at some variables and the effect they have on tone.

Material

Picks are made from various materials, and they all have a functional purpose. You can find Nylon, Celluloid, Delrin, stone, and even metal picks amongst the various choices available.

Nylon is soft and flexible, which produces a mellower, warmer tone. These picks also have friction coating that is easy to hold. While there are many different thicknesses available for nylon picks, for any thickness, you will notice they are far more flexible than other plastics.

Celluloid was the original alternative to tortoiseshell (banned since 1973) and was designed to provide a similar feel and tone. Celluloid is more flexible than tortoiseshell but much stiffer than nylon. Celluloid generally has a pearl-like texture or is made to emulate the look of tortoiseshell.

Delrin is commonly known as Tortex (as made by Dunlop) and is a popular pick material that enhances the top-end sonic characteristics similar to tortoiseshell with the added benefit of an easy-to-grip powdery texture. The unique texture of Delrin provides one of the best grips, even under conditions of excessive sweating. The friction coating also translates against the strings while playing, giving a unique pick response.

Wood picks are less commonly used, and perhaps more novelty or aesthetic. Wood picks are dark-sounding and produce a mellow tone. They are generally quite thick and suited more to particular playing styles and techniques.

Metal picks are quite different from the lot. Virtually no give, hard on your strings, and loud. They can produce a lot of additional noise and harmonics- which may be desired for some players.

Thickness

Most manufacturers offer a wide range of thicknesses for different pick lines. You may see everything from a super thin 0.4mm to a super heavy 2mm and beyond.

Thin (.60mm and less)

A thinner pick provides a lighter tone with more "give," which many players love for acoustic or fast strumming. Thin picks generally produce more trebles and less volume than a medium or heavy pick.

Medium (.60-.80mm)

The thicker the pick, the less flex or "give" it has. A thicker pick will produce more volume and attack on the string, while also accentuating more bass and midrange frequencies. Medium picks are the most versatile and are often favoured by both rhythm and lead guitarists to play everything from riffs to leads to rhythm parts accurately.

Heavy (.80mm and over)

Heavy picks will produce the most bass, midrange, and volume- at the cost of little or no "give." For example, if strumming a guitar with a heavy pick, it will produce a big sound but will take much more work to do so. Heavy picks are a favourite to jazz and metal players simply because the pick has a solid attack on the strings and produces great tone.

Shape

The shape of a pick will affect its playability, but this is very much a personal consideration. Some picks such as Dunlop Jazz III will have a pointed tip, whereas the common shaped guitar pick will have more of a rounded tip. Many players like the addition of a point on the tip as they feel it allows for better note articulation and speed, whereas others will prefer the standard shapes. Try a few and see what you prefer.

TROUBLESHOOTING

String Buzz, Rattle, & Noise

Problem: Strings buzzing.

- Are the strings old or worn out? Replace strings.

- Have you set the neck relief? Is the neck too straight? Adjust the truss rod for more relief.

- Is the string height too low? Adjust the strings higher using the examples given.

- Is it more of a rattle or vibration? Check bridge saddle hardware for rattles. Check that the tuners are torqued down. Check that no hardware is loose.

- Is the string hitting the pickup(s)? Check pickup height and adjust as necessary.

Problem: Strings buzz when playing certain frets only.

- Is the neck back-bowed? Adjust the truss rod for more relief.

- Is there an inconsistent fret height in that area? Is there low, worn, or raised frets? Raise the string height for better clearance. If the problem persists or is too difficult to work around, the solutions for in-depth fretwork go beyond the scope of this guide - seek professional advice.

- Is the neck warped? Site neck from the butt-end. Can you see any twists, raises, or humps in the fretboard? Raise the string height for better clearance. If the problem persists or is too difficult to work around, the solutions for in-depth repair go beyond the scope of this guide - seek professional advice.

Problem: Strings buzz when playing open strings only.

- Is the neck back-bowed? Adjust the truss rod for more relief.

- The nut slot(s) may be cut too low or wide. Shim, fill & recut, or replace the nut.

Problem: Strings buzz when playing open strings only but sounds more like a vibration.

- Put gentle pressure on the string behind the nut. If the vibration stops, the string slot may be too wide. Fill & recut, or replace the nut.

- Firmly press down on the string behind the nut. If the buzzing goes away, you may need more downward string angle behind the nut. Use more windings around the string post to push the string angle down lower. Ensure the nut slots are cut at the proper angle. Install string trees if necessary.

Problem: Strings buzz when playing on the first few frets only.

- Adjust the strings higher.

- Is the neck too straight or back-bowed? Adjust the truss rod for more relief.

- Is the neck warped? Site neck from the butt-end. Can you see any twists, raises, or humps in the fretboard? Raise the string height for better clearance. If the problem persists or is too difficult to work around, the solutions for in-depth repair go beyond the scope of this guide - seek professional advice.

Common Tuning Issues

Problem: Won't stay in tune.

- Have you thoroughly stretched the strings?

- Are there adequate windings around the tuning posts (2-3 for wound strings, more for plain strings)?

- Are the strings getting stuck in the nut slot? Is there a pinging sound when you tune the strings? File the nut slot for the specific string gauge and/or add a lubricant to the slots.

- Do you have a Floyd Rose or double-locking tremolo system? If there is a nut clamp, make sure it's firmly locked down (but not over-tightened). Check for grooves in nut clamp. Change if necessary. Check nut mounting bolts are tight. Check for wear or marring at the bridge posts. Check the tremolo moves freely up and down uninhibited.

Problem: String won't tune to pitch, keeps slipping.

If you are experiencing the string slipping as you try to tune it to pitch, this points to a problem at either the ball end of the string or at the tuning peg winding. The first place to check would be the bridge. Is there anything in the string guide hole preventing the ball end from making complete contact with the bridge. It can be especially true on acoustic guitars when the string is not pulled tight after reinserting the bridge pin.

If the string-to-bridge contact is solid, check the windings around the tuning post. Are the windings neat and together with no overlaps? Is the string threaded through above the windings? If the answer to either of these questions is no, that could be the source of the string slipping. Unfortunately, strings are difficult to re-straighten without problems after they have been wound around the tuning peg, so in most circumstances, this would require a new string to be fitted. You could try to take the existing string off and reuse it, but if you can't get a neat winding, you may need to replace it and start over.

In extreme circumstances, this issue can be caused by an issue with the gear inside the tuning peg. If applying an oil-based mechanical cleaning product does not resolve this, you will need to consider installing a replacement tuner. On lower-end guitars, this is more common as the tuning pegs and their mechanisms are often made from softer metals that wear out quickly.

Have you remembered to tune up to pitch? Are the strings adequately stretched? Is the nut slot lubricated?

Problem: Strings keep breaking at the bridge/saddle.

Many string breakages that occur at the bridge or saddle are commonly linked to a sharp edge wearing into the bridge. This kind of breakage is common on Gibson-style guitars, where the bottom of the saddle can become sharp from string wear and has the effect of pinching at the string until eventually snapping.

If the saddle has a sharp edge, repeated use will wear through the string and compromise its strength. To address this, you run a piece of fine sandpaper or a specially designed bridge/nut file through the saddle to remove the sharp edge. Any qualified luthier will also be able to perform this task.

If the issue persists, replacement saddles and bridges are relatively inexpensive components and may be a good option.

Problem: Strings go out of tune immediately.

Strings that go immediately out of tune are usually the result of the string either being incorrectly installed, or not being stretched correct. Sudden drops in pitch are usually due to the string contact points at the tuning peg and bridge not being fully tight. If there is a gap in these areas when tension is applied to the string, it can pop out of tune due to the tension.

If this happens, retune and stretch your strings, and it should solve the issue.

Problem: Strings go out of tune after a few minutes.

If you have tuned up to pitch and stretched your strings and the guitar slips after a few minutes of playing, this could be a mechanical issue. If you have a Fender-style guitar with a vintage tremolo or a Floyd Rose-style equipped guitar, check the tremolo position is level. Tremolos are prone to pulling strings sharp or flat after use if they are not correctly tensioned balanced.

For non-locking tremolo guitars or Gibson-style guitars, check for any binding points at the nut or the bridge. If there are any sharp edges, they could be causing the string to catch. If you find an edge that the string is catching on, this can be resolved by filing the area with the correct size bridge or nut file or by taking it to a professional luthier.

Guitars, much like people, are sensitive to temperature changes. Any environmental fluctuations can influence tuning stability. As the guitar's temperature increases and decreases, the wood will expand and contract accordingly, and this will apply or remove tension on the strings causing a loss in tuning. For example, taking a guitar out of a cold vehicle, into a warm building will affect the instrument's tuning considerably.

In less dramatic settings, the guitar will change temperature, simply after it's been played. The metal of the strings will expand and contract in response to being played and as the temperature increases.

> *NOTE: It is always best to leave the guitar in its case to reacclimatise after being moved between temperature extremes.*

Have you remembered to tune up to pitch? Are the strings adequately stretched? Is the nut slot lubricated?

Problem: It's tuned, but the chords sound out-of-tune.

If the open strings are in-tune, but chords sound out of tune, this may be due to the intonation needing adjustment. Intonation is the overall tuning of the string across its length and is set by moving each bridge saddle backwards or forward to compensate. Check out the section on **Intonation** in the **Guitar Setup** section for further details.

Common Bridge & Saddle Problems

Problem: Tremolo bridge angle too high. Can't adjust the bridge plate to sit flat or parallel to the body.

-Adjust tremolo spring claw towards the body. If it is maxed against the tremolo cavity wall and the bridge is still too high, install more springs. If you cannot install more springs, a lighter string gauge or tuning must be used.

Problem: Saddle height adjustment screws are maxed out, but string height is still too low.

- Have you set the neck relief? Is the neck too straight or back-bowed? Adjust the truss rod for more relief.

- The neck angle may need adjustment. Remove the neck (bolt-ons) and check for debris or shims. Remove shims, reattach neck and test. If there is no improvement, try adding a shim to the front of the neck pocket. If the problem persists or is too difficult to work around, the solutions for in-depth repair go beyond the scope of this guide - seek professional advice.

Problem: Saddle height adjustment screws are bottomed out, but string height is still too high.

- Have you set the neck relief? Does the neck have too much bow? Adjust the truss rod for more relief.

- The neck angle may need adjustment. Remove neck (bolt-ons) and install shim(s) in the neck pocket. Reattach neck and test. Use enough shim material to create an adequate neck angle for saddle height adjustment. See "How to Adjust Neck Angle."

Problem: Can't adjust saddle height, adjustment screws are corroded and stuck.

- Remove strings and apply 3-in-One oil or WD-40 to the rusted adjustment screws. Allow enough time to penetrate and unthread screws completely to assist in cleaning the threads. Reinstall and adjust string height.

Common Truss Rod Issues

Problem: Can't turn the truss rod.

- Is the truss rod wrench making direct contact with the nut?

- Does the truss rod nut appear worn or have rounded edges? The nut may be stripped.

- Are you using the correct truss rod wrench designed for the guitar model? Verify the size is correct.

- Is the truss rod wrench turning, but the nut isn't? The truss rod nut may be stripped.

Problem: Can't tighten the truss rod, feels stuck.

- Have you first assessed the neck relief with strings on the guitar, tuned to pitch? Is an adjustment needed?

- Have you tried loosening the truss rod nut first? Try and back off the truss rod nut completely to assess the adjustment range. If possible, remove the nut and lubricate with Vaseline. Reinstall and test again.

- Is the truss rod nut already as tight as it can go? Back off the truss rod nut completely to assess the adjustment range and response in neck relief.

- If none of the above apply, the truss rod nut may be seized. Seek professional assistance.

Problem: Can't loosen the truss rod, feels stuck.

- Have you first assessed the neck relief with strings on the guitar, tuned to pitch? Is an adjustment needed?

- Is the truss rod nut already completely backed off and as loose as it will go? Try and tighten the truss rod nut a few turns to assess the adjustment range and response in neck relief.

- If none of the above apply, the truss rod nut may be seized. Seek professional assistance.

Problem: The truss rod wrench turns, but nothing happens.

- Is there a rattle in the neck when shaken? The truss rod nut may be dislodged, unthreaded, or broken.

- If possible, loosen the truss rod nut completely and inspect it for stripped threading.

- The truss rod nut may be stripped. Seek professional assistance.

Problem: Truss rod nut spins freely. It doesn't do anything.

- The truss rod nut may be stripped. Seek professional assistance.

- The truss rod may have become dislodged in the neck. Seek professional assistance.

Problem: Truss rod wrench doesn't fit.

- Is the truss rod wrench making direct contact with the nut?

- *Does the truss rod nut appear worn or have rounded edges? The nut may be stripped.*

- *Have you verified that the truss rod wrench is the correct size and designed for the exact guitar model? Verify the correct size.*

- *Is the truss rod wrench turning, but the nut isn't? The truss rod nut may be stripped.*

Problem: Truss rod is tightened, but there's still too much relief in the neck.

- *Have you first assessed the neck relief with strings on the guitar, tuned to pitch?*

- *Is it possible that the truss rod can be tightened further?*

- *Have you changed the gauge of strings to a higher tension? Temporarily de-tune the guitar strings and completely loosen the truss rod nut to relax the neck overnight. Does the neck bow relax and straighten out when there isn't any string tension? Leave it for another day if needed and check again. When ready, tighten the truss rod as far as it will go (without the string tension). Finally, retune the strings to pitch and check if there is any difference in relief from where you started. If the neck bow has fluctuated during your testing, but there is no difference when strung to pitch, the neck is not able to withstand the tension from the strings. This can result from a multitude of reasons. Change to a lighter gauge.*

- *If all the previous steps have been checked, the neck may be warped. Seek professional assistance.*

Problem: Truss rod is loosened all the way, but the neck does not have enough relief- or it's back-bowed.

- *Have you first assessed the neck relief with strings on the guitar, tuned to pitch?*

- *Is it possible that the truss rod can be loosened further?*

- *Have you changed the gauge of strings to a lower tension? Is the neck straight or back-bowed when there is no string tension?*

- *If all the previous steps have been checked, the neck may be warped. Seek professional assistance.*

Problem: Neck relief is too high or low on one side of the neck.

- *Have you first checked the neck relief while the strings are tuned to pitch?*

- *Are you using a hybrid gauge set of strings that may exert unbalanced force in the neck? Change to a balanced set and check again.*

- *Some guitar necks may have a slight twist (warp), which gives one side of the neck more relief than the other.*

Problem: The neck relief on the low E side is perfect, but there's too much relief on the high E side.

Problem: The neck relief on the high E side is perfect, but there's not enough relief on the low E side.

- ***Corrective Actions***

- *Option 1: Adjust the relief for the low E string as straight as possible (without excessive buzz) to compensate.*

- Option 2: Use a hybrid set of strings with heavy bottoms and light tops to compensate.

- Option 3: Take it to a luthier for treatment/repair.

Problem: The neck relief on the low E side is perfect, but there's not enough relief on the high E side.

Problem: The neck relief on the high E side is perfect, but there's too much relief on the low E side.

- Corrective Actions

- Option 1: Adjust the relief for the low E string with a little extra bow to compensate.

- Option 2: Use a hybrid set of strings with regular bottoms and heavier tops to compensate.

- Option 3: Take it to a luthier for treatment/repair.

Problem: When I turn the truss rod nut, I hear a creaking sound.

- If tightening, STOP.

- If loosening, go slow. If the noise doesn't disappear after half a turn, STOP.

Hearing creaking noises while adjusting the truss rod can suggest wood compressing or decompressing, but it can be associated with structural issues within the neck as well. Overtightening a truss rod nut can lead to a guitars' certain death. Loosening a truss rod is generally a low-risk endeavour.

Always remember: Never force anything.

Problem: Where is the truss rod nut at all? I can't find it.

- Classical (nylon string guitars) generally do not have truss rods, although not without exception.

- Some vintage guitars do not have adjustable truss rods, or truss rods at all.

- Some acoustic guitars have the truss rod adjustment hidden up underneath the guitar top body (through the soundhole), at the end of the neck and can be difficult to see without the use of a flashlight and small mirror.

Common Electronics Issues

Problem: Guitar sounds weird. Single notes sound "warbly," out of tune.

- Lower pick up height and check intonation.

Problem: The pickup selector switch makes static noise or cuts in and out.

- Possibly a dirty switch. Try cleaning with contact cleaner.

- Check all hardware is tightened firmly and not loose.

- Check wiring for any possible shorts and check all connections are intact on the switch itself.

- Possibly old and worn-out switch. If cleaning doesn't improve, replace it.

Problem: Volume/tone control makes static noise or cuts in and out.

- Possibly a dirty potentiometer. Try cleaning with contact cleaner.

- Check wiring for any possible shorts and check all connections are intact.

- Check hardware is tightened firmly and not spinning freely.

- Possibly old and worn-out pot. If cleaning doesn't improve, replace it.

Problem: Guitar signal intermittently cuts out while playing.

- Check the guitar cable and all connections to the amplifier.

- Check output jack hardware is tightened and not spinning freely.

- Check output jack wiring is intact.

- Look for any ground connections near output jack that may be interfering. Jacks commonly ground out on cavity shielding (black shielding paint or metallic tape), which is also wired to ground.

- Check wiring for any possible shorts and check all other connections are intact.

- Check all other hardware is tightened firmly.

- Check guitar cable while plugged into output jack that it has no side-to-side play. Jack terminals may need to be bent into position, or a replacement may be needed.

Problem: Static noise emanating while playing (static electricity).

- Static electricity buildup on the guitar. Wipe down the underside of any plastic pickguards or parts with a dryer sheet and insert it into the electronic cavity (if possible). Static electricity can build up on guitars, just like on your clothes.

Problem: Loud hum present while playing guitar.

- Possible ground problem. Missing or broken ground wire.

- Check output jack connections, and electrical component ground wiring is intact.

- Check bridge-to-string ground wire is connected.

Problem: Loud hum present when hands are on strings, disappears when hands are off.

- Output or ground wires have become reversed in the circuit. Recheck pickup wires and wiring diagram for fault.

Problem: Loud hum present when hands are off the guitar, disappears when hands are on the guitar.

- Some guitars make much more noise than others. The ground noise should be lower once the hands are on the guitar strings. Turn off any stompboxes and hi-gain settings when not in use. Turn the volume down when not in use.

Problem: Loud hum present depending on where the guitar is pointed in the room.

- This kind of noise is RF interference, which is generated from lights, radio waves and other electronic devices. Some guitars pick this up more than others. It can be heard as noise that fades in and out, radio broadcast signals, and loud hum.

- Use a quality guitar cable. Higher-end guitar cables will provide better shielding as well as a quieter, truer sound.

- If upgrading your cables doesn't work, shield the guitar electronics. (check our website for instructions at blackwoodguitarworks.com)

Problem: Loud hum intermittently comes and goes.

- This could be a loose ground or an RF problem. Ground hum is generally loud and doesn't change in frequency or tone. It is a similar sound as unplugging a guitar cable and leaving it on the ground, with the amplifier turned on. RF noise generally wavers in and out and is heard just behind the guitar signal, but heard the most obviously when the guitar strings are not being played.

- See previous troubleshooting recommendations for fixes.

Other Problems

For other problems you may encounter, contact us through the website at blackwoodguitarworks.com, and we'll do our best to find you a solution!

TOOL TEMPLATES

Cut the following templates out with an X-Acto knife or scissors and paste them onto a piece of cardboard such as an old cereal box, etc. Use them for all aspects of guitar setup like measuring the fretboard radius, string height, and more. They can also be downloaded and printed from *www.blackwoodguitarworks.com* under the **RESOURCES** page.

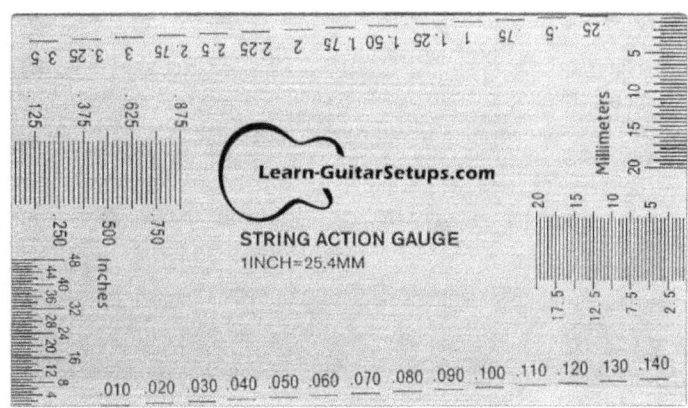

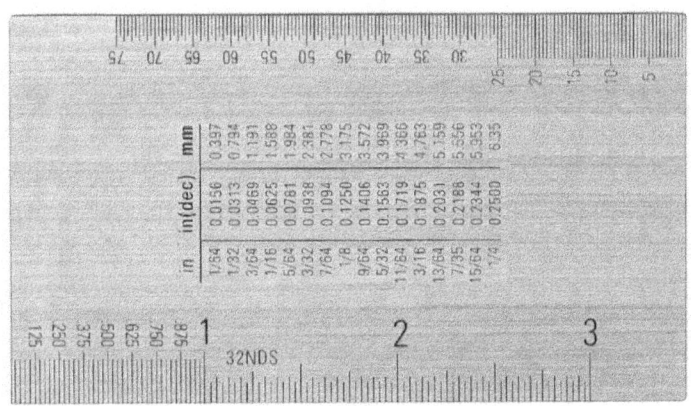

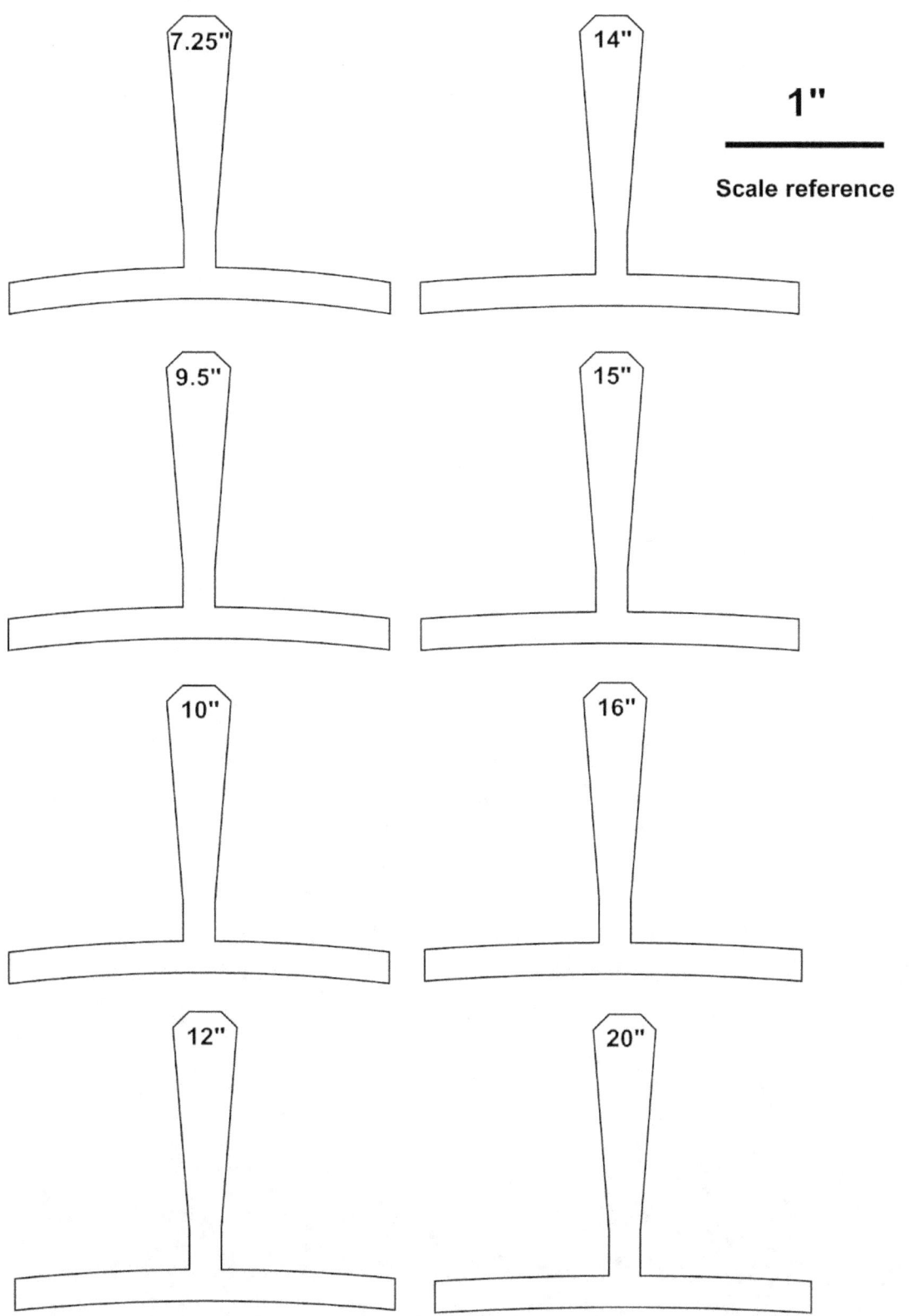

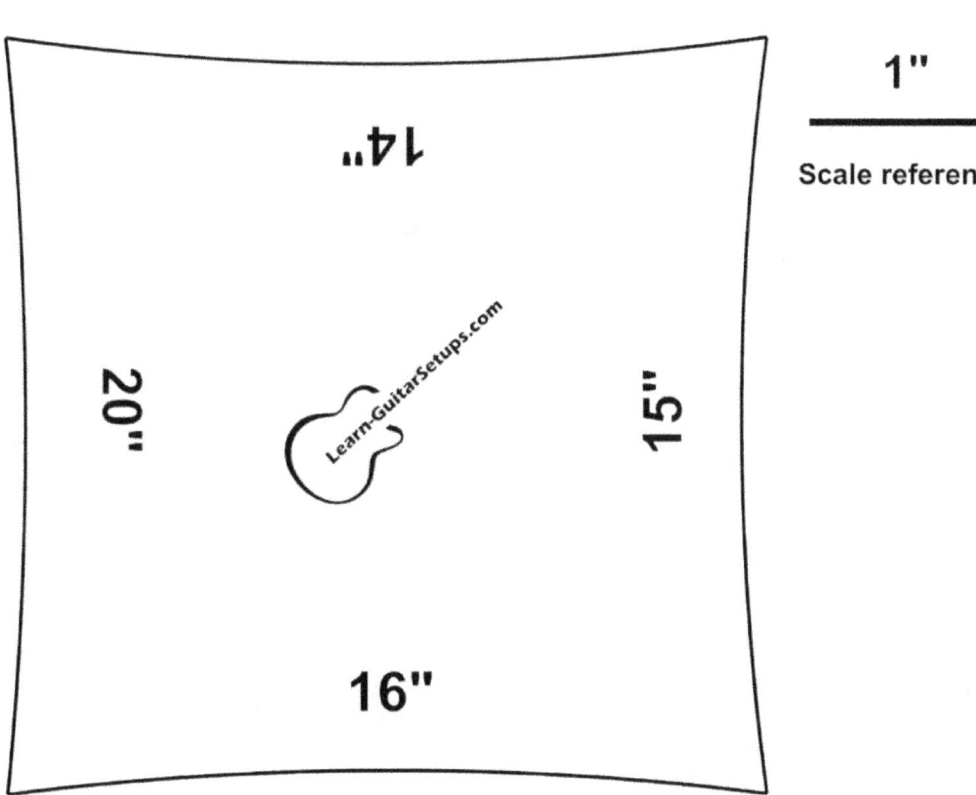

1"
Scale reference

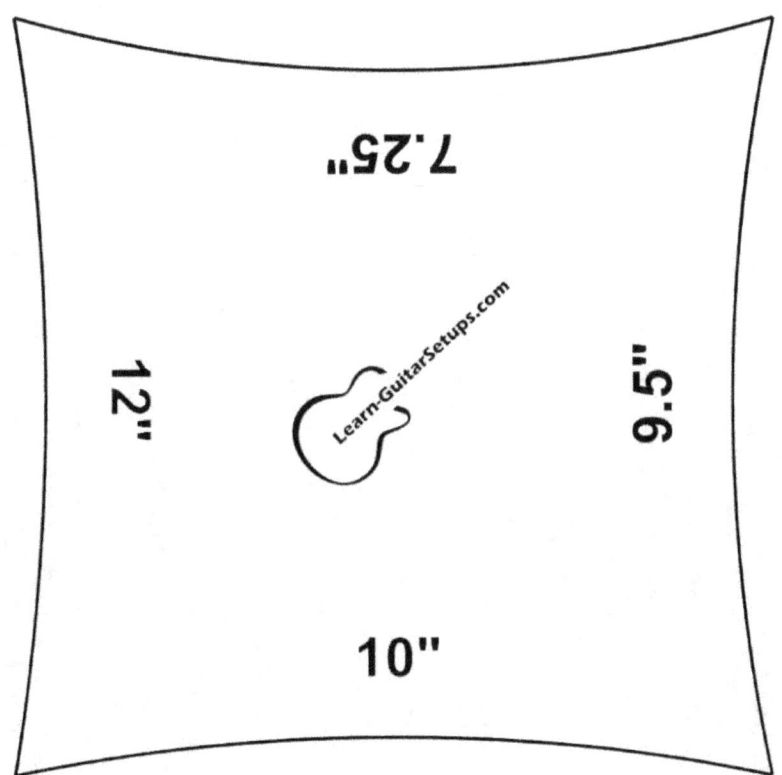

149

HOW TO USE RADIUS GAUGES

Radius gauges can be used for many different jobs on the guitar bench. Use them to measure the fretboard radius, the bridge and nut radius, the string height, and much more.

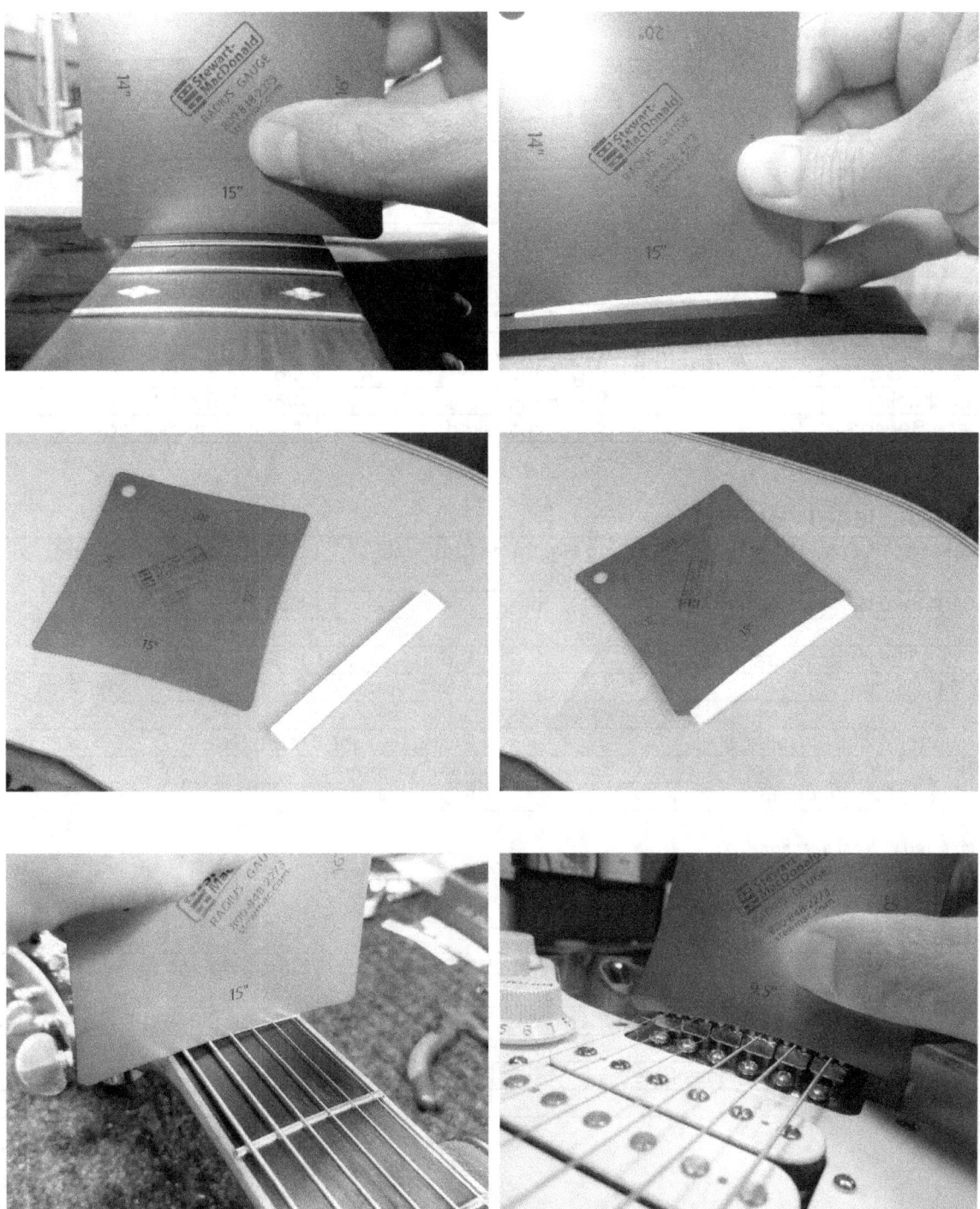

SETUP SPEC SHEETS

Electric Guitars

Fender Electric Guitars

Radius	Relief at 8th Fret	String Height at 17th Fret, Bass Side	String Height at 17th Fret, Treble Side
7.25"	.012" (.3 mm)	5/64" (2 mm)	4/64" (1.6 mm)
9.5" to 12"	.010" (.25 mm)	4/64" (1.6 mm)	4/64" (1.6 mm)
15" to 17"	.008" (.2 mm)	4/64" (1.6 mm)	3/64" (1.2 mm)

Pickup Height Model	Bass Side	Treble Side
Texas Specials	8/64" (3.2 mm)	6/64" (2.4 mm)
Vintage Style	6/64" (2.4 mm)	5/64" (2 mm)
Noiseless Series	8/64" (3.2 mm)	6/64" (2.4 mm)
Standard Single Coil	5/64" (2 mm)	4/64" (1.6 mm)
Humbuckers	4/64" (1.6 mm)	4/64" (1.6 mm)
Lace Sensors	As close as desired	As close as desired

Gibson Electric Guitars

Relief at 7th Fret	String Height at 12th Fret, Bass Side	String Height at 12th Fret, Treble Side
.010" to .012"	*5/64" (2 mm)	*3/64" (1.2 mm)

String Height at 1st Fret, Bass Side	String Height at 1st Fret, Treble Side
2/64" (.8 mm)	1/64" (.4 mm)

Pickup Height, Bass Side	Pickup Height, Treble Side
Bridge - 4/64" (1.6 mm)	4/64" (1.6 mm)
Neck - 6/64" (2.4 mm)	6/64" (2.4 mm)

*Measured with 1st fret barred

Gretsch Electric Guitars

Relief at 8th Fret	String Height at 12th Fret, Bass Side	String Height at 12th Fret, Treble Side
.008"	4/64" to 5/64" (1.6 mm - 2 mm)	4/64" to 5/64" (1.6 mm - 2 mm)

String Height at 1st Fret, Bass Side	String Height at 1st Fret, Treble Side
.020" +/- .002" (.5 mm)	.018" +/- .002" (.45 mm)

SETUP SPEC SHEETS
Electric Guitars

Guild Electric Guitars

Relief at 5th Fret	String Height at 12th Fret, Bass Side	String Height at 12th Fret, Treble Side
.006" +/- .002"	4/64" to 5/64" (1.6 mm - 2 mm)	4/64" to 5/64" (1.6 mm - 2 mm)

String Height at 1st Fret, Bass Side	String Height at 1st Fret, Treble Side
.020" +/- .002" (.5 mm)	.018" +/- .002" (.45 mm)

Ibanez Electric Guitars

Relief at 7th Fret	String Height at 14th Fret, Bass Side	String Height at 14th Fret, Treble Side
.008" to .020" (.2 mm - .5 mm)	.079" (2 mm)	.059" (1.5 mm)

Jackson/Charvel Electric Guitars

Relief at 8th Fret	String Height at 17th Fret, Bass Side	String Height at 17th Fret, Treble Side
.007" - .008"	4/64" (1.6 mm)	3/64" (1.2 mm)

Pickup Height, Bass Side	Pickup Height, Treble Side
Single Coil – 5/64" (2 mm)	4/64" (1.6 mm)
Humbucking – 4/64" (1.6 mm)	4/64" (1.6 mm)
EMG/ Active - As close as desired	As close as desired

General Electric Guitars (Author's specs)

Model	Relief at 7th Fret	String Height at 12th Fret, Bass Side	String Height at 12th Fret, Treble Side
Generic	.008" to .010"	*.063" (1.6 mm)	*.051" (1.3 mm)
Gibson - Les Paul	.008" to .010"	*.066" (1.7 mm)	*.038" (.97 mm)
Generic - Low action	.008" to .010"	*.052" (1.3 mm)	*.037" (.94 mm)
Heritage - Les Paul*	.005" to .007"	*.047" (1.2 mm)	*.047" (1.2 mm)
Gretsch - Electromatic	.005"	*.041" (1 mm)	*.041" (1 mm)

String Height at 1st Fret, Bass Side	String Height at 1st Fret, Treble Side
.030" +/- .002" (.76 mm) Heritage & Gretsch	.018" +/- .002" (.46 mm) Heritage & Gretsch
.010" +/- .002" (.25 mm)	.005" +/- .002" (.13 mm)

*Measured with 1st fret barred

SETUP SPEC SHEETS
Bass Guitars

Fender Bass Guitars

Radius	Relief at 8th Fret	String Height at 17th Fret, Bass Side	String Height at 17th Fret, Treble Side
7.25"	.014"	7/64" (2.8 mm)	6/64" (2.4 mm)
9.5" to 12"	.012"	6/64" (2.4 mm)	5/64" (2 mm)
9.5" to 12" (5 or 6 string)	.014" (at 'B' string)	6/64" (2.4 mm)	5/64" (2 mm)
15" to 17"	.010"	6/64" (2.4 mm)	5/64" (2 mm)

Pickup Height, Model	Bass Side	Treble Side
Vintage style	8/64" (3.2 mm)	6/64" (2.4 mm)
Noiseless	8/64" (3.2 mm)	6/64" (2.4 mm)
American Std.	6/64" (2.4 mm)	5/64" (2 mm)
Lace Sensors	As close as desired	As close as desired

Guild Bass Guitars

Relief at 5th Fret	String Height at 12th Fret, Bass Side	String Height at 12th Fret, Treble Side
.006" +/- .002"	6/64" (2.4 mm)	5/64" (2 mm)

String Height at 1st Fret, Bass Side	String Height at 1st Fret, Treble Side
.022" +/- .002" (.56 mm)	.020" +/- .002" (.51 mm)

Ibanez Bass Guitars

Relief at 7th Fret	String Height at 14th Fret, Bass side	String Height at 14th Fret, Treble Side
.012" to .020" (.3 mm -.5 mm)	.098" (2.5 mm)	.079" (2 mm)

Jackson/Charvel Bass Guitars

Relief at 8th Fret	String Height at 17th Fret, Bass Side	String Height at 17th Fret, Treble Side
.012"	6/64" (2.4 mm)	5/64" (2 mm)

Pickup Height, Bass Side	Pickup Height, Treble Side
Vintage Style – 8/64" (3.2 mm)	6/64" (2.4 mm)
Seymour Duncan – 6/64" (2.4 mm)	6/64" (2.4 mm)
EMG/ Active - As close as desired	As close as desired

General Bass Guitars (Author's specs)

Relief at 7th Fret	String Height at 12th Fret Bass Side	String Height at 12th Fret, Treble Side
.014" to .016"	*.095" (2.4 mm)	*.075" (1.9 mm)

*Measured with 1st fret barred

SETUP SPEC SHEETS
Acoustic Guitars

Fender Acoustic Guitars

Radius	Relief at 8th Fret	String Height at 14th Fret, Bass Side	String Height at 14th Fret, Treble Side
9.5" – 12"	.010"	6/64" (2.4 mm)	5/64" (2 mm)

Gibson Acoustic Guitars

Relief at 7th Fret	String Height at 12th Fret, Bass Side	String Height at 12th Fret, Treble Side
.012"	6/64" to 7/64" (2.4 mm - 2.8 mm)	4/64" to 5/64" (1.6 mm - 2 mm)

String Height at 1st Fret, Bass Side	String Height at 1st Fret, Treble Side
2/64" (.8 mm)	1/64" (.4 mm)

Taylor Acoustic Guitars

Relief at 7th Fret	String Height at 12th Fret, Bass Side	String Height at 12th Fret, Treble Side
.004" to .007"	6/64" (2.4 mm)	4/64" (1.6 mm)

String Height at 1st Fret, Bass Side	String Height at 1st fret – Treble Side
.025" (.64 mm)	.019" (.48 mm)

Guild Acoustic Guitars

Relief at 5th Fret	String Height at 12th Fret, Bass Side	String Height at 12th Fret, Treble Side
.006" +/- .002"	5/64" to 6/64" (2mm - 2.4 mm)	4/64" to 5/64" (1.6 mm- 2 mm)

String Height at 1st Fret, Bass Side	String Height at 1st Fret, Treble Side
.022" +/- .002" (.55 mm)	.020" +/- .002" (.5 mm)

Ibanez Acoustic Guitars

Relief at 7th Fret	String Height at 14th Fret, Bass Side	String Height at 14th Fret, Treble Side
.008" to .020" (.2 mm - .5 mm)	.090" (2.3 mm)	.066" (1.7 mm)

SETUP SPEC SHEETS
Acoustic Guitars

Martin Acoustic Guitars

Relief at 7th to 9th Fret	String Height at 12th Fret, Bass Side	String Height at 12th Fret, Treble Side
.010"	6/64" to 7/64" (2.4 mm - 2.8 mm)	4/64" to 5/64" (1.6 mm - 2 mm)

String Height at 1st Fret, Bass Side	String Height at 1st Fret, Treble Side
.024" max (.6 mm)	.016" min (.4 mm)

General Acoustic Guitars (Author's specs)

Relief at 7th Fret	String Height at 12th Fret, Bass Side	String Height at 12th Fret Treble Side
.010" to .012"	*5/64" (2 mm)	*4/64" (1.6 mm)

Nylon Stringed Guitars**

Relief at 7th Fret	String Height at 12th Fret, Bass Side	String Height at 12th Fret, Treble Side
.003" to .010"	*8/64" (3.2 mm)	*7/64"
Ibanez Factory	.145" (3.7 mm)	.118" (3mm)
Taylor Factory	.125" (3.2 mm)	.080" (2 mm)

*Measured with 1st fret barred

**Classical or Flamenco style guitars are commonly set with higher action to accommodate the playing style. Higher action has the additional benefit of producing more volume.

User Specs

Model	Relief at 7th Fret	String Height at 12th Fret, Bass Side	String Height at 12th Fret, Treble Side

String Height at 1st Fret, Bass Side	String Height at 1st Fret, Treble Side

MANUFACTURER PICKUP HEIGHT SPECS

Note: Active pickups have less magnetic pull and may be adjusted closer to the strings than passive pickups.

Make	Model	Bass Side	Treble Side	Specification
Fender	Texas Specials	8/64" (3.2 mm)	6/64" (2.4 mm)	
	Vintage style	6/64" (2.4 mm)	5/64" (2 mm)	
	Noiseless™ Series	8/64" (3.2 mm)	6/64" (2.4 mm)	
	Standard Single-Coil	5/64" (2 mm)	4/64" (1.6 mm)	
	Humbuckers	4/64" (1.6 mm)	4/64" (1.6 mm)	
	Lace Sensors	As close as desired (allowing for string vibration)		
Gibson	generic	4/64" (1.6 mm)	3/32" (2.4 mm)	
PRS	Humbucker/Soapbar	3/32" (2.4 mm)	5/64" (2 mm)	
	Singlecoil	4/32" (3.2 mm)	2.5/32"	Neck
		4/32" (3.2 mm)	3.5/32"	Middle
		4/32" (3.2 mm)	2/32" (1.6 mm)	Bridge
Ibanez	Generic	1/16" (1.6 mm)	5/64" (2 mm)	Neck
		1/8" (3.17 mm)	5/64" (2 mm)	Middle
		1/32" (.8 mm)	5/64" (2 mm)	Bridge
Jackson	Humbucker	4/64" (1.6 mm)	4/64" (1.6 mm)	
	Singlecoil	5/64" (2 mm)	4/64" (1.6 mm)	
	Noiseless Singlecoil	8/64" (3.6 mm)	6/64" (2.4 mm)	
G&L	generic	1/16" (1.6 mm)	1/32" (.8 mm)	
Gretsch	generic	6/64" (2.4 mm)	4/64" (1.6 mm)	
	Bass	4/32" (3.2 mm)	3/32" (2.4 mm)	
ESP	Max height gtr	3/32" (2.4 mm)	4/64" (1.6 mm)	
	Max height bass	9/64" (3.5 mm)	3/32" (2.4 mm)	
Fralin Pickups	Set and fine-tune by ear	1/8" (3.17 mm)	1/16" (1.6 mm)	
Yamaha	generic	5/64" (2 mm)	4/64" (1.6 mm)	

MEASUREMENT CONVERSION CHART

Conversion Table
1 Inch = 25.4mm
1 Millimeter = .0394 Inches

Fraction	Decimal	Millimeter
1/64"	0.0156"	0.3969mm
1/32"	0.0313"	0.7938mm
3/64"	0.0469"	1.1906mm
1/16"	0.0625"	1.5875mm
5/64"	0.0781"	1.9844mm
3/32"	0.0938"	2.3813mm
7/64"	0.1094"	2.7781mm
1/8"	**0.1250"**	**3.1750m**
9/64"	0.1406"	3.5719mm
5/32"	0.1563"	3.9688mm
11/64"	0.1719"	4.3656mm
3/16"	0.1875"	4.7625mm
13/64"	0.2031"	5.1594mm
7/32"	0.2188"	5.5563mm
15/64"	0.2344"	5.9531mm
1/4"	**0.2500"**	**6.3500m**
17/64"	0.2656"	6.7469mm
9/32"	0.2813"	7.1438mm
19/64"	0.2969"	7.5406mm
5/16"	0.3125"	7.9375mm
21/64"	0.3281"	8.3344mm
11/32"	0.3438"	8.7313mm
23/64"	0.3594"	9.1281mm
3/8"	**0.3750"**	**9.5250m**
25/64"	0.3906"	9.9219mm
13/32"	0.4063"	10.3188m
27/64"	0.4219"	10.7156m
7/16"	0.4375"	11.1125m
29/64"	0.4531"	11.5094m
15/32"	0.4688"	11.9063m
31/64"	0.4844"	12.3031m
1/2"	**0.5000"**	**12.7000m**

Fraction	Decimal	Millimeter
33/64"	0.5156"	13.0969m
17/32"	0.5313"	13.4938m
35/64"	0.5469"	13.8906m
9/16"	0.5625"	14.2875m
37/64"	0.5781"	14.6844m
19/32"	0.5938"	15.0813m
39/64"	0.6094"	15.4781m
5/8"	**0.6250"**	**15.8750m**
41/64"	0.6406"	16.2719m
21/32"	0.6563"	16.6688m
43/64"	0.6719"	17.0656m
11/16"	0.6875"	17.4625m
45/64"	0.7031"	17.8594m
23/32"	0.7188"	18.2563m
47/64"	0.7344"	18.6531m
3/4"	**0.7500"**	**19.0500m**
49/64"	0.7656"	19.4469m
25/32"	0.7813"	19.8438m
51/64"	0.7969"	20.2406m
13/16"	0.8125"	20.6375m
53/64"	0.8281"	21.0344m
27/32"	0.8438"	21.4313m
55/64"	0.8594"	21.8281m
7/8"	**0.8750"**	**22.2250m**
57/64"	0.8906"	22.6219m
29/32"	0.9063"	23.0188m
59/64"	0.9219"	23.4156m
15/16"	0.9375"	23.8125m
61/64"	0.9531"	24.2094m
31/32"	0.9688"	24.6063m
63/64"	0.9844"	25.0031m
1"	**1.0000"**	**25.4000m**

WIRING DIAGRAMS

Standard Strat

(Fender switch)

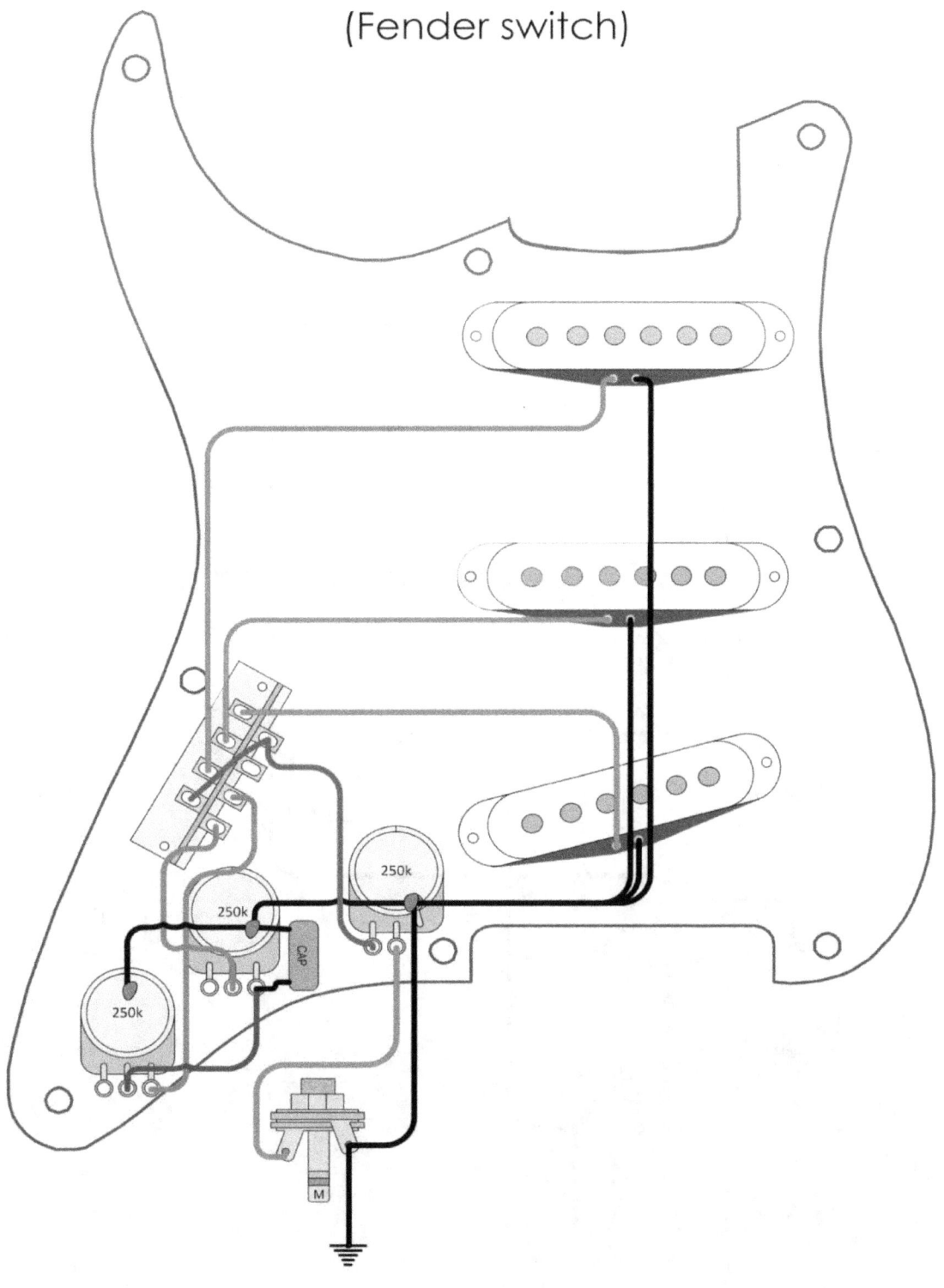

Standard Strat
(blade switch)

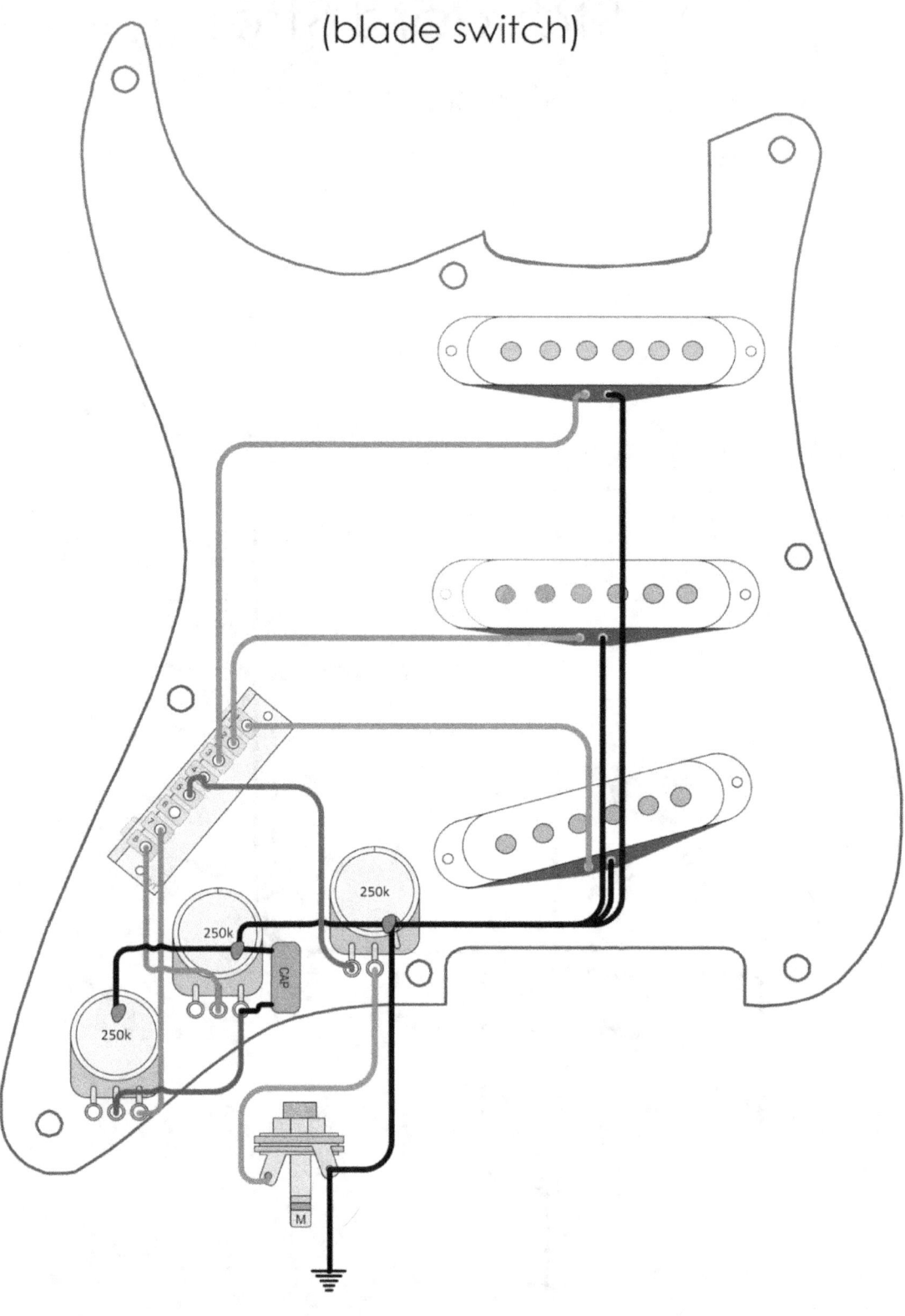

Strat HSS

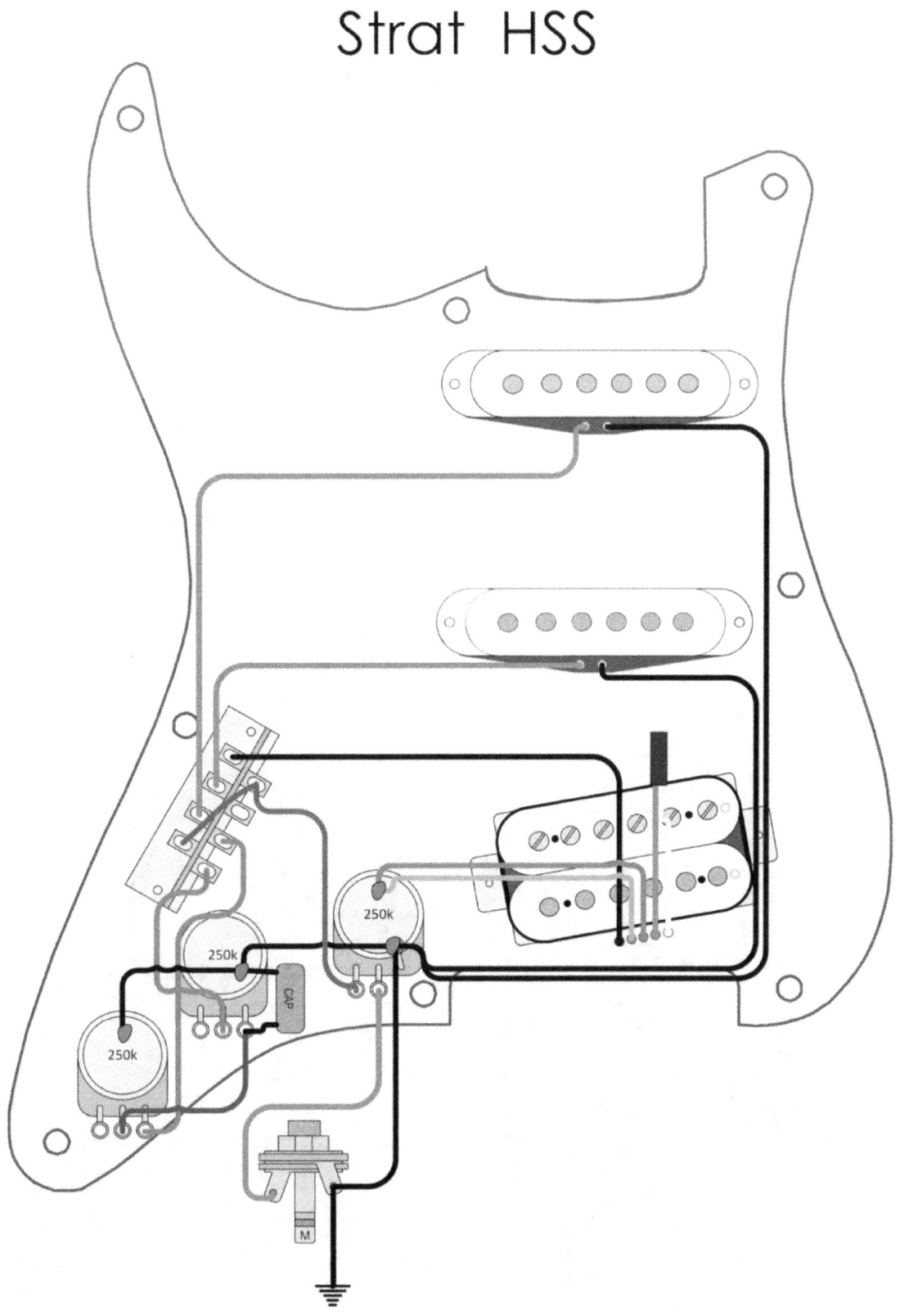

Strat HSS
(Coil Tap)

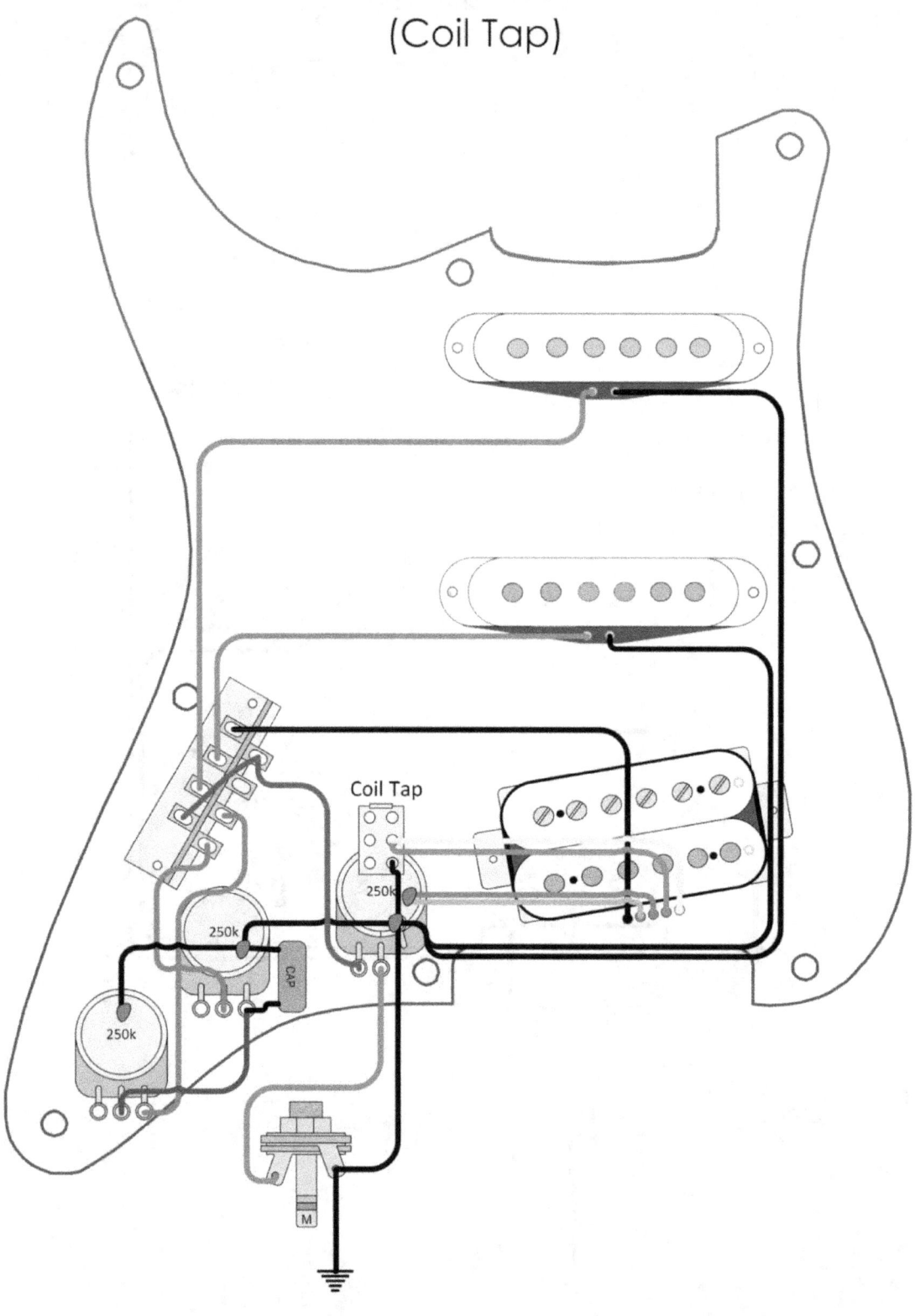

Strat HSH

Strat HSH
(Coil Tap)

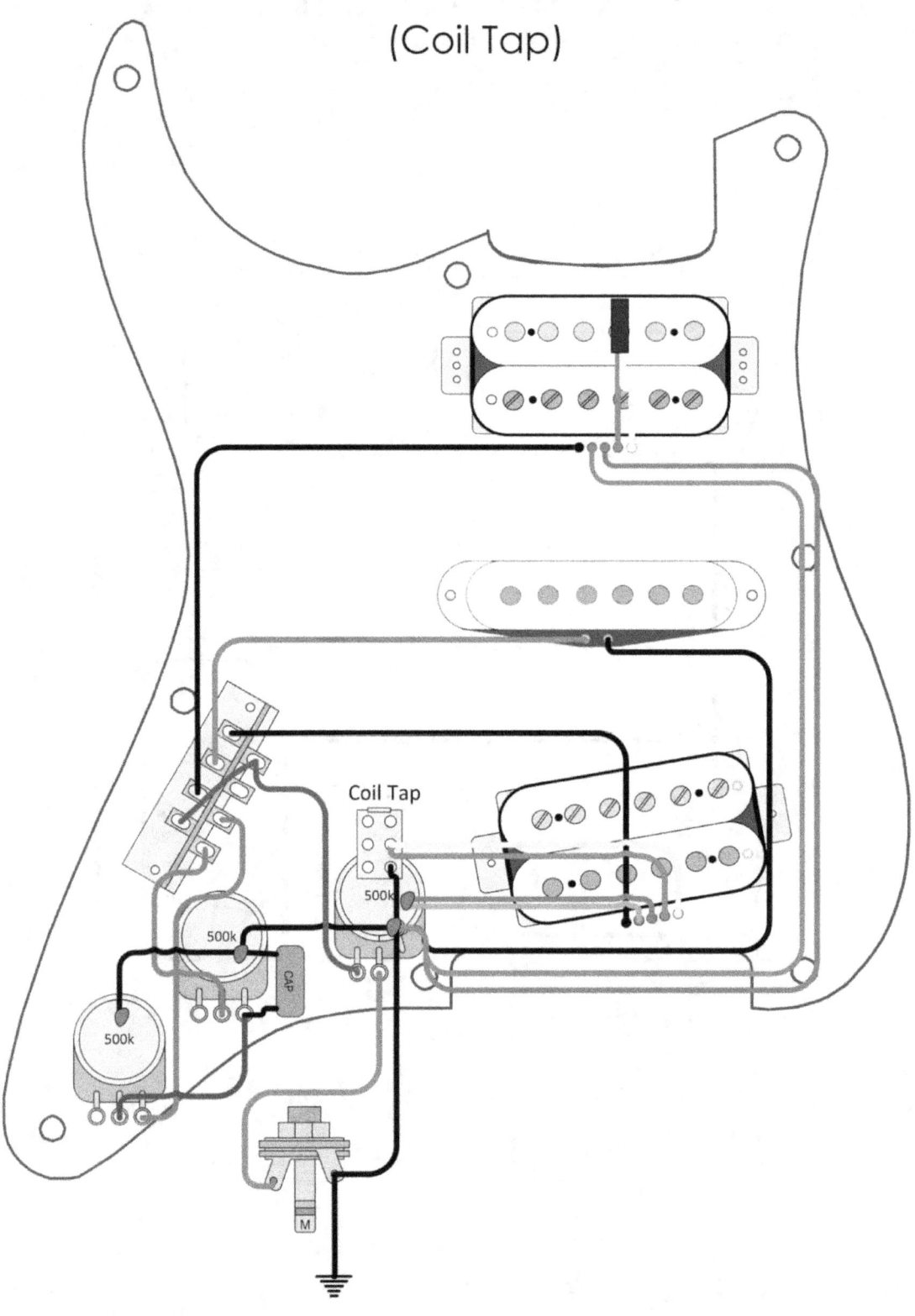

Standard Tele

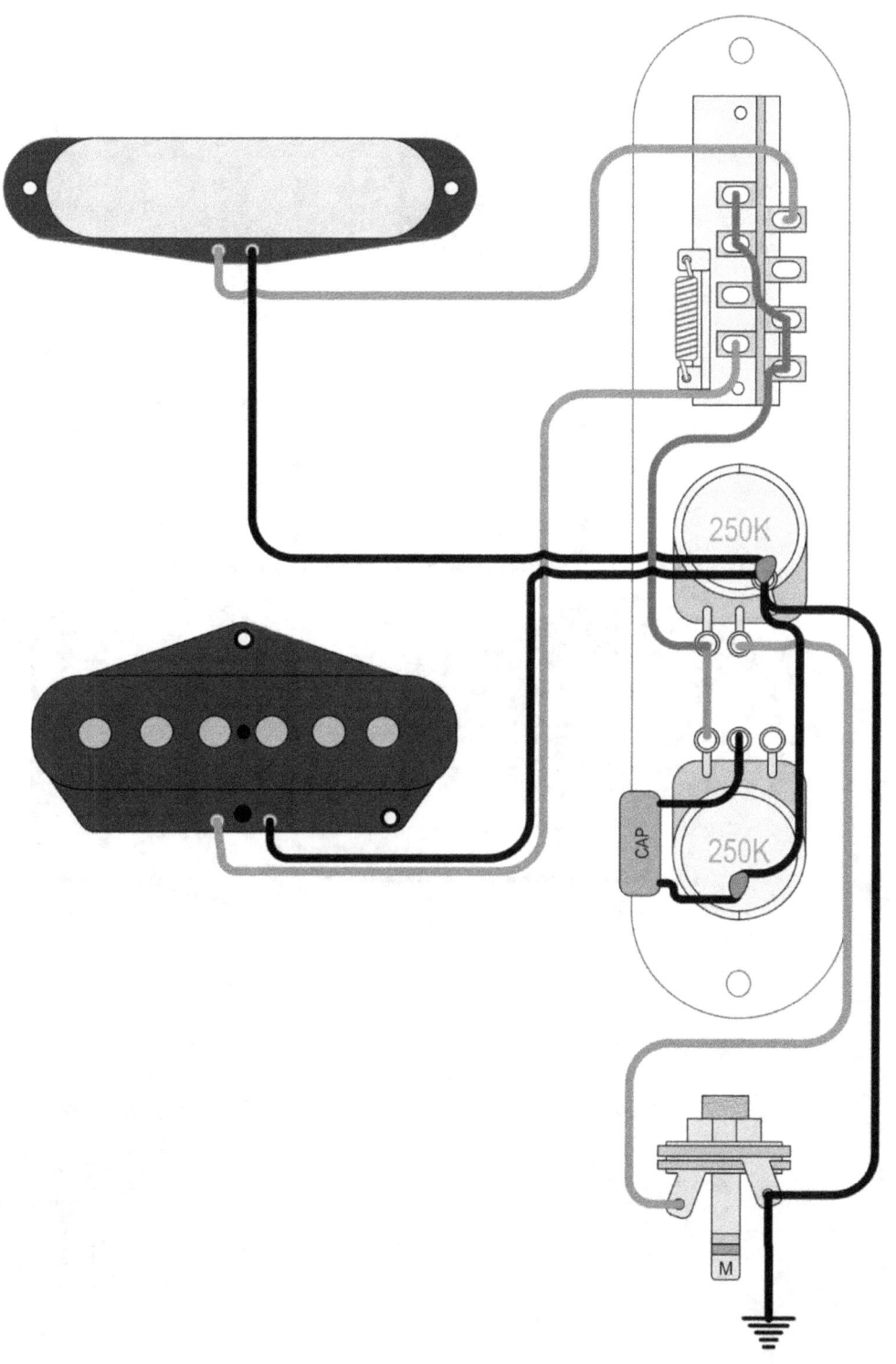

Tele HS

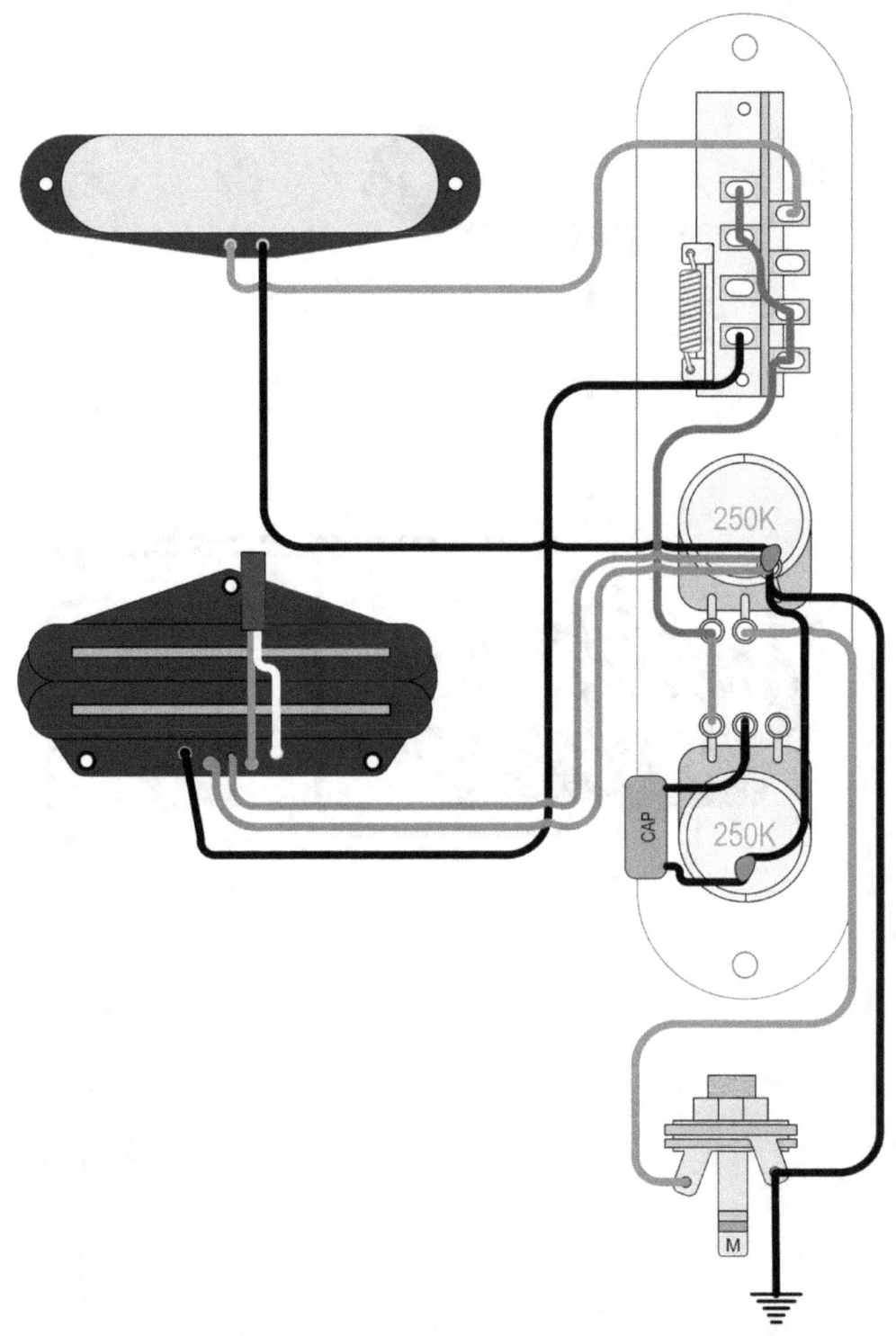

Tele HS
(Coil Tap)

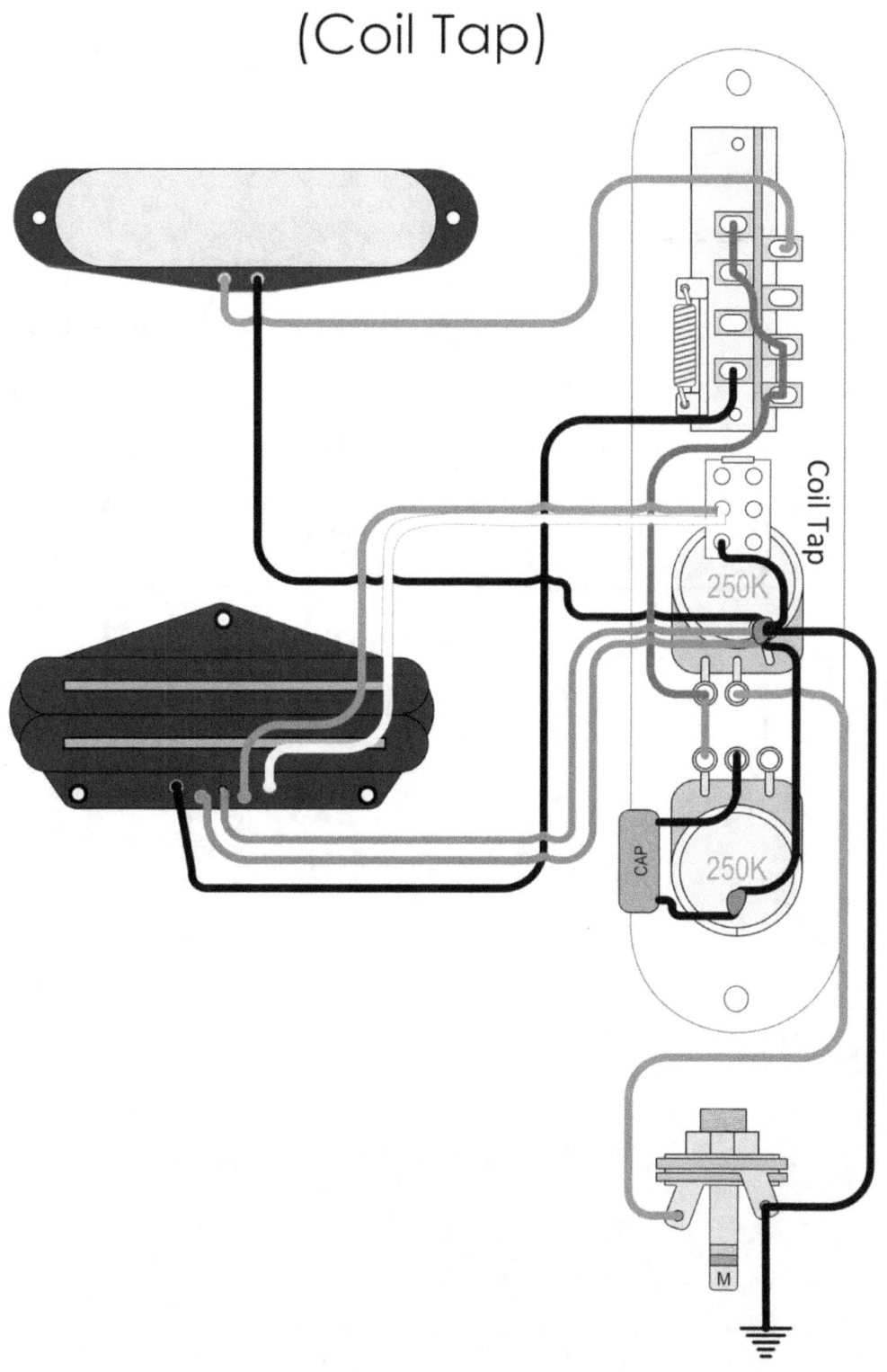

Standard LesPaul

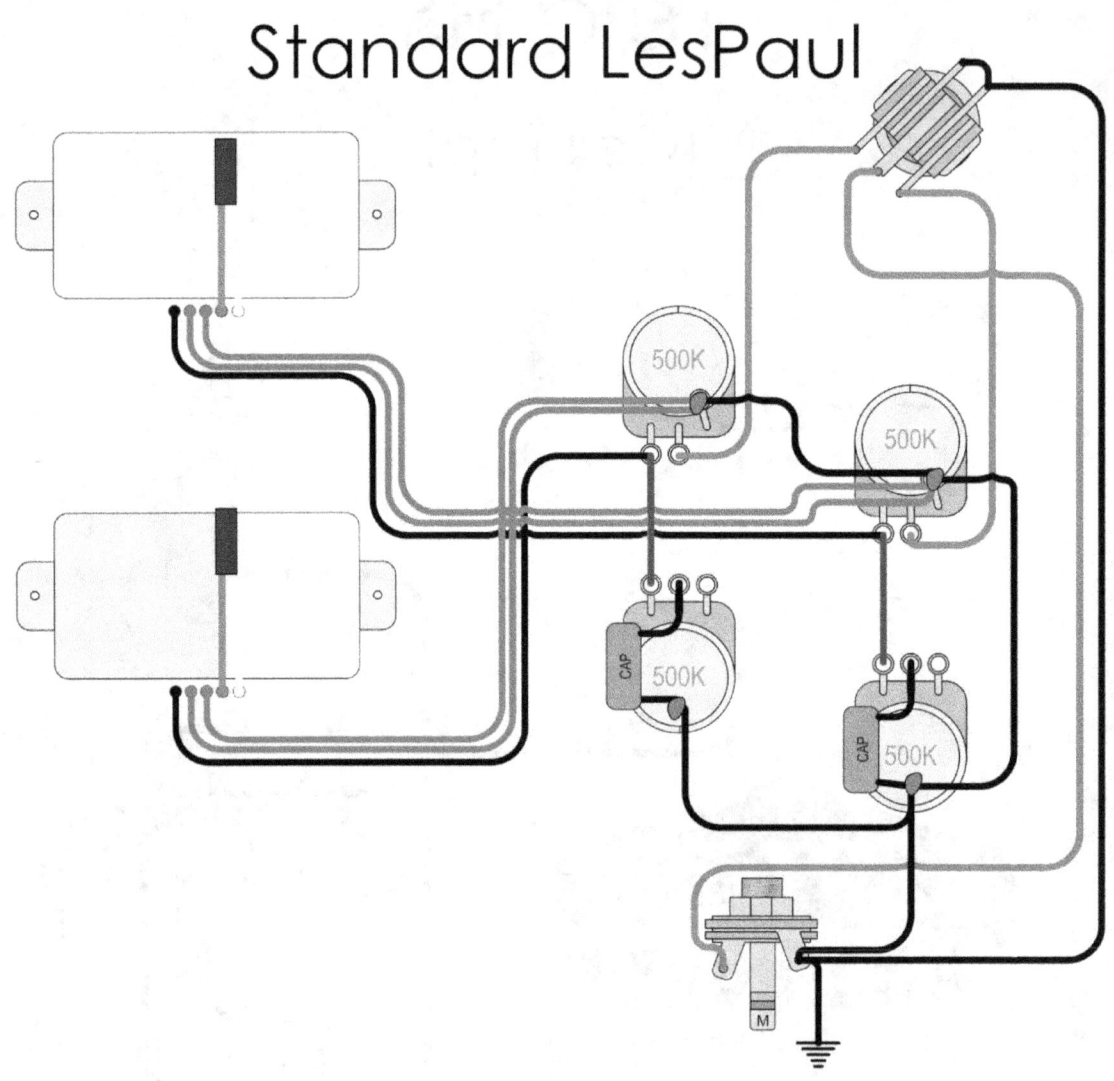

LesPaul Junior

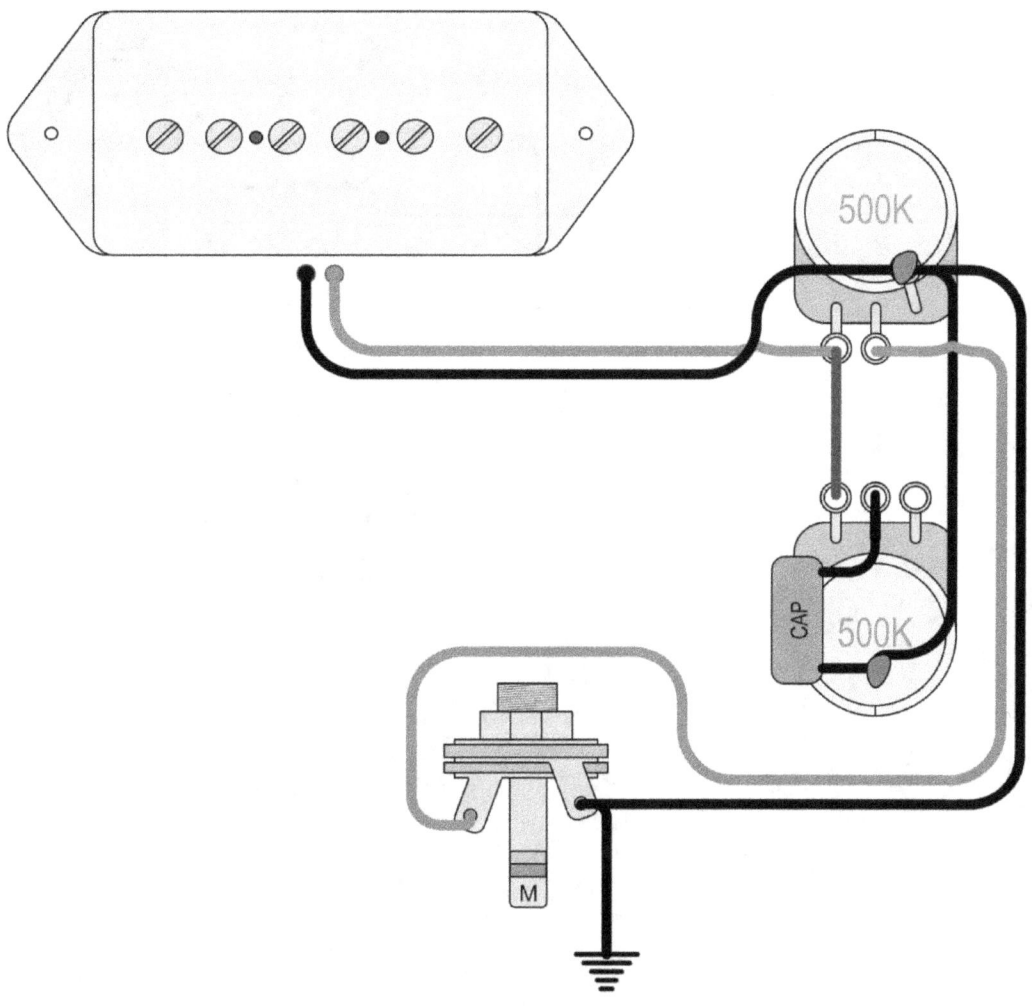

Gretch style p90

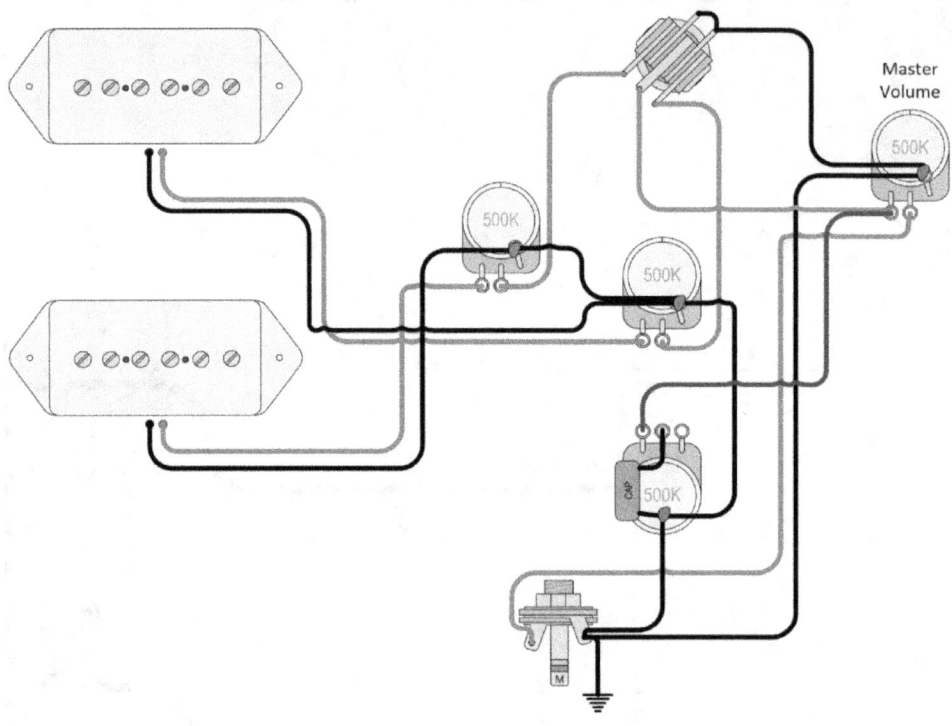

FURTHER RESOURCES

Training
- Summit School of Guitar Building & Repair Inc. - http://www.luthiers-international.com
- Gallop School of Guitar Building & Repair - http://www.galloupguitars.com/school.htm
- Stewart MacDonald's Intl. list of Lutherie Schools - http://www.stewmac.com/freeinfo/Reference/i-8010.html

Information & Tools
- Online guitar setup calculator, guitar setup & repair articles, and more – http://www.learn-guitarsetups.com
- Parts, tools & information - http://www.stewmac.com
- Luthiers supplies & tools - http://www.lmii.com

Further Reading
- Guitar Player Repair Guide – Dan Erlewine
- How to Make Your Electric Guitar Play Great – Dan Erlewine
- Guitar Setup and Maintenance – Hal Leonard
- The Fender Stratocaster Handbook – Paul Balmer
- How to Build Electric Guitars – Will Kelly
- Mel Bay Guitar Setup – John LeVan
- Electric Guitar Setups – Hideo Kamimoto
- Complete Guitar Repair – Hideo Kamimoto

Online Restringing Guides
Accessible at https://www.blackwoodguitarworks.com/resources

ABOUT THE AUTHOR

Jonny Blackwood has been a guitarist and repair tech for over two decades.

His love of guitars began in his youth on Vancouver Island, BC, Canada, where his interests in guitar electronics and customization eventually led to building guitars.

In his early 20s, he started working in a guitar store owned by a highly respected luthier, who's tech credits include INXS, Metallica, Bryan Adams, Kd Lang and Aerosmith. From this time forward, he began learning the craft of setup and repair by a true master.

Over the years he has worked on thousands of guitars, studying all aspects of the trade and becoming an authorized technician for every major brand in the industry and awarded several factory designated certifications.

Since 2009, he has been teaching guitar repair and maintenance through group and private classes, corporate staff training, client literature, and his popular books, including the Amazon best-selling title, "*How to Setup Your Guitar Like A Pro: An Easy Guide for Beginners.*"

He is currently writing and publishing new material that breaks down the barriers between repairing, maintaining, and playing the guitar.

Learn more at www.blackwoodguitarworks.com

ONE LAST THING

If you found this book useful, would you be kind enough to leave a short review? I depend on reviews to get the word out about my books! I also read all the reviews personally so that I can get feedback about how to make this, or future books even better. I'd love to hear how it's helped you.

Let's stay connected- find me on Facebook (www.facebook.com/blackwoodguitarworks), Instagram (@blackwoodguitarworks) or through my website (www.learn-guitarsetups.com) and let me know how it's worked out.

- J.B.

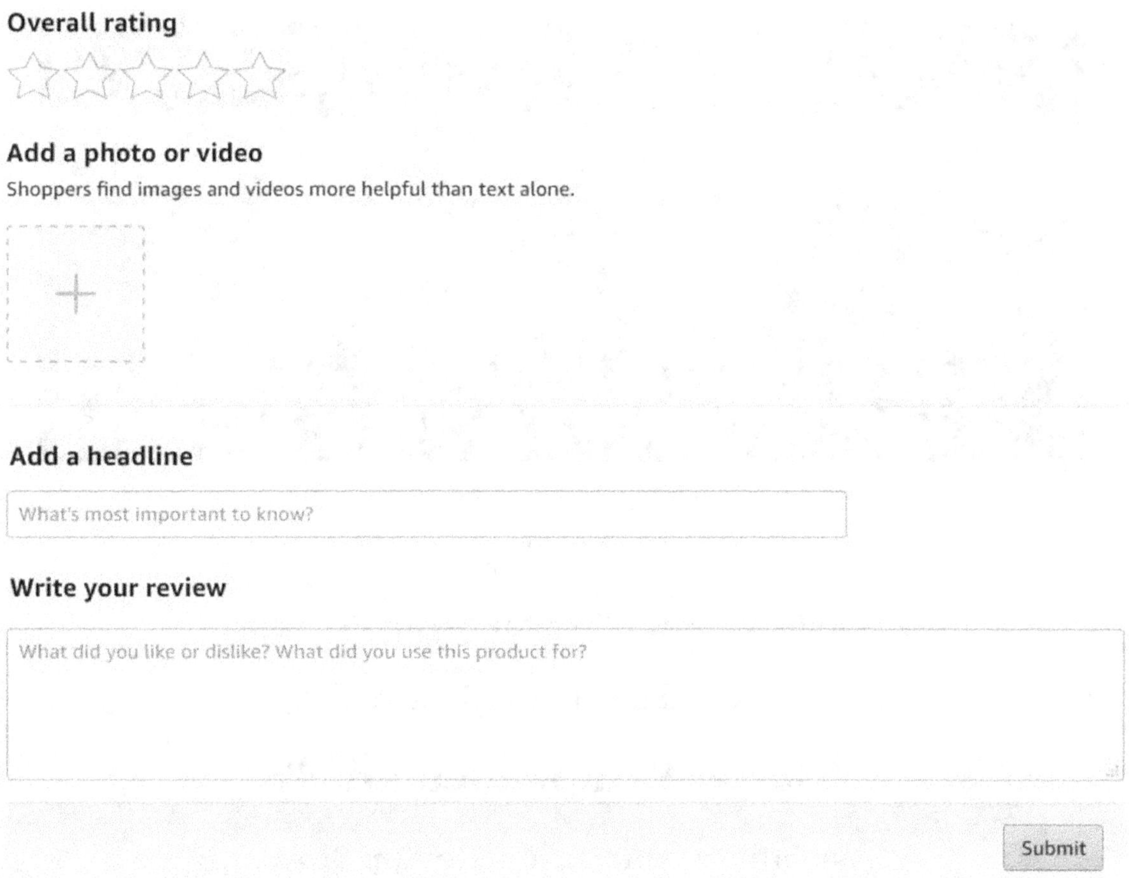

Overall rating

☆☆☆☆☆

Add a photo or video

Shoppers find images and videos more helpful than text alone.

[+]

Add a headline

[What's most important to know?]

Write your review

[What did you like or dislike? What did you use this product for?]

[Submit]

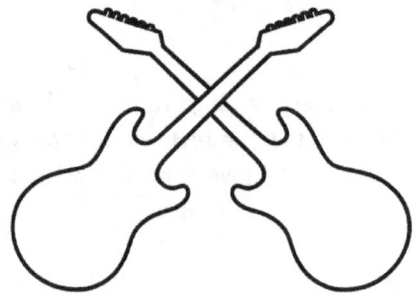

Blackwood Guitarworks

Discover other books available from the author

(paperback and digital editions):

 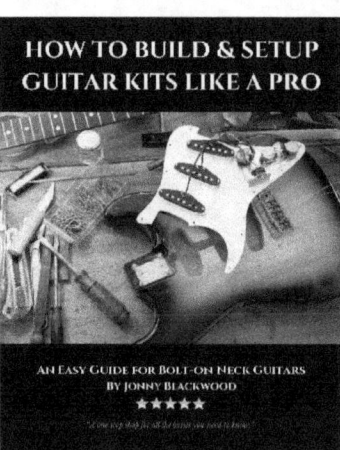 

* * * * *

Also, discover the "Guitar Setup Pro" app,

featuring our exclusive

"Guitar Setup Calculator".

Available at your favourite App Store.

* * * * *

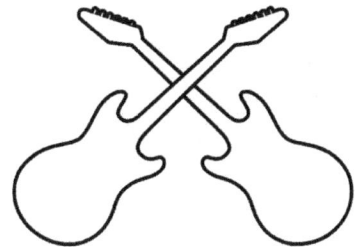

Blackwood Guitarworks
www.blackwoodguitarworks.com

Have a group of friends interested in

learning guitar setups?

Interested in hosting

a Group Guitar Setup or

repair Class in your area?

Contact us

THROUGH OUR WEBSITE

for more details

www.ingramcontent.com/pod-product-compliance
Lightning Source LLC
Chambersburg PA
CBHW081357070526
44583CB00020B/2583